Becoming President

Becoming President

The Bush Transition, 2000–2003

John P. Burke

LYNNE
RIENNER
PUBLISHERS

BOULDER
LONDON

Published in the United States of America in 2004 by
Lynne Rienner Publishers, Inc.
1800 30th Street, Boulder, Colorado 80301
www.rienner.com

and in the United Kingdom by
Lynne Rienner Publishers, Inc.
3 Henrietta Street, Covent Garden, London WC2E 8LU

Library of Congress Cataloging-in-Publication Data
Burke, John P., 1953–
    Becoming president : the Bush transition, 2000–2003 / John P. Burke.
        p. cm.
    Includes bibliographical references and index.
    ISBN 1-58826-292-8 (alk. paper)
    1. Bush, George W. (George Walker), 1946– 2. Bush, George W. (George
Walker), 1946—Influence.   3. Political leadership—United States—Case
studies.   4. United States—Politics and government—2001—Decisionmaking.
5. United States—Foreign relations—2001—Decisionmaking.
6. Presidents—United States—Biography.   I. Title.
    E903.3.B86 2004
    973.931'092—dc22

                                                                    2004001255

British Cataloguing in Publication Data
A Cataloguing in Publication record for this book
is available from the British Library.

Printed and bound in the United States of America

The paper used in this publication meets the requirements
of the American National Standard for Permanence of
Paper for Printed Library Materials Z39.48-1992.

5   4   3   2   1

Contents

v

Why Transitions Matter

My purpose in researching and writing this book is to continue the analysis of how presidents prepare to take office and its relationship to the unfolding of their early administrations. This is a topic I first explored in the book *Presidential Transitions: From Politics to Practice,* which examined in depth the four presidential transitions from Jimmy Carter through Bill Clinton and their effects on their respective presidencies.[1] My aim now is to extend that analysis by focusing on the transition and early presidency of George W. Bush. Examination of the Bush transition is important in extending our understanding of transitions and presidencies, as they can become enriched by the experiences of the most recent occupant of the office. But what occurred in the 2000 transition is also interesting in its own right: the most unique transition at least since that of Rutherford B. Hayes in 1876, whose election to the presidency was also mired in a controversy over electoral votes. So too with the subsequent Bush presidency: presidential leadership within a divisive political environment, the loss of his party's control of the Senate in June 2001, and the challenges raised by the terrorist attacks of September 11 and their aftermath. Few presidents have faced such a myriad of difficulties so soon in their administrations.

Why Is Analysis of Presidential Transitions Important?

Since the advent of the modern presidency under Franklin Delano Roosevelt (FDR), the actions that presidents-elect undertake before inauguration day have been seen by scholars, journalists, other observers, and even presidents themselves as critical in determining their successes—and failures—once in office. A successful transition enables a new administration to "hit the ground running," as James P. Pfiffner has so well phrased it.[2] By contrast, mistakes during the transition can lead them to "hit the ground stumbling," creating an inauspicious debut from which it can be difficult to recover.

For FDR, his transition to office was a crucial time for assembling his "brain trust" of close advisers and crafting a number of the policy proposals that he hoped would lead the country out of the depression. After inauguration day, this effort set the stage for his landmark "100 days," during which Congress quickly passed much of what he wanted into law. Almost fifty years later, in 1980, Ronald Reagan and his advisers also experienced a transition to office that has generally been regarded as successful, one that facilitated their ambitious first-year program of tax and budget cuts and the rebuilding of the U.S. military.

Other presidents-elect have been less successful. Jimmy Carter's transition to office in 1976 was plagued by internal feuding among his team. White House organization and operations were poorly planned. Carter also failed to develop a coherent policy agenda, which soon generated opposition in Congress. In 1992, Bill Clinton used the time before he took office to plan his program of economic recovery and deficit reduction. But he failed to recognize the need to plan more effectively for his White House staff and to develop orderly procedures and processes for policy deliberations. Not surprisingly, his first six months as president were rocky (in fact, it took almost two years to develop a White House staff system that functioned well). Years later, he would reflect that choosing a number of important White House staff positions only days before he was inaugurated was the "biggest mistake" of his first term.[3]

The importance and impact of presidential transitions has also increased over time. Since FDR, expectations have mounted about early presidential performance. Indeed, evaluation of this performance begins during the transition itself. Media attention to what is occurring (and often to what fails to occur) has increased markedly. No longer are just cabinet appointments the prime preoccupation. Journalists and political pundits focus on a range of matters, and how well presidents-elect and their associates accomplish their tasks is often taken as a harbinger of future presidential competence and expertise. Once in office, early "honeymoon" periods and the first 100 days have become benchmarks for the media and other presidency watchers in their evaluations and assessments of new presidents. Policy initiatives are expected, as are the marks of some success with Congress. Presidents who fail to do well have a lot to dig themselves out of, and presidents-elect who fail to plan well during the transition are unlikely to do well once in office. Recent presidents are at a further disadvantage. Tax and budget issues have been central parts of their political agendas. Yet given the budget cycle under which Congress works, they must immediately have proposals ready, especially if they choose to give the traditional February economic address before a joint session of Congress—roughly a month after inauguration day.

The roughly 75 days that predate the new administration's succession to office can be a crucial window of opportunity for effectively lengthening the 100-day postelection time frame and getting the new administration up and running by inauguration day rather than February or March—perhaps even later—as the clock ticks away. Especially with respect to an administration's policy agenda, while presidents benefit over time from a "cycle of increasing effectiveness," as Paul Light has noted, they also are hindered by a "cycle of decreasing influence."[4] Transitions, therefore, are crucial in taking advantage of the political capital that usually accrues to an administration in its early days.

Getting the resources on hand to assist the president in political efforts and policy deliberations is a central part of the task. The size of the cabinet has increased. John F. Kennedy had nine cabinet-level department positions to fill in 1960, George W. Bush had fourteen (his successor will have fifteen with the recent addition of the Department of Homeland Security). Cabinet departments have also increased in organizational complexity, with increasing numbers of presidential appointees at the top of their organizational hierarchies. As Paul Light has observed, there has been a thickening at the top of most federal departments—more assistant secretaries, undersecretaries, deputy assistant secretaries, and so on—all of whom are presidential appointees and all of whom are now subject to an increasingly lengthy process of personal and financial scrutiny.[5]

But arguably more important in developmental change is the White House staff. Since FDR, the size and complexity of the staff have grown over time; this too complicates the tasks of presidential transitions. The size of the staff has grown from a mere handful of aides to over 500 in the White House Office alone, with some 2,000 more in the larger Executive Office of the President. Most are presidential appointees who are expected to leave office once the new administration takes power. This sets up a monumental personnel task in finding their replacements. It also creates a mammoth organizational dilemma. Few statutory restrictions exist governing how the various units of the White House staff should be organized; for most, even their size is left to the discretion of the new president. This is especially so for the White House Office, the unit closest to the president in physical and functional proximity. Should the president have a chief of staff? And if so, what will be his or her duties and responsibilities? How will domestic and economic policy staffs and the staff of the National Security Council be organized? Will there be cabinet councils linking the policymaking of the White House and cabinet departments? How will media and communications operations be staffed and structured? Are units needed for outreach to interest and other constituency groups? How will the president's lobbying and liaison relations with Congress be undertaken?

These are merely a few of the relevant questions that must be asked and answered. For presidents, they must be resolved quickly, and the transition period is the time for this to occur. As I note in *Presidential Transitions:*

> Unlike a new chief executive officer of a private corporation, presidents do not enter a new office with an old organization still largely intact, with an ongoing level of activity, or with easily accessible data about past activities and performance; the needed management changes cannot be made slowly, at will, and in a more deliberate fashion. Rather, every new president encounters a "corporate headquarters" in which all the top positions are vacant and most offices empty. Basic information no longer exists or has been carted away to await the opening of the predecessor's presidential library.[6]

Analysis of presidential transitions and early presidencies is also important because it is useful not just for scholarly inquiry but also for practical purposes. The historical reconstruction of what happened and the lessons to be drawn are an important base of data for those who are themselves involved in transitions. Very little of what has been termed "institutional memory" gets carried over from one White House to another (witness the difference between the new president and the hypothetical new CEO noted above). Some of this memory can be reconstructed by contacts with persons who occupied those positions or oversaw similar responsibilities in prior administrations. Some have availed themselves of this opportunity well: in the 1988 transition of George H. W. Bush, for example, there was a rich dialogue between many of the new Bush appointees and their counterparts who had served under Ronald Reagan. Where there have been long gaps between administrations of the same party (the twelve years between Carter and Clinton) or where the president-elect and close associates come from outside the Washington Beltway and have fewer links to those in past administrations, the dialogue may be more attenuated.

But whether closely linked or more distant in knowledge and familiarity, scholarly work is useful. It can fill in the gaps, as well as provide a broader base of comparative data and analysis. This occurred in the "friendly" Reagan-to-Bush takeover in 1988: at the Bush Sr. presidential library at Texas A&M University, there is a shelf of books by historians and political scientists that Chase Untermeyer, the head of Bush Sr.'s preelection transition and then its personnel director, immersed himself in. In the 2000 transition, to take but one example, the White House 2001 Project, which Martha Joynt Kumar directed, provided a wealth of material to Clay Johnson, who headed the Bush preelection effort, starting in the summer of 2000, through the transition, and then into the early days of the new administration (material was also provided to the Gore preelection transition group). As she and her project codirector Terry Sullivan note in *The White House World,* a book-length compilation of some of the materials they assembled, their efforts "found a receptive and appreciative audience." And, if I might be permitted a bit of authorial pride, among the items Kumar submitted over the summer were the page proofs of my book *Presidential Transitions*. As Kumar and Sullivan note in their introduction: "John Burke in his *Presidential Transitions: From Politics to Practice* completed the century by updating our understanding of individual transitions, including those of Presidents Carter, Reagan, Bush and Clinton. . . . And, by the accounts of the Bush transition staff, John Burke's book, read in manuscript, was an important source of information about those transitions they were particularly concerned about. . . . Based on our discussions with those involved in the transition planning, the Bush transition staff paid special attention to the Burke manuscript, using it as a source of information on those transitions they had already identified as critical examples for them."[7]

Why Is Analysis of the Bush Transition and Early Presidency Important?

The Bush transition and early presidency is an important subject for research for a number of reasons. First, it had the potential for a disaster in the making given that the election outcome was not settled until December 13, 2000 (following the Supreme Court's decision to halt the Florida recount and, shortly thereafter, Al Gore's concession speech). In the interim, roughly half the time of the normal transition period, from election day to inauguration day, had passed. Bush, moreover, faced a potential crisis of political legitimacy: he was the first president-elect to receive fewer popular votes than his opponent since Benjamin Harrison in 1888 *and* he was the first president since Rutherford B. Hayes in 1876 to attain an electoral vote majority based on contested results.

Yet a disaster did not occur. In fact, Bush and his advisers quickly announced key appointments, in many cases doing so earlier than their Clinton counterparts had eight years previous. By inauguration day, the top levels of the White House staff were in place and the cabinet was awaiting confirmation. During the early months of the new administration, few mistakes or missteps occurred that could be traced to a faulty transition. Bush avoided the problems that had beset Carter and Clinton, and the transition to office resembled that of the successful Reagan effort in 1980. In some respects, it was an even smoother transition than the "friendly takeover" of Bush Sr. in 1988. The story and analysis of what transpired in the preelection period, during the postelection Florida controversy, and after December 13 until inauguration day are important, especially in contrast with the experiences of recent presidential transitions, which not only took place in less trying political climes, but also were often fraught with difficulties and a variety of mistakes and errors.

Second, the Bush transition is an important object of study given its somewhat unique nature. It was not the "friendly takeover" of the White House by a vice president of the same party as the outgoing president. That had occurred with Bush Sr. in 1988 (the last sitting vice president elected to the presidency before that had been Martin Van Buren in 1836).[8] Nor was George W. Bush a political outsider coming to power with more attenuated links to the political folklife and workways of Washington, as had been the case (to varying extent) with fellow governors Carter, Reagan, and Clinton. Bush was a governor, but he was also the son of a former president, had participated in his father's transition to office, and had observed from time to time the inner workings of his father's presidency. Bush thus had the opportunity to reach back into his father's presidency (and, as it turned out, those of Presidents Reagan and Ford) for advice, information, and in some instances nominees and appointees with experience. At the same time, he had the opportunity to meld in his own loyal, disciplined, and agenda-committed team from Austin. Both groups bring their own advantages, although most political outsiders elected to office are tempted to place their trust in the latter (Reagan is perhaps the most noticeable exception). Familial circumstance placed George W. Bush in the position of availing himself more easily of both, but with the challenge of making that combination work.

Third, the Bush transition and subsequent presidency is of interest given the internal organization of the White House staff. An interesting and somewhat unique division of labor was created at the top of the White House among Bush's principal aides: Chief of Staff Andrew Card, Senior Adviser Karl Rove, and Counselor Karen Hughes. Not only did Bush not follow the usual pattern of selecting a strong chief of staff with singular control and responsibility, but concern for political strategy and impact (Rove) and communications and media relations (Hughes) were elevated to the top of the White House hierarchy as well. Other facets of the Bush White House are also of interest. Discipline, loyalty, and teamwork were emphasized in the selection process during the transition and permeated the organizational culture of this White House.

Fourth, Bush's early legislative agenda is notable (whatever one thinks about its substantive merits). He did have the advantage, at least initially, of being the first Republican president since Eisenhower to enjoy a majority (albeit quite narrow) in both houses of Congress (Reagan had only the Senate). The circumstances of his electoral victory, however, could have substantially hampered him. Yet Bush resisted calls for a coalition government, and he proceeded as if the election had delivered him a popular mandate. Questions about the legitimacy of Bush's presidency were also quickly pushed aside. He pursued an ambitious political agenda, resembling that of a new president who had been elected with a substantial popular and electoral vote margin. While the record of immediate success was mixed, his domestic proposals certainly exceeded those of his own father and his approval ratings were higher than those of Bill Clinton at comparable points in their early presidencies.[9] At the same time, Bush once again faced a unique challenge: the May 2001 defection of Vermont senator James Jeffords from the Republican Party (GOP) in a Senate that was then evenly divided fifty-fifty and Jeffords's decision, now as an independent, to caucus with the Democrats and give them Senate control in June. No other modern president has had their party lose its control of a house of Congress in such a manner. And it occurred at a critical point early in the Bush presidency.[10]

Finally, analysis of the Bush transition and early administration is important in another very important way. The events of September 11, 2001, presented a challenge unique to any recent presidency so early in its tenure. Conventional wisdom suggests that it caused a transformation in this presidency and in this president. At some level, this is undoubtedly true, and it is a topic I will explore. But it is also important to consider how what had transpired before—during the transition and before September 11—affected what occurred after. Was there a "new Bush" and a new Bush presidency? If so, transitions may be less consequential in the long run (at least) than I have argued. Or, did the Bush transition and early presidency have an impact upon how the administration responded to this challenge? The Bush presidency before and after September 11 thus offers an important test of the causal impact and significance of presidential transitions in the long run. It is an important question that I shall explore.

Outline of the Book

Chapters 2 and 3 explore the Bush transition up through inauguration day. Chapter 2 explores the transition planning that took place in the preelection period and the efforts that were under way, often behind the scenes, from election day through the final resolution of the Florida controversy by the Supreme Court and Al Gore's concession on December 13, 2000. Chapter 3 focuses on events after that date, particularly selection of the cabinet and the organization and appointment of a White House staff. Chapter 3 also examines another important set of tasks for a presidential transition: moving from campaign promises to a more concrete and tailored policy agenda, developing a political strategy, and building bridges and creating support with Congress, constituency groups, and the American public. The next three chapters examine the unfolding of the early Bush presidency. Chapter 4 looks at the Bush team in office, particularly the unique division of labor among Bush's top aides—Andrew Card, Karl Rove, and Karen Hughes—as well as the impact of the cabinet and the cabinet councils. Chapter 5 focuses on President Bush, particularly his distinct decisionmaking and leadership styles and their relationship to the staff arrangements and decision processes of his presidency. Chapter 6 explores the early Bush policy agenda, its strategic implications, and its policy consequences. Chapter 7 examines the post–September 11 Bush presidency, through 2003, both in its continuities with what had transpired earlier and in the new challenges it faced. The concluding chapter offers lessons from the Bush transition and presidency, especially in comparison with its recent predecessors.

Notes

1. Burke, *Presidential Transitions.* For earlier twentieth-century transitions, through 1952, see Henry, *Presidential Transitions.* Other sources on transitions include Brauer, *Presidential Transitions* (Eisenhower through Reagan); Pfiffner, *The Strategic Presidency;* Jones, *Passages to the Presidency;* Felzenberg, *The Keys to a Successful Transition;* Abshire, *Report to the President-Elect 2000;* and Kumar and Sullivan, *The White House World.*

2. Pfiffner, *The Strategic Presidency.* The phrase comes from the subtitle of the book.

3. Drew, *Whatever It Takes,* p. 257.

4. Light, *The President's Agenda,* pp. 36–37.

5. Light, *Thickening Government.*

6. Burke, *Presidential Transitions,* p. 395.

7. Kumar and Sullivan, *The White House World,* pp. xvi, xiii–xiv.

8. Had Vice President Al Gore prevailed in the Florida recount, it would have been a case parallel to that of Bush Sr., which would have provided some interesting basis of comparative analysis. One might argue that friendly takeovers might also be extended to include members of Congress or other Washington-based officials who are elected president and continue their party's control of the White House. Interestingly, there are none among modern presidents (FDR and his successors); and for the whole of the twentieth century, there are only two cases where cabinet members of the outgoing administration were elected (Taft in 1908 and Hoover in 1928), and no cases where members of Congress were elected.

9. From February through early September, Clinton's Gallup poll "presidential approval" rating was at its highest (59 percent) in early March, and at its lowest (37 percent) in early June. For Bush, the highest rating was 62 percent, in late April, and the lowest was 51 percent, right before September 11. Although the surveys for each were undertaken on different dates, Bush's approval ratings were all higher than Clinton's during similar time periods. See www.gallup.com.

10. Some elected presidents in their first terms have, of course, found themselves facing a Congress controlled by the other party: in the twentieth century, Nixon in 1969 (both Senate and House), Bush Sr. in 1989 (both Senate and House), and Reagan in 1981 (House but not Senate). During his first term in office, Eisenhower also faced a Senate divided between forty-seven Republicans, forty-eight Democrats, and one independent, Senator Wayne Morse of Oregon. Morse had been a Republican, but he still chose to cast his vote with the GOP when the Senate was organized in January. According to the account provided by the Senate Historian's Office at the official U.S. Senate website, "Rebuffed by his colleagues at the [1952] Republican National Convention, he cast an absentee ballot for Adlai Stevenson, the 1952 Democratic presi-

dential candidate. At that time, Morse resigned from the Republican party and started campaigning for Stevenson. When the 83rd Congress commenced in 1953, Morse listed himself as an independent. As the only third-party member on the Senate floor, he did not know where to sit, and set up a folding chair in the aisle between the Republican and Democratic sections. Eventually, he settled on the Republican side of the aisle. On February 17, 1955, Morse joined the Democratic party, and helped the Democrats take control of the Senate." Both in January 2001 and January 1953, the vice president cast the tie-breaking vote to organize the Senate with his and the president's party in control. See www.senate.gov.

2

Starting Early

At one level, George W. Bush's transition to the presidency was unique and without much precedent as a guide. Unlike the situation facing his modern predecessors, Bush's "official" postelection transition did not begin until December 14, 2000 (the day after Vice President Al Gore's concession speech), when the General Services Administration (GSA), the agency in charge of the federal government's transition funds and logistics, finally handed over the keys to transition headquarters. Roughly half the time of a normal transition had been lost as the controversy over the Florida vote dragged on.

The reality, of course, was that transition planning had been well under way in the Bush camp. Richard Cheney, Bush's vice-presidential candidate, was at the helm of a not-quite-official (but clearly operational) Bush transition since the day after the election, and he would open a privately funded transition headquarters on November 27, the day after Florida secretary of state Katherine Harris "certified" Bush's victory. Andrew Card had also operated as de facto chief of staff since election day (his appointment—as well as several others—would be announced on November 27 following certification). And Governor Bush himself faced the delicate task of appearing to be the victor but without presuming quite yet to being president-elect.[1]

But here too modern presidential history presented no guide. Throughout the period from November 8 through December 13, Bush and his advisers faced the unique challenge of preparing for a new presidency but within their own context of an unsettled election outcome. The nearest historical reference was the far reach of the Rutherford Hayes and Samuel Tilden contest in 1876, when Hayes won the presidency by the exact number of electoral votes needed and following a challenge of the election outcome in three states (one of which was Florida).[2] But even that election offered little in the way of lessons. There was little in the way of a White House staff to organize and fill, and the cabinet was much smaller. Nor was much expected in the way of a legislative agenda. There was no expectation of a "100 days" legislative

11

benchmark (this would come with Franklin Delano Roosevelt [FDR]). Congress and the political parties ruled the political day to a greater extent than would be the case from FDR on.

Yet despite the seeming uniqueness of its situation, recent presidential history would come strongly into play for Bush and his associates. The Bush transition offers the best example to date of an effort that was aware of the experiences of prior transitions, recognized the value of the lessons to be learned, and generally was prepared to reap the positive benefits of its predecessors' experiences but avoid the pitfalls.

Before November

As has been the case for all transitions since 1976, Bush began early to plan for his presidency. He delegated the job to Clay Johnson, a longtime friend. Both Bush and Johnson had attended Phillips Academy Andover and later roomed together at Yale.[3] In the summer of 1994, still campaigning for governor, Bush told his old friend that he believed he might win and wanted Johnson to oversee appointments to state boards and commissions. "I want someone whose primary interest is me—George W. Bush," he told him, "who doesn't hope to parlay this into something and isn't trying to curry favor with this one and that one. . . . I'll take care of the politics," Bush emphasized. "You go find the best people."[4]

By 1999, Johnson was serving as Bush's appointments director, advising the governor on over 4,000 state positions. In the spring, when he announced his candidacy for president, Bush moved his then–chief of staff, Joseph Allbaugh, over to his campaign and appointed Johnson to replace him. But Bush also had an additional job for Johnson: he asked him to think about planning for a possible Bush presidency.[5] "I would like you to figure out what we need to do starting the day after the election," Bush told him. "Come up with a plan—talk to people who have done this before, read what you can get your hands on, confer with people, pick their brains and come up with a plan."[6] At a May 2, 2001, panel discussion at Harvard's Kennedy School of Government on the Bush transition, Johnson recalled that George W. Bush, "as was his custom," had charged him to "put together a plan for the transition; what should our goals be; how do we organize; how do we accomplish those goals and so forth."[7]

Bush's preparation was early but not unique among his recent predecessors. Jimmy Carter's effort began in the spring of 1976 when he asked a young aide, Jack Watson, to begin planning for his presidency. Although some prior presidential candidates had done some preparation before election day, Carter was the first to invest significant staff resources and money in the effort. The practice of significant preelection planning continued under Reagan, Bush Sr., and Clinton.

Although George W. Bush broke the record for beginning early, an early start was not the only important feature of his preelection effort. Bush's selection of Johnson to undertake the task was also important. As a longtime friend and associate of Bush, Johnson knew his principal. Questions about how Bush made decisions, delegated authority, dealt with staff, digested information, and organized his workday were familiar territory for Johnson. So, too, with what Bush valued in appointees.

As has been the case for all preelection efforts beginning with Carter's in 1976, efforts have been made to keep any preelection planning away from the campaign war room, lest the latter become preoccupied with future spoils rather than the electoral task at hand. So too with the Bush effort in 2000. As Johnson would later reflect: "Campaign leaders should not be in charge of the [preelection] transition. Campaigns are about winning while transitions are about preparing to govern. Campaign leaders are unlikely to have any time to work on the transition before the election as is necessary."[8] Yet Johnson took steps to keep the Bush campaign team—Karl Rove, Karen Hughes, Joe Allbaugh and Don Evans—informed. "Starting about maybe the spring or early summer of 2000, I sat down with them and told them what my thinking was and kind of what I thought we needed to do before the election. . . . And I wanted them to be aware of it."[9]

That Johnson could easily communicate with the top levels of the campaign team and was himself a member of the Bush inner circle brought an element of trust. Individuals and groups who might otherwise be concerned about who had the candidate's ear presidency-wise or might have a hand in future jobs after election day would be reassured. Like Edwin Meese (who oversaw preelection transition planning for Reagan in 1980) and Chase Untermeyer (who was Johnson's counterpart in 1988 for Bush Sr.), Johnson was already a known commodity and valued member of the candidate's team. His selection for the task was not likely to generate jealousy and infighting. By contrast, in 1976, although Jack Watson had worked for Carter in a number of capacities, he was only indirectly connected to the Carter inner circle and his efforts almost immediately generated tensions with the Carter campaign staff. So too with Bill Clinton's selection of Mickey Kantor in 1992. In both cases, conflicts would spill over into the postelection period, and in Carter's case even into his early administration.

Johnson, moreover, proceeded with discretion. There was little media attention about his work until shortly before election day. Again, the Bush preelection effort was in contrast to those of 1976 and 1992, when newspaper stories reported on the operations of the preelection planners, much to the consternation of their campaign war rooms. For Karl Rove, Bush's chief campaign strategist, Johnson's activities presented no problem and his discretion was welcomed: he was "separate and apart" from the campaign, but this was desired. "We necessarily wanted it to be so. We also wanted it be very low visibility, which it was. . . . Clay worked for months before anybody discovered him."[10]

Johnson did his homework. He immersed himself in the literature on past transitions and sought to learn their lessons, especially so that past mistakes would not be repeated. Johnson was particularly cognizant of the difficulties that Clinton had encountered in 1992. "I think the Clinton administration transition did not go particularly well, I think by everybody's admission, even the Clinton people," he later recalled.[11]

Johnson operated on his own through 1999 and into 2000, but Bush would periodically oversee and direct his efforts. "Every couple of months [I would] chat with the governor for a little bit of time and tell him what I was doing," Johnson would later recall. Bush would then tell him: "You ought to call this guy or that guy or this person." So Bush provided direction? "Yes. He said be sure to call Jim Baker [a former secretary of state and treasury and White House chief of staff]. Be sure to call George Shultz [a former secretary of state, treasury, and labor]. Be sure to do this and that." Often Bush's instructions and queries were more detailed: "I would pay more attention to this person than that person. . . . One of the things I wonder about is how do you organize a White House? . . . How do you make sure this cabinet department and that cabinet department don't get in conflict with each other?" According to Johnson, "There were things that [Bush] would wonder about, about as president how do you prevent this from happening or make sure that happens. As I visited with people I would inquire about or raise those kinds of issues."[12]

Johnson began to contact a range of former Bush Sr. and Reagan administration officials:

> I went out to Palo Alto [to meet with George Shultz] and he introduced me to a bunch of his Hoover [Institution] folks who had been involved in the Bush and or Reagan administrations. I picked some of their brains. I visited with Condi Rice when I was out there. I went over to Houston to visit with Jim Baker. I visited with Ed Meese and Ed Fuelner [head of the Heritage Foundation in Washington].

Baker and Shultz were particularly influential sources of advice:

> But most importantly with Jim Baker and George Shultz: it was ten key things to be looking for in setting up a White House; and also the kinds of people to be looking for in a secretary of state or a secretary of defense. Qualities to look for and how they all relate to each other and the role of cabinet secretaries versus the [national] security adviser.

These meetings occurred "before Dick Cheney was chosen [as vice-presidential candidate] and definitely before Andy Card was chosen [as chief of staff]." But Cheney and Card also "brought firsthand knowledge too. And they just dittoed a whole lot of the input that I had gotten separately and earlier from Shultz and Baker and the like. So we had an abundance of wise counsel."[13]

How a successful transition might be organized was also part of Johnson's effort during this period. He met with "a number of people to understand what some of the big issues are in a transition and how do you try to deal with them, how do you try to prevent the problems from rearing their ugly head and take advantage of the opportunities that you have during the seventy-some days of a typical transition."[14]

Two members of the 1988 Bush transition and, later, the Bush Sr. administration were important sources of knowledge: Chase Untermeyer, who directed (like Johnson) its preelection planning and later headed up the transition personnel operation and then the White House personnel unit (both of which Johnson would also do), and C. Boyden Gray, who became the 1988 transition's legal counsel and then Bush Sr.'s White House legal counsel. According to Johnson, "Chase helped us set up the personnel operation in Austin when the governor came in 1995 and we appointed Chase to the state board of education. So I spent a lot of time with Chase off and on." So too with Boyden Gray: "I visited with Boyden at the convention at Philadelphia, about the clearance operation, about the White House counsel, and what kind of person to be looking for White House counsel." Johnson also met with Pendleton James, his counterpart in the 1980 Reagan preelection transition, who also became the Reagan White House personnel director.[15] These three figures—James, Untermeyer, and Gray—had played central roles not only in their respective preelection planning efforts, but they also held central positions during these earlier postelection transitions and, later, on the White House staff: personnel director and legal counsel, both critical to the success of a smooth appointment and vetting process.

Although Johnson's preelection work involved a range of activities, personnel planning was perhaps one of the most important. The latter included an assessment of types of backgrounds that might be well suited for particular positions, as well as the assembling of the names of potential nominees:

> I talked to policy people and senior officials from previous administrations about the types of people we should be looking at for the different cabinet secretary positions and specific people we might consider. I did not contact anyone to express our interest or determine theirs, but I collected about 200 names with which to begin the discussions with the president- and vice president-elect when appropriate.[16]

Preparation before election day, in Johnson's view, was essential:

> The primary things that we tried to do based on everything we read and people we had talked to was that we wanted to prepare to make a lot of important personnel decisions very, very quickly. There was no way that the president or vice president were going to be inclined to sit down prior to the election and make cabinet secretary decisions because they were going to be

actively involved in the campaign. But there was work we could do in identifying the kinds of qualities, based on people who had been there before, the
kinds of qualities we should be looking for. . . . And then if we were going
to have ten or fifteen names to start thinking about . . . who are those ten or
fifteen names?[17]

In August, Johnson traveled to Wyoming to meet with Dick Cheney. It
was a visit that was particularly important, because, by that time, not only had
Cheney been picked as the vice-presidential candidate, but Bush had made the
decision that Cheney would head up transition operations after election day:

> I had been collecting those names and so I was picking Dick Cheney's brain
> about people. Thinking about people for this and that and so forth, getting
> his reaction to the names that had been suggested so far. So we did a little
> brain storming about names, a little about types of people to be looking for
> and about how to organize a transition. All that was after the convention,
> after he had been selected. Mid or late August.[18]

Johnson also was in contact with Martha Joynt Kumar, who headed the
White House 2001 Project, a group of scholars who prepared essays on tran-
sition-related topics and extensive analyses of the principal White House
offices. Kumar and her associates also undertook over seventy-eight interviews with former White House officials. As Johnson recalled:

> In the summer or late spring of 2000, Martha Kumar made contact with me
> or somebody did. So she made me aware of what they were doing and as
> they started compiling their interviews, she would feed me drafts of some of
> the material as quickly as they had it. As far as institutional memory, that
> was helpful to get people's reflections on what worked and didn't work in
> presidential personnel or the counsel's office or some other White House
> office. Some of that wasn't available until the fall. But it was very helpful
> when we got it.[19]

Learning Lessons, Setting Goals

Johnson learned the lessons of prior transitions, especially so that past mistakes would not be repeated. By June 2000, Johnson had developed a list of
tasks and priorities that were needed for a successful Bush transition. These
were then honed in August following discussions with Cheney:

- Pick a chief of staff early, preferably before election day.
- Try to identify cabinet secretaries by mid-December, but also recognize that it is more important to select senior White House staff by this
  time.
- Proceed with hiring based on the new administration's policy priorities.

- Identify the qualities needed for key positions and identify prospective candidates before opening up discussions with particular individuals, especially in order to counterbalance the political pressure to make certain appointments.
- Brief cabinet nominees on "department priorities, issues, and facts, and the campaign promises related to each."
- Develop a clear set of policy goals, "otherwise you will have your goals set for you."
- Develop a 20-day, 100-day, and 180-day preliminary schedule for the president.
- Prepare to present the administration's budget proposal by mid-February.
- Review executive orders and other regulatory matters requiring immediate attention.
- Recognize that Congress and career executives pay attention to how a new administration reaches out to and communicates with them.
- Take steps to reach out to Congress and a variety of constituency groups: "We especially wanted to establish a strong working relationship with Congress."
- Recognize that the public is attentive to how the president-elect acts prior to inauguration day, as this will begin to indicate what kind of president he will be.
- "Clearly communicate that we are aggressively preparing to govern, that we are operating without hubris or triumphant partisanship, that we are experienced and not neophytes."[20]

By the end of summer, Johnson had also settled on a number of organizational and housekeeping steps that needed to be taken before election day to ensure a smooth transition:

1. Creating a postelection website for job applications and for general information on the Bush transition. Commitments were made for the software in August. Johnson would later estimate that some 95 percent of job applications were received online. "It made a huge difference. We had been in the people-picking business not in the data-entry business as a result of that."[21]
2. Establishing a budget for the transition, estimated at $8.5 million, about what the Clinton transition had spent in 1992. This figure was $4 million over the federal allocation, so efforts were also undertaken to prepare a direct-mail campaign to Bush donors to cover the additional costs.
3. Drafting of letters and e-mails that might be used after election day to contact supporters, job seekers, members of Congress, and others,

especially concerning how to apply for positions or make recommendations on behalf of others.

4. Deciding that "we wanted only small teams to prepare briefing books for, and interact with, each cabinet department rather than assemble large 'transition teams.'"[22]

A Unique Case: A Robust Mandate but Without Contention

Johnson's close and direct connection to Bush was especially beneficial in the way that it allowed him to proceed on a variety of fronts in preparing for a possible Bush presidency. His mandate was broad and encompassed not just organizing a personnel process (the focus of the preelection planning in 1980 and 1988), but it also involved such activities as discussions with Bush about a variety of matters, contacts with former transition and administration principals, and discussions (but not selection) of possible nominees to a variety of positions. That Johnson pulled it off with a minimum of tension and publicity suggests, first, that a more ambitious and successful preelection operation is possible. It is the first such case: the 1980 and 1988 preelection efforts were largely limited to setting up a personnel operation. The 1976 and 1992 efforts, which are generally regarded as less successful by comparison, were more ambitious in scope. Second, the fact that Johnson was closely connected to Bush both as someone who knew him as an executive and decisionmaker *and* that he had the confidence of others in the Bush inner circle and campaign may have generated a degree of trust, permitting a great deal of latitude and a more robust mandate than occurred in 1976 or in 1992.

Early Decisions Before Election Day

Johnson's close relationship to then-candidate Bush also enabled him to make sure that Bush was prepared to put some of the lessons he had learned into practice. Bush heeded his counsel. Most important, the selection of Andrew Card as chief of staff was settled before election day. As well, the decision was made right after the Republican convention that Cheney would serve as the transition's chairman presuming a Bush victory.[23] Both Card and Cheney came well equipped for the task at hand. Both had served in key White House positions, both had headed cabinet departments, and both had been in charge of outgoing transitions for the administrations in which they served (Cheney for Ford in 1976, Card for Bush Sr. in 1992). Clay Johnson's postelection appointment as executive director of the transition rounded out the top team. Their collective knowledge and experience surpassed that of their counterparts in earlier transitions: Jack Watson and Hamilton Jordan in 1976, Ed Meese in 1980, Robert Teeter and Craig Fuller in 1988, and Warren Christopher and Vernon Jordan in 1992.

The selection of Cheney to head the postelection transition and Johnson to serve as its executive director (with major duties in the appointments process) also avoided a major problem that beset the Clinton transition. In 1992, Clinton named Warren Christopher (a prominent Los Angeles lawyer who had served in the Kennedy, Johnson, and Carter administrations) as transition director, and Governor Richard Riley of South Carolina as the head of its appointment talent search. Yet both were soon tapped to head cabinet-level departments—Christopher as secretary of state and Riley as secretary of education—leading them to focus a good part of their attention on preparing for their confirmation hearings and assuming their offices after inauguration day. With Cheney and Johnson occupying key positions in Bush's 2000 transition, by contrast, their efforts focused on the job at hand. Cheney needed little preparation to assume the vice presidency, while Johnson's position neatly tracked into his postinaugural duties as director of the White House personnel office.

Card's selection as chief of staff before election day was especially crucial. As Johnson later recalled:

> One of the primary things we did in the transition—and has borne fruit during the first 100 days—we got the president to do what most people running for the presidency do not want to do [and that is] to decide who their chief of staff is to be and ask him to be the chief of staff before the election. It was critically important that Andy Card had been asked and accepted and was on the ground prior to the election and beginning to have conversations with Governor Bush.[24]

During Johnson's periodic conferences with Bush, Bush sometimes reflected on the jobs he might have to fill if he were elected. Bush was especially clear about what kind of chief of staff he wanted and it was his call that led to Card's selection as chief of staff. As Johnson observes:

> [Bush] did not want someone to be chief of staff who was over-territorial, or was a control freak, or felt like they had to control the content or the recommendations that flowed to the president. He wanted somebody who was more a facilitator, an orchestrator, and a tie breaker; as they say an honest broker. . . . The president's knowledge about the way he likes to work led him to choose Andy Card.[25]

Bush's own gubernatorial experiences and practices, as well as lessons drawn from his father's presidency, were also factors. As governor, Bush never called his chief of staff "chief of staff":

> He called him an executive assistant for that reason. So he wanted somebody who was comfortable with that role and Andy is very much that way. And the president knew that and had worked around him enough to know that that was the kind of person he was. It was totally the president's decision. I didn't know Andy and I didn't recommend him to the president. The president knew him. . . . The vice president knew him and thought highly of Andy.[26]

Card's selection and the time he was selected were very crucial:

> I think the selection of Andy Card was very important. Not only him as a
> person but when he was selected. And I think a lot of the study [of transi-
> tions] indicated the importance of that. So I was pretty insistent with the
> president [then still a candidate] that he needed to do that. Whoever it was—
> he could pick whoever—I didn't have anything to do with that—he had a
> better sense of who he could work with as chief of staff and who he wanted
> as chief of staff and knew a lot more people than I did, but I was pretty insis-
> tent that it had to be before the election. And the selection of Andy was great
> and when he was selected was great. Those had huge, huge benefits to the
> start of this administration.[27]

Initially, Bush was reluctant to think about the job of chief of staff when
Johnson broached the subject in the summer of 2000, particularly emphasizing
to Bush the importance of having a senior White House staff in place "within
days after the election; and the only way you you're going to do that is to have
your chief of staff committed to be your chief of staff before the election."
Bush demurred, telling him, "God dang, I'm running for office, I can't." But
he then added, "Well, we'll talk about it later." In September, Johnson brought
the matter up again and Bush was more receptive; so receptive in fact that by
early October he had settled on Card and Card had accepted the position. Card
"was on the ground before the election and began to have conversations with
people about staff. And that was so very important. I read about the Clinton
transition, and Mack McLarty was not on board until mid-December. Well, by
mid-December, Andy already had the senior staff done."[28]

According to Hughes, Bush told her that he was thinking of asking Card
to serve as chief of staff on the day of his third and final debate with Al Gore.
"He's a great guy, a team player; he's fair and everyone respects him. He
knows Washington and how the White House works," Bush explained to her.
But Bush then went on to signal that Hughes too would have an important
place in his White House should he win: "I want you involved in everything
and I want you to have direct access to me."[29]

By election day, the Bush camp was well prepared to begin a transition
to the presidency. Indeed, of all modern presidencies, it was best poised to hit
the ground running with a postelection transition.

Waiting on Florida: A Transition
Not Quite a Transition

Election night was a roller coaster of events for both the Bush and Gore
camps. Shortly before 8:00 P.M., the networks declared Florida for Gore, and
given the electoral votes each candidate was projected to win, it looked

unlikely that Bush could arrive at the magic number of 270. However, the exit polling on which the Florida call had been made proved faulty and, two hours later, Florida was subtracted from the Gore column. At 2:16 A.M., Fox News declared Florida for Bush; the other networks quickly followed.[30] Based on the Florida vote, Bush had a bare majority of the electoral votes needed to make him president. Shortly thereafter, Gore called Bush to concede and then proceeded by motorcade to the hall in Nashville where he was to address his waiting supporters. Yet while he was en route, staffers notified him that the raw vote totals had narrowed (the exit polling had again been faulty), and Gore once again called Bush, now to tell him that he was not conceding.

By early morning the vote totals narrowed to 1,784 in Bush's favor, a number that triggered a recount (but not necessarily a hand recount) under Florida election law. As well, reports began to surface of confusing ballots in Palm Beach County, where 3,500 Gore voters might have mistakenly voted for Pat Buchanan, the presidential candidate of the Reform Party. Questions were also raised about 19,000 spoiled ballots, on which voters had voted twice for a presidential candidate.

With Florida's vote in dispute, the Gore campaign immediately chartered a plane from Nashville to Florida, carrying seventy-five lawyers and political advisers, to begin contesting the results.[31] Gore also sent Warren Christopher, Clinton's former secretary of state, to Florida to head up efforts to look into voting irregularities; he was later joined by campaign chairman William Daley (brother of Chicago mayor Richard M. Daley, son of former Chicago mayor Richard J. Daley) and Clinton's former secretary of commerce. The Bush campaign, in turn, dispatched campaign chairman Don Evans to Florida, but then bolstered their efforts by sending in James Baker, a former secretary of state and treasury and White House chief of staff. The heavy hitters had arrived.

By the end of the week, the nation's attention was riveted on Florida. By Friday, the machine recount had Bush's margin at a mere 327 votes. But the Gore camp demanded hand recounts in several Florida counties. The recount process would continue off and on over the next several weeks, a period marked by litigation, new questions about the validity of absentee ballots and ballots sent from overseas by military personnel, and a delay in the deadline for certifying votes ordered by the Florida Supreme Court. Throughout the period, however, Bush's narrow lead held.

The two principals carried on differently during this period. On Thursday, November 9, Roy Neel (Gore's transition head) announced that all transition planning by the Gore camp had been suspended.[32] Al Gore, for his part, was portrayed as deeply involved in the Florida controversy, in constant touch with his lieutenants by computer, Palm Pilots, and telephone. By contrast, Bush was more detached from the events in the Florida. He went about gubernatorial business and, more important, continued with aides to plan for a new administration.

The day after the election, reports surfaced in the press indicating that Bush's transition planning was under way in Austin. Cheney was reported to be heading up the transition team. And Bush aides reportedly said that he was prepared to name Colin Powell as secretary of state and Andrew Card as his chief of staff. On November 10, Bush spent part of the day with Card. Bush also had lunch with Cheney and Lieutenant Governor Rick Perry, who would face a transition of his own should Bush win.

Reporters were also invited to witness an Oval Office–like setting where Bush was seated with Cheney, Condoleezza Rice, economic adviser Larry Lindsey, and Card. Bush told them: "I understand that there are still votes to be counted, but I am in the process of planning, in a responsible way, a potential administration. . . . There have been a series of ongoing meetings that [Cheney] and I have had on a variety of subjects, so that should the verdict that has been announced be confirmed, we'll be ready . . . to assume office and be prepared to lead."[33]

The mantra in the Gore camp about what was transpiring in Austin was that Bush was being "presumptuous." The strongest words come from campaign chairman William Daley, who criticized transition planning under way in Austin: "I believe that their actions to try to presumptively crown themselves the victors, to try to put in place a transition runs the risk of dividing the American people and creating a sense of confusion." Roy Neel also took the Bush transition effort to task: "It is mind-boggling to me that they would be so presumptuous."[34] They were joined by an editorial in the *Washington Post,* which made similar criticisms: "The Bush campaign shouldn't be leaking purported news about its transition plans and otherwise giving the impression of measuring for new curtains in the Oval Office."[35]

But Bush and his associates were not deterred and continued to plan for his presidency, albeit with a good measure of circumspection. Although it was clear that work was under way, the Bush team carefully avoided claiming that Bush was indeed the president-elect, lest it politically backfire. At the same time, they also recognized that some transition planning needed to proceed lest valuable time be lost.

The time frame allowed Bush and his associates to further narrow their list of choices, especially for cabinet positions. Some names had surfaced before election day (some 200 or so by Clay Johnson's recollection). The next few weeks allowed them to further narrow their list of potential nominees. This effort proved useful, according to Johnson, because once Florida was settled, "We were able to get into the meat of some of these [cabinet] secretary decisions because there was something on the blackboard; there was not an empty blackboard."[36]

Card was also at work organizing and staffing the Bush White House. According to Johnson, Card was "busy with people about their interests and what kind of role they might want to have in the White House. He was also thinking about how he wanted to structure the presidency. And so he was doing that during Florida."[37]

A More Public Transition: After Certification

Following Bush's certification as the winner of the Florida vote (by a margin of 253 votes)[38] by the Florida secretary of state's office, which had been delayed by the Florida Supreme Court until November 26, the Bush transition became more open in its efforts and took on more the appearance of a traditional transition. The legal challenges raised by the Gore camp, however, would continue. And it would set in motion a complex legal battle that would culminate with the U.S. Supreme Court's historic decision in Bush's favor on December 12 and Gore's concession on December 13.[39]

But certification did offer an opportunity for the Bush camp to move forward and also to more firmly entrench the perception of Bush as the presumptive president-elect. Still, an element of caution prevailed. In the view of one Bush adviser: "What you're balancing here is a very imperative need to move forward with the process of governing while avoiding any sense of presumption. . . . We're dealing with an extraordinary set of circumstances that have not been dealt with in this country in more than a century. So you have to move at a pace and with a demeanor that is different from all recent transitions."[40]

At 9:00 P.M. on the evening of the vote certification, Bush addressed the nation from the state capitol in Austin. "Now that the votes are counted, it is time for the votes to count," Bush stated. Pledging to "work to unite our great land," Bush noted that "the election was close but tonight after a count, a recount, and yet another recount, Secretary Cheney and I are honored to have won the state of Florida, which gives us the needed electoral votes to win the election." Bush also added, "I respectfully ask" that Gore reconsider further contesting the Florida results.

Bush took the opportunity to more firmly establish his position as president-elect, adding that he would begin "preparing to serve as president." He announced that Cheney would direct the transition's operation in Washington and that Card had been selected as his chief of staff (both, of course, were already well at work at their designated tasks). Cheney, he said, had been asked to "work with President Clinton's administration to open a transition office in Washington." Bush also briefly sketched out a legislative agenda including education reform, social security reform, Medicare reform and a prescription drug benefit for seniors, and lower taxes.

But Cheney's efforts to move operations into the federal facility in Washington, D.C., designated for the presidential transition and to receive federal funding were quickly denied by the General Services Administration, which oversees transition operations.[41] Before election day both campaigns had been in contact with the GSA to ensure a smooth postelection operation. In the view of June Huber, director of presidential transition support at the GSA, "Both sides are doing a pretty good job of preplanning."[42] According to another report, by the end of October, "hundreds of desks are in place, the computers are ready, the software they each intend to use has been installed and the telephones have dial tones."[43] The GSA also set up an Internet site to provide links to telephone directories, maps, and relocation information. "Technology is going to make a difference on how the transition operates," Huber confidently predicted a few days before the election. "Everything will happen faster."[44]

Yet Florida threw a wrench into the works: the certification of a Bush victory had not settled the issue of who had won Florida's crucial electoral votes, at least in the eyes of the federal government. The Gore camp's legal challenges remained. On the evening of the vote certification, Beth Newberger of the GSA announced, "There is not an apparent winner and the outcome is unclear."

At 4:00 P.M. on Monday, November 27, Cheney held a press conference. He stressed the need for a Bush transition to begin, and he was critical of the Clinton administration for withholding $5.3 million in federal funds. In his view, the GSA's announcement to that effect was "regrettable." He also criticized Gore for contesting the election: "That is unfortunate, in light of the penalty that may have to be paid at some future date if the next administration is not allowed to prepare to take the reins of government."[45]

Cheney noted that he, Bush, and other advisers had already undertaken discussions of potential cabinet nominees and that some appointments might be announced even before the courts were finished with their work. "We believe it is time to get on with the business of organizing the new administration." He also revealed that Clay Johnson would serve as executive director of the transition and that Ari Fleischer would be press spokesperson.[46] On Tuesday, November 28, Bush held another well-publicized meeting with Card on transition planning, while Cheney, appearing on NBC's "Today Show," emphasized that the Bush team is "rapidly running out of time to put together that new administration."[47]

The issue of who had decided not to have the GSA "recognize" the validity of the Bush transition immediately captured media attention and figured into the ongoing wrangle over the Florida vote. According to one story in the *Washington Times,* the order did not come from the GSA's administrator, David J. Barram, but from White House Chief of Staff John Podesta. According to a Podesta memo, the GSA and other federal agencies were ordered not to proceed with any transition activities "until the time when the election is decided. . . . Because of the uncertainty over election results, no president-elect has been identified to receive federal funds and assistance under the Presidential Transition Act of 1963. . . . Until a president-elect is clearly identified, therefore, no transition assistance as contemplated under the Transition Act is available."[48] Another account noted that the Clinton administration was merely following Congress's intent. According to one administration official, congressional debate during passage of the act indicated that "lawmakers were concerned that the head of the GSA, with the authority to disburse transition money, would wield too much power in deciding who would be president. That led to language that says 'when the election is in doubt, the administrator must wait until it is clear' who has won."[49] President Clinton also weighed in on the controversy. At a cabinet meeting on Monday, November 27, he said that he had not been involved in the decision made by the GSA and, that if it were up to him, he would offer transition aid to both Bush and Gore.[50]

The dispute fueled antipathies, present and past. In the view of one Bush adviser, "If the Clinton administration chooses that course, there are other options we'll pursue. . . . If the administration wants to play politics, that's entirely their prerogative."[51] At his November 27 press conference, Cheney pointedly announced that Card had tried to contact Podesta, but his phone call was never returned. Podesta told reporters the next day that Card had called at 3:08 P.M., at a time when Podesta was shown live on television sitting at a cabinet meeting. Podesta tried to call Card back but only got his answering machine.

For Clinton's aides, it was payback time for their own 1992 transition difficulties: "It is clear that in addition to the law, some old grudges are playing out. Mr. Clinton's aides bitterly maintain that the administration of Mr. Bush's father did little to help the incoming Clinton team at the end of 1992, after a hard-fought campaign. They arrived, they say, to a White House lacking even basic office supplies," an article in the *New York Times* noted. John Podesta ordered every department to prepare briefing books, but the briefings, according to one Clinton aide, "are more than we ever got in 1992." The Gore camp also got in their licks. According to Gore's transition chief, Roy Neel, "We haven't been so presumptuous as to ask for the keys until the thing is finally decided."[52]

Although Cheney's efforts were rebuffed by the Clinton administration, a Bush transition proceeded nonetheless. At his November 27 press conference, Cheney also announced that the Bush team would set up their own transition office near Washington and raise private funds for the transition.[53] Two days later, the "Bush-Cheney Presidential Transition Foundation, Inc." had leased 21,000 square feet of office space in McLean, Virginia. By Thursday, November 30, the rudiments of a transition operation had begun; fifteen paid staffers were at work plus some fifty volunteers. Ten of those staff members, including Clay Johnson, had flown quickly up from Austin. On December 3, the announcement was made that Karl Rove, Bush's chief political adviser and strategist, would be joining them. On December 4, the transition website (www.bushcheneytransition.com) was up and running, with job information and downloadable personnel forms.

The centerpiece of the new headquarters the first couple of days was a Formica table staffed by women collecting resumes. "Applicants must sign in on a white pad, give their name, Social Security number, address, phone number, then drop their resumes. The women file them in one of two plastic bins—one for those interested in getting paid for their labor, the other for those content with volunteer work."[54]

The White House also began to soften its position a bit, but in a way that indicated that Gore was not out of the game, that two transitions were under way, and that the electoral outcome still remained to be settled. On Tuesday, November 28, the White House announced that it would offer to meet with the transition directors for both Bush and Gore and that Bush would receive the same daily intelligence briefing as the vice president. The announcement also indicated that they had asked for a legal opinion from the Justice Department about whether the Federal Bureau of Investigation (FBI) could begin background checks for prospective nominees. The Bush camp immediately accepted the offer, but did not set a time for a meeting. Podesta spoke to both Card and Neel by phone: "I had virtually duplicative conversations with Card and Roy Neel." In his view, "We're trying to ensure that we have a professional, efficient transition no matter who takes over. There's certain things we can do now. There's other things we can do later."[55]

That same week, the White House and the Justice Department reevaluated their position on whether the FBI could begin background checks. Justice Department officials now ruled that they did in fact have legal authority to begin background checks. In the opinion of Attorney General Janet Reno: "I think we will try to be in a posture, when we receive requests, to be able to deal with it. The principles that I am operating under are: We want to be fair, and we want to make sure that we are responsive . . . in terms of preparing for a new administration."[56] White House press spokesman Jake Siewart also announced that letters asking for resignations went to some 3,000 Clinton appointees, with the exception of inspectors-general and the heads of independent agencies. The White House also held a meeting of its own transition team, with Podesta presiding, and it included representatives from the FBI, the GSA, and the Internal Revenue Service (IRS).

Although still locked out of the official transition facility, the Bush transition proceeded on course, but with little of the panoply associated with prior transitions. As one account noted, Bush and Cheney "accelerated and formalized" their transition efforts, but "they did so in muted tones, without any sense of political revelry."[57] Reports indicated that Bush had made some cabinet selections and had developed short lists for other posts, and that Cheney had been contacting prospective appointees for interviews and background materials.

Clay Johnson would later recall that the effort had been more cautious: Bush and Cheney "began to have conversations . . . about cabinet secretaries. We didn't approach anybody, but we began to get the [preelection] lists of ten or fifteen people down to one or two, so that when it became official, we would agree that we were going to try to get this person in first for an interview and talk to them. We were going to do some background checking or whatever."[58]

One nomination was clear, that Colin Powell would be secretary of state. Powell, however, demurred from a public announcement of his selection until the legal challenges in Florida ended. But he did agree to meet with Bush at the latter's ranch in Texas in late November, during which both national security policy and possible appointments were reported to be the subject of their conversations. During the visit, Bush took the opportunity to emphasize to the press that his transition was well under way: "Dick [Cheney] has opened up our office there in Washington, D.C.—we're open for business. Andy [Card] has been spending time with me and getting our White House team in place." As for Powell and other nominees: "We'll make those announcements at the appropriate time." Press spokesman Ari Fleischer was asked whether the visit was designed to create an "aura of inevitability"; Fleischer responded that it was more appropriate to term it an "aura of responsibility."[59]

Both Cheney and Card continued to work during this period at fleshing out their own responsibilities. On December 7, Bush announced that he was ready to name White House staff, an obvious indication that Card was nearing completion of his task of assembling the top levels. Cheney quickly built a transition staff, reaching out to former Pentagon aides, including David J. Gribbin (who was placed in charged of congressional relations) and I. Lewis Libby, as well as his daughter, Liz Perry, and his campaign chief of staff, Kathleen Shanahan.[60]

Cheney also enlisted the services of Fred Fielding to lead the vetting and clearance process, a role he had in the 1980 transition and later as Reagan's first White House counsel. According to Clay Johnson: "We were very knowledgeable once clearance became something we had to deal with because Fred Fielding was there and he was an invaluable resource and a big part of our transition operation." Fielding assembled his own team of vetters, but "he personally did all of the interviews and so forth with an early assessment of the cabinet secretary people, then set up an operation for doing it for the sub-cabinet folks and senior White House people."[61]

Because of the time constraints, Fielding's expertise and close involvement were crucial: "Fred would tell us whether he was confident that there were no clearance problems or not. . . . There's some risk . . . when it's all verbal, you don't have forms to look at and so forth. But it turned out that, you know, we were talking to pretty public people, and there was a pretty good track record, and they had been in the public's eye, and so if there were problems there, they probably would have had a chance to surface." As a result, "We were able to show a lot of movement on the people front, even though we got a thirty-some-odd day late start."[62]

Other parts of the transition process were also settled by mid-December. A plan for creating policy coordinating groups was set up. Three to six policy experts were tapped for each, and their job was to brief Bush's cabinet nominees on his campaign promises and act as liaison to the Clinton administration. The effort was led by Joshua Bolten, Bush's chief domestic policy aide during the campaign. The groups were officially unveiled on December 15, two days after Gore's concession.

The Florida period also allowed them to fine-tune other parts of the departmental outreach process. Beginning with the Carter transition, extensive efforts have been made to set up teams for each cabinet department in order to gather information, prepare new cabinet officers, establish new priorities, and set new agendas. The track record of these operations has often been mixed; a number of the Reagan cabinet members, in particular, found them not particularly useful. In 2000 the decision was made not to create the large teams that have often been assigned to each department and agency but to go with smaller groups.[63] On December 19 the departmental and agency teams were formally announced.[64] At the same time, the transition did not want to foreclose any advice that might come from a variety of sources, so they created "transition advisory teams" who would not work directly with the departments and agencies but would serve as a conduit for advice. On December 29 the names of 474 members of these teams were publicly announced. Interestingly, however, no teams for defense or state were announced. The *Washington Post* dubbed it "Bush's amazing holiday gift to K Street."[65]

Cheney own role as head of the postelection transition, however, may have been the most important factor in moving the Bush transition forward despite the delay over Florida. According to Johnson:

> I am not a political person, but I think selecting Dick Cheney as the chair was very important because of his credibility in Washington, knowledge of Washington, and he was here. He is of Washington but not of Washington. He could alleviate a lot of anxiety about who are these people coming to town. Are they going to be easy to work with or whatever? There was a lot reaching out and a lot of communication that only somebody like a Dick Cheney could have done as effectively as he did. And we set up a congressional relations operation early on with Dave Gribbin heading it up and so there was a whole lot of outreach, and facilitation, and coordination with Congress and that was very important. So Dick's selection as chair was very important.[66]

But Cheney's central role was not without its pitfalls. According to one press report, "The post-election period has raised questions about a Bush presidency, or more accurately re-raised old questions. His general invisibility, contrasted with Cheney's regular news conferences and television interviews, has prompted questions about whether Bush will be too disengaged from the machinery of governing." Yet according to one Republican Party official, Bush's stance during this period was both necessary and strategic: "The strategy is to low-key it and not let Bush be damaged in this period, so that when he is president-elect, he can mount a charm offensive and start to talk to Democrats."[67]

Meanwhile, a Gore Transition?

Although the Gore camp had publicly labeled the unfolding Bush transition as presumptuous, by the third week in November they too began to turn to transition matters.[68] In a public address on November 22, following a favorable ruling by the Florida Supreme Court, Gore himself inserted language in his remarks signaling that he was now prepared to resume transition planning.[69] The person in charge of the effort was Roy Neel, a close associate of Gore, who had been his legislative director when Gore entered the House, then was his chief of staff in the Senate and in the vice president's office.

Like Johnson, Neel had been tapped to begin work during the preelection period. He began in the spring of 2000, but it was not until September that he took an unpaid leave from his job as the head of the United States Telecom Association. Gore specifically instructed Neel "to keep it extremely quiet, no discussions with anybody in the media, and for that matter no discussions with individuals who . . . might have a vested interest in joining a Gore administration." Drawing on his own experience in the 1992 Clinton transition, Neel knew that discussion about possible jobs "is rarely kept secret or in confidence." Neel was particularly cautious before election day not to distract the campaign staff from the job of winning the election. As he would later recall:

> Before the election, we didn't do as much outreach as it sounds like Clay [Johnson] did for a variety of reasons. One of which is that we felt like, particularly from our experience in '92, that the most important thing was to keep all activity out of the heads of the campaign staff, but yet at the same time make them feel like no one was filling in office charts. . . . So we knew not to do too much specific planning about people.[70]

Neel did, however, draw up an organizational chart for a possible postelection transition, and he began to recruit Clinton and Gore loyalists to staff it. Since the spring, Neel had also begun collecting material on past presidential transitions, and he too had been in contact with Martha Joynt Kumar, director of the White House 2001 Project, and had received some of the same material as had been provided to Clay Johnson. But, unlike Johnson, Neel did not meet frequently with his principal; in fact, he would later note that only one meeting took place with Gore and Senator Joseph Lieberman (D-CT), the vice-presidential candidate, before election day.

Following election day, the Gore camp turned its attention to Florida rather than to a possible Gore transition. Gore, of course, had the luxury as a sitting vice president of having firsthand knowledge of the inner workings of the presidency, and the task of a "friendly takeover" was less daunting than the one Bush faced. Yet as Neel would later observe, the period also brought some "real disadvantages": "The Bush campaign had done an extremely good job in creating the dynamic that George Bush was the presumptive president-elect. . . . We never did plant a seed in the public's mind that Gore was truly the winner."[71]

Perhaps to change that dynamic—or to begin planting that seed—Gore, Lieberman, and Neel assembled a small group of trusted aides and associates (including Labor Secretary Alexis Herman; Gore's current vice-presidential chief of staff, Charles Burson; Kathleen McGinty, an adviser on environmental policy and former head of the White House Council on Environmental Quality; and Leon Fuerth, Gore's national security adviser). They began to turn their attention more fully to a possible Gore presidency in late November. In some ways, they felt more of a need to be circumspect about their activities than did the Bush camp. According to Neel, "given the politics of the situation, they [Bush] were able to do more and be able to do more things publicly."[72] Preliminary lists of nominees for top positions were drawn up, although no further action was taken. Gore and Lieberman did, however, discuss appointments with the Reverend Jesse Jackson and AFL-CIO president John Sweeney. And they began to think about creating a Gore "Citizen Advisory Committee."[73]

The media began to pick up on the new activity in the Gore camp. On November 23, Thanksgiving Day, the *New York Times* reported that Neel had been sounding out people for possible cabinet positions, including holding over Commerce Secretary Norman Mineta and Treasury Secretary Larry Summers. Clinton's chief domestic and economic advisers, Bruce Reed and Gene Sperling, were also reported interested in positions, as were Alexis Herman, former senator George Mitchell, William Daley, and a number of others.[74] The next day, the *New York Times* reported that Gore had met at his residence with Lieberman, Daley, Herman, Fuerth, and Neel to continue transition planning. According to Neel, Gore was focusing on more than just cabinet appointees and was examining policy goals and what kind of legislation might be crafted in light of a divided Congress. "He is looking at how to reach out to Republicans, what kind of legislative agenda makes sense with a divided Congress. . . . You can't sit around doing nothing but watch CNN."[75]

In addition to beginning preparations for a possible Gore presidency, the *Times* article also noted that it served a useful political purpose in the election recount battle, since it sent signals to Democrats that Gore was not giving up and to Republicans that he was thinking about a more bipartisan approach to legislation. According to one adviser: "I know he's been talking to a number of people on how to reach out to Republicans, how a Democratic president in this odd climate we're facing can begin to build bipartisan solutions to key issues."[76] Yet by the end of the first week in December, the Gore transition effort appeared to stall as the end game drew near in Florida. According to one aide who was tasked with drawing up lists of potential nominees for national security positions, "It was like playing fantasy football."[77]

Within the Gore camp, the circle drew ever tighter: many of his campaign aides were described as having been "sidelined," with Gore turning to his family, Lieberman, and a few aides. According to the *New York Times,* "One result is that Mr. Gore is forging forward, driven by his conviction, unchallenged by those around him, that he is the rightful winner." According to one former consultant, "Al Gore is flying solo and not even willing to listen [to other points of view]. There is no Plan B and there is no talk of 2004."[78]

We obviously have no way of knowing how a subsequent Gore transition might have panned out if events had gone differently. But we do know that, a year later, Neel spoke admiringly of his counterparts' work:

> I thought the Bush-Cheney operation, especially after December 12th, was breathtakingly successful. It was quite extraordinary what they were able to do, putting together that team and making those announcements, almost in a zero-defect way. I think I can say this because I am not looking for a job in that administration. But it was quite remarkable, and I think given the difficulty of it all and having an incoming president with a bit of a muddled victory, it may have been the best transition that I've seen, even beyond the 1980 Reagan transition, which was, up to that point, the high water mark for transitions.[79]

December 12 and 13: The Supreme Court Speaks and Gore Concedes

But a Gore transition was not to be. The Bush legal team was successful in pressing its case that the Florida Supreme Court had exceeded its constitutional authority and that continuation of the recounts violated the equal protection clause of the U.S. Constitution. On Monday, December 11, oral argument in the case of Bush versus Gore took place before the U.S. Supreme Court, and the next day, at 10:00 P.M., the Court issued its ruling. By a 7–2 vote the Court acknowledged that there were equal protection problems in the recount order of the Florida Supreme Court. And by a narrower 5–4 vote the Court essentially said that a proper recount, including acceptable standards for determining the validity of disputed votes, could not be done in a timely fashion to meet deadlines (that very day at midnight according to the Court's majority) so that Florida's electors could cast valid electoral college votes: "It is obvious that the recount cannot be conducted in compliance with the requirements of equal protection and due process without additional work."[80] With the recounts shut down, Bush's certification as the winner of Florida's electoral vote stood and with it came the presidency (by 1 more electoral vote than the 270 required). The next day, Gore conceded.[81]

*   *   *

The unsettled electoral context faced by the Bush transition will hopefully not be one his successors will have to deal with. Yet its transition activities, both before election day and through mid-December, offer important lessons. Clay Johnson's work, stretching over a year and a half, is a model for how pre-election transitions can effectively operate. Johnson touched base effectively with a range of knowledgeable individuals, drew appropriate lessons from past transitions, and was ready on election day to have a transition operation up and running. Most important, he had successfully pressed then-candidate Bush to select his chief of staff and to make a range of other decisions that would lead to a smooth transition. After election day, the skilled and experienced team of Cheney, Card, and Johnson—plus Bush—used the period until Florida was resolved to proceed with a range of transition activities, without making Bush appear too presumptuous of the outcome. The challenge ahead was whether the truncated time left for a "normal" transition—from mid-December to inauguration day—would allow the Bush transition team to puts its plans and decisions into action.

Notes

1. In fact, the Florida delay may have had a positive side to it: it enabled Bush and his advisers to do transition planning but without the media spotlight and other pressures that normally occur.

2. On the 1876 election controversy, see Morris, *Fraud of the Century.* Like Bush in 2000, Hayes also lost the popular vote.

3. Johnson, the son of a Fort Worth rancher and businessman, later obtained an MBA degree from MIT, then worked for Frito-Lay and Wilson Sporting Goods (both divisions of the Pepsi-Cola Company) before joining the Horchow mail-order catalogue company and eventually ending up as the chief operating officer of the Dallas Museum of Art.

4. Lois Romano, "George W.'s Inner Circle," *Washington Post National Weekly Edition,* October 9, 2000.

5. Telephone interview with Clay Johnson, September 20, 2001.

6. James Bennet, "The Bush Years: CEO, USA," *New York Times Magazine,* January 14, 2001.

7. Clay Johnson, panel discussion, "President Bush's First 100 Days," Kennedy School of Government, Harvard University, May 2, 2001.

8. Johnson, "The 2000–01 Presidential Transition," p. 51.

9. Clay Johnson, panel discussion, "Bush Transition to the Presidency: Planning and Implementation," American Enterprise Institute, Washington, D.C., December 11, 2001.

10. Karl Rove, "A Discussion with Karl Rove," American Enterprise Institute, Washington, D.C., December 11, 2001.

11. Johnson, panel discussion, "Bush Transition to the Presidency."

12. Telephone interview with Clay Johnson, September 20, 2001.

13. Ibid.

14. Johnson, panel discussion, "Bush Transition to the Presidency."

15. Telephone interview with Clay Johnson, September 20, 2001.

16. Johnson, "The 2000–01 Presidential Transition," p. 52.

17. Johnson, panel discussion, "President Bush's First 100 Days."

18. Telephone interview with Clay Johnson, September 20, 2001.

19. Ibid. Some of the materials and essays that Kumar and her associates compiled were later published in Kumar and Sullivan, *The White House World.* Information about the White House 2001 Project can be located online at www.WhiteHouseTransitionProject.org.

20. Johnson, "The 2000–01 Presidential Transition."

21. For further analysis of the Bush effort with an online nomination process as well as some of the issues and problems involved in the scrutiny and vetting of potential candidates for positions, see Sullivan, "Nomination Forms Online," pp. 13–15; Sullivan, "Already Buried and Sinking Fast," pp. 31–33; and Mackenzie, "The Real Invisible Hand."

22. These are adapted from two sources: Dana Milbank, "Tome for the Holidays: A Transition Reading List," *Washington Post,* December 19, 2000; and Johnson, "The 2000–01 Presidential Transition," p. 51.

23. Telephone interview with Clay Johnson, September 20, 2001.

24. Johnson, panel discussion, "President Bush's First 100 Days."

25. Telephone interview with Clay Johnson, September 20, 2001.

26. Telephone interview with Clay Johnson, September 20, 2001.

27. Johnson, panel discussion, "President Bush's First 100 Days."

28. Johnson, panel discussion on the "Bush Transition to the Presidency."

29. Hughes, *Ten Minutes from Normal,* p. 181.

30. NBC declared the state for Bush at 2:17 A.M. (Eastern Time), CNN and CBS at 2:18, and ABC at 2:20. Kaplan, *The Accidental President,* p. 12.

31. The effort was led by Ron Klain, Gore's former chief of staff. Jack Quinn, another former Gore chief of staff and a former Clinton White House legal counsel, was involved in the Nashville end of the effort.

32. Richard Berke, "Two Strategies But One Goal," *New York Times,* November 10, 2000.

33. "Excerpts from Bush's Remarks About Election," *New York Times,* November 11, 2000.

34. Ibid.

35. Editorial, *Washington Post,* November 10, 2000.

36. Johnson, panel discussion, "Bush Transition to the Presidency."

37. Telephone interview with Clay Johnson, September 20, 2001.

38. At 7:30 P.M. on Sunday, November 26 (some two and a half hours after the deadline set by the Florida Supreme Court), Florida secretary of state Katherine Harris announced the results and certified George W. Bush as the victor in Florida. Bush received 2,912,790 votes to Gore's 2,912,253. Harris did not include partial results from Palm Beach County (which had been unable to finish by the 5:00 P.M. deadline)

or the results from the partial Miami-Dade recount, which had been suspended. Had those additional votes been included, plus several hundred missing votes in Nassau County, Gore would have garnered an additional 426 votes, and the Bush lead would have dropped to only 101.

39. For analysis of the events throughout the 2000 election, see Caeser and Busch, *A Perfect Tie;* Dionne and Pomper, *The Election of 2000;* Jamieson and Waldman, *Electing the President, 2000;* and Wayne and Wilcox, *The Election of the Century.* On the events in Florida, see Kaplan, *The Accidental President;* Sabato, *Overtime;* Tapper, *Down and Dirty;* and Toobin, *Too Close to Call.* On the legal and constitutional issues raised, see Dionne and Kristol, *Bush v. Gore;* Dworkin, *A Badly Flawed Election;* Greene, *Understanding the 2000 Election;* and Posner, *Breaking the Deadlock.*

40. Frank Bruni, "Quietly but Confidently, Bush Pushes Ahead," *New York Times,* November 28, 2000.

41. In 2000, $4.2 million in federal funds were available for transition support and an additional $1 million was added to compile a directory of transition information and support an orientation program for the new administration's fifty top appointees. The federal facility, at 1800 G St., Washington, D.C., NW, had previously been the headquarters of the government's Y2K task force.

42. Stephen Barr, "Administrations Come and Go," *Washington Post,* November 5, 2000.

43. Al Kamen, "Hoping to Ease the Shift in Power," *Washington Post,* November 1, 2000.

44. Stephen Barr, "Administrations Come and Go," *Washington Post,* November 5, 2000.

45. "Excerpt from Statement by Cheney on Transition," *New York Times,* November 28, 2000.

46. Ibid.

47. Edward Walsh, "For Bush Campaign It's Full Steam Ahead," *Washington Post,* November 29, 2000.

48. George Archibald, "White House Puts Transition on Hold," *Washington Times,* November 22, 2000.

49. Al Kamen, "Hoping to Ease the Shift in Power," *Washington Post,* November 1, 2000.

50. David E. Sanger and Marc Lacey, "Federal Agency Denies Bush Team Access to Money and Office for Transition," *New York Times,* November 28, 2000.

51. Al Kamen, "Hoping to Ease the Shift in Power," *Washington Post,* November 1, 2000.

42. David E. Sanger and Marc Lacey, "Federal Agency Denies Bush Team Access to Money and Office for Transition," *New York Times,* November 28, 2000.

53. Cheney announced that the Bush team would accept up to $5,000 in direct and in-kind contributions to pay for the effort.

54. Kevin Merida, "From the Ground Up," *Washington Post,* December 1, 2000.

55. Marc Lacey, "White House Arranges Sessions for Both Sides," *New York Times,* November 29, 2000.

56. David Wise and Ben White, "Reno Ready for Dual Checks," *Washington Post,* December 1, 2000.

57. Frank Bruni, "Quietly but Confidently, Bush Pushes Ahead," *New York Times,* November 28, 2000.

58. Johnson, panel discussion, "Bush Transition to the Presidency."

59. Mike Allen, "Powell Meets with Bush, Cheney in Texas," *Washington Post,* November 30, 2000.

60. Eric Schmitt, "Planning Presidential Team from Across the Potomac," *New York Times,* December 5, 2000.

61. Telephone interview with Clay Johnson, September 20, 2001. Fielding covered both professional and personnel matters, culminating with what has come to be known as the Fred Fielding question: "Is there any other information about you or your family that could possibly be a source of embarrassment to you or to the president if it ever became publicly known?" Al Kamen, "Instant Cabinet: Add Clearance Counsel, Sir," *Washington Post,* January 5, 2001.

62. Johnson, panel discussion, "Bush Transition to the Presidency."

63. According to Clay Johnson, "We were not going to have those large department teams descend upon the department of whatever; forty, fifty people with puffed-up chests and kind of, you know, scare people and probably violate ethics laws and so forth." Instead, "we were going to have small groups of six or eight go in there, meanwhile still have all the advisers that wanted to provide advice, put them on an advisory team, but not have them be the people that went into the departments. . . . We sort of thought through that and better organized all of that." Johnson, panel discussion, "Bush Transition to the Presidency." According to one press report, "Bush aides initially considered skipping the transition advisory process because of time constraints, transition insiders said. But advocates of the idea won out, arguing that business representatives with deep Washington experience can draw maps of each agency's minefields—depicting the regulatory and legal controversies set for detonation—that the Bush team would never get from career agency officials." John Mintz, "Transition Advisers Have Much to Gain," *Washington Post,* January 17, 2001.

64. The heads of the department teams included: Zalmay Khalilzdad, a Pentagon official under Bush Sr., for Defense; William Hansen, a former Education Department official, for Education; Anne Klee, chief GOP counsel at the Senate Energy Committee, for Interior; Paul McNulty, legislative director for Majority Leader Dick Armey (R-TX), for Justice; John Bridgeland, former chief of staff for Representative Rob Portman (R-OH), for Labor; Joel Shin, Bush campaign foreign policy adviser, for State; Jack Schenendorf, a top aide on the House Transportation and Infrastructure Committee, for Transportation; John Cogan, deputy director of the Office of Management and Budget under Bush Sr. and a Stanford economist, for the OMB; David Johnson, former general counsel to the Senate Agriculture Committee, for Agriculture; Theodore Kassinger, former trade counsel to the Senate Finance Committee, for Commerce; Andrew Lundquist, staff director of the Senate Energy and Natural Resources Committee, for Energy; Sally Canfield, a Bush campaign policy adviser and aide to Representative Jim McCrery (R-LA), for Health and Human Services; Robert Woodson Jr., a Bush campaign adviser, for Housing and Urban Development; Timothy Adams, an economist and former aide to Lawrence Lindsey, for Treasury. The groups were led by Gary Edson, deputy director for policy in the transition office (Edson also led the Veterans Affairs and GSA teams). It is interesting to note that the composition of the team leaders included Bush campaign advisers but also a large number with congressional staff experience, giving them both substantive knowledge as well as prior oversight information about their respective departments.

65. Mike Allen, "Bush Enlists Cast of 474 Insiders," *Washington Post,* January 1, 2001.

66. Telephone interview with Clay Johnson, September 20, 2001.

67. Dan Balz, "Analysis: Bush Effort Gets Mixed Reviews," *Washington Post,* December 3, 2000.

68. Their shift followed a November 21 ruling of the Florida Supreme Court that mandated that partial tallies from manual recounts then under way be included in vote

totals; as well, the time for certification of the Florida vote on November 26 was drawing near.

69. "Because we know that this process is going to take more time, I believe it's now appropriate for both of us to focus on the transition," Gore said. Katherine Q. Seelye and John Broder, "Gore Has Decided to Start Engines of His Transition," *New York Times,* November 23, 2000.

70. Roy Neel, panel discussion, "Bush Transition to the Presidency: Planning and Implementation," American Enterprise Institute, Washington, D.C., December 11, 2001.

71. Ibid.

72. Ibid.

73. Ceci Connolly, "Roy Neel, Gore's Maybe Man," *Washington Post,* December 2, 2000.

74. Katherine Q. Seelye and John Broder, "Gore Has Decided to Start Engine of His Transition," *New York Times,* November 23, 2000.

75. Katherine Q. Seelye, "Pressing On with Plans, Gore Begins Laying the Foundation for His White House," *New York Times,* November, 25, 2000.

76. Ibid.

77. Al Kamen and Steven Mufson, "Gore Planners Shift Transition into Second Gear," *Washington Post,* December 10, 2000.

78. Melinda Henneberger, "With No Dissent in Inner Circle, Gore Hasn't Discussed Conceding," *New York Times,* December 1, 2000.

79. Neel, panel discussion, "Bush Transition to the Presidency."

80. In addition to a number of criticisms that legal scholars raised concerning both the Court's intervention and its jurisprudential reasoning, some legal scholars questioned the Court's view that the putative deadline for determining who Florida's electors were was, under federal law, December 12 (that very day at midnight), as the majority argued in shutting down the recounts immediately. The electoral college did not formally meet until December 18. The majority opinion also led Justice John Paul Stevens to issue one of several forceful dissents: "Time will one day heal the wound to that confidence that will be inflicted by today's decision. One thing, however, is certain. Although we may never know with complete certainty the identity of the winner of this year's election, the identity of the loser is perfectly clear. It is the nation's confidence in the judge as an impartial guardian of the law."

81. Despite the Supreme Court's decision, Gore was reportedly still considering the possibility of some appeal, perhaps to the Florida Supreme Court, to which the U.S. Supreme Court had technically remanded its decision for further action. But prominent Democrats began to close the door on further legal appeals; they reportedly included Senator Robert Torricelli (D-NJ), Democratic National Committee chairman Ed Rendell, and Gore's own lawyer, Harvard law professor Laurence Tribe. By 9:00 A.M. the next day, Gore was still mulling over his options. But by 10:00 A.M. William Daley, his campaign chairman, announced that Gore would deliver a concession speech that evening. Gore delivered his address at 9:00 P.M., which was followed by an address by President-Elect Bush from the chamber of the Texas House of Representatives.

3

After December 13:
A Transition Unveiled

The electoral vote controversy in Florida placed the Bush team in the most difficult circumstance of any modern transition. The tasks it faced in the remaining weeks before January 20, 2001, were daunting. Selecting a cabinet, picking a White House staff, and organizing internal operations are trying even under normal circumstances. Carter and Clinton both experienced difficulties in effectively meeting the tasks before them, especially in organizing and staffing the White House. For Bush, the test was even greater. Would the efforts undertaken before election day and during the "quiet transition" through mid-December pay off?

Picking a Cabinet

Following Gore's concession, Bush and his advisers (principally Cheney, Card, and Johnson) quickly moved to fill his cabinet. Bush did not appear to be in a position to match the pace of cabinet nominations set by his predecessors, although in the end he got very close. In 1976, the first Carter nominee was unveiled on December 3 and the last on December 23. In 1980, the first Reagan nominee was announced on December 11, with all but one named by December 23 (the last nominee—secretary of education—came on January 6). In 1988, Bush Sr. announced the nomination of James Baker for secretary of state two days after the election, with all but one named by December 24 (the last nominee—secretary of energy—came on January 12).[1] In 1992, Clinton announced his first appointments on December 10 and his last on December 24.[2]

The first Bush nominee, announced on December 16, came as no surprise: Colin Powell as secretary of state. The last three announcements were made on January 2 (thus Bush finished ahead of Reagan and Bush Sr., but behind Carter and Clinton).[3] Seen from another perspective, however, Bush rolled out his cabinet picks in three weeks from the time his official transition started on December 13, rather than in the eight to ten weeks it took his pred-ecessors since Carter. The work that Johnson and Cheney undertook in the preelection period in beginning to develop lists of nominees, then the work of Cheney, Card, and Johnson during the Florida recount period, had enabled them to move quickly.

Although Bush had made no public pronouncements about picking a cab-inet that "looked like America," as Bill Clinton had proclaimed eight years before, ethnic and gender diversity remained a concern. At a news conference on November 27, the day after certification, Cheney registered this: "I think diversity will be an important consideration." In the view of one Bush adviser, Bush and Cheney are "on a real talent hunt for minorities and women. They are really beside themselves to find diversity."[4]

In 2000, political diversity was more strongly added to the mix, and there was much speculation in the press about need to appoint Democrats to the cabinet given the divided result of the election. Cheney noted the issue, stat-ing at his November 27 press conference that Governor Bush's actions "are likely to be influenced by the fact that it's been a close election, that the nation is, if anything, evenly divided, if you will."[5] But here, the eventual Bush cab-inet did not really meet initial speculation: it only had one Democrat in the end (Transportation Secretary Norman Mineta).

The Bush cabinet that emerged was notable for its gender and racial diversity: two African Americans (Colin Powell at State and Roderick Paige at Education), one Hispanic male (Mel Martinez at Housing and Urban Devel-opment [HUD]), one Hispanic female (Linda Chavez, the initial nominee at Labor), one Asian American male (Mineta at Transportation), one Arab Amer-ican (Spencer Abraham at Energy), and three women (Ann Veneman at Agri-culture, Gale Norton at Interior, plus Chavez at Labor).[6] From a political per-spective, it was a mix of moderate and conservative Republicans (with the exception of Mineta, a Democrat), several seasoned corporate executives, a number of Washington insiders (ten of the fourteen had prior experience in the federal government), as well as outsiders with a strong connection to Bush and allegiance to the Bush policy agenda.

It was clearly not the coalition government some Democrats had pushed for in the aftermath of the divided election. The names of a number of promi-nent Democrats surfaced in the press as possible cabinet appointees. The pos-sible appointment of former senator Sam Nunn (D-GA) as secretary of defense had been prominently mentioned, but on November 29, Nunn took himself out of consideration. Former governor Jim Hunt, a Democrat from North Carolina, also indicated he was not interested in serving in the Bush cabinet as education secretary. William Gray III, a former Democratic mem-ber of the House and president of the United Negro College Fund, was another name mentioned for that job.[7] In late November, the office of Senator John Breaux (D-LA) confirmed that Bush representatives had approached him about serving as energy secretary. But Breaux, who met with Bush on December 15, told him he planned to remain in the Senate. There was even speculation that Bush might keep Larry Summers on as treasury secretary.[8] The close division in both the House and Senate also was a factor that potentially excluded some candidates from both sides of the aisle, such as Breaux as well as Representative Henry Bonilla, a Texas Republican who might have been a leading candidate for HUD secretary.

It was also a cabinet appointment process that had comparably few leaks and a number of surprise nominations. One of those surprises was the nomination of Donald Rumsfeld for defense secretary, a position that he held in the Ford administration. In part, Rumsfeld's name emerged following something of an impasse between Powell and Cheney, who were each backing different candidates. Powell favored Governor Tom Ridge (R-PA) and had reportedly raised his name with Bush at their late November meeting at the Bush ranch, while Cheney backed Paul Wolfowitz, who had been his undersecretary of defense for policy planning in the Bush Sr. administration.[9] A third candidate, former senator Dan Coats (R-IN), emerged, but Bush was reportedly not satisfied with his interview with Coats, who had strong support among conservatives in the Senate. Bush wanted someone with strong management skills in the position.[10] Tellingly, it was Bush himself who rejected Coats. Moreover, Powell was not told that Rumsfeld was under consideration until after Bush had interviewed him, and even then the task to tell Powell about Rumsfeld was left to a subordinate. Powell reportedly had some reservations but in the end "saluted." According to one Bush insider, "Powell wasn't asked whether he thought this was a good choice. But he is delighted with the choice."[11]

Like his father before him, Bush faced pressure from the right wing of the Republican Party (GOP), particularly Christian fundamentalists concerned about potential nominees' positions on abortion and other lifestyle issues.[12] Reverend Jerry Falwell was especially critical of the possible appointments of Governor Christie Todd Whitman (R-NJ) and Governor Ridge. While Ridge decided to remain as Pennsylvania's governor, Whitman was tapped to head the Environmental Protection Agency and was given cabinet rank. But religious conservatives were able to derail the possible nomination of Governor Marc Racicot (R-MT) as attorney general, and they played a key role in the selection of Senator John Ashcroft (R-MO), who had just lost his reelection bid, for that post. Bush aide Karl Rove, moreover, served as the conduit for their concerns.[13] Conservatives were also delighted with the nomination of Gail Norton, a former attorney general of Colorado, as secretary of interior. Both the nominations of Ashcroft and Norton raised some controversy, although both were eventually confirmed by the Senate.[14]

The one major stumble was Bush's nomination of Linda Chavez as labor secretary, which ran into trouble over her assistance to an illegal immigrant. Yet it was quickly over and done with (within fifty-five hours from the time the accusations against her surfaced). Unlike the prolonged battle over the nomination of John Tower as secretary of defense that had plagued his father's first months in office, and Clinton's difficulties with his first two nominees for attorney general (Zoe Baird and Kimba Wood and the ensuing "Nanny gate" controversy), Bush quickly dumped Chavez and announced a replacement, Elaine Chao, an Asian American and the wife of Senator Mitch McConnell (R-KY).

Subcabinet

As the cabinet selection process neared completion, the Bush transition—principally Cheney and Johnson—turned their attention to subcabinet appointments. They avoided Carter's error in 1976 of abandoning these selections to the incoming cabinet members. But they also did not exercise the more forceful control of the Reagan transition in 1980, which erred in the opposite extreme: cabinet members forced to accept subcabinet appointees with whom they were not happy or had not been consulted about. The mantra in the Bush camp, as press spokesman Ari Fleischer explained to the press on January 2, 2001, was: "We have a motto at the transition, and that is, 'Do it with them, not to them.'"[15]

The same exact phrase was used by Clay Johnson in an interview with the *New York Times.* According to the *Times,* Johnson and Cheney acknowledged that cabinet members would play a major role. "But they also described the process . . . as a joint effort with Bush officials, mixing and matching personnel to get the right blend of personal chemistry, expertise, diversity and loyalty to form a team that can win approval from the Senate." According to Johnson:

> It's identifying what kind of person we are looking for; what's the universe of names to consider for each position; and who best matches up to the specifications and who best fits with everyone else, personality-wise and style-wise. It's not a beauty contest, it's not who writes the most letters or gave the most money. . . . We get concurrence with the cabinet secretaries on those jobs, and then start reviewing with them their suggestions and our suggestions.[16]

A year later, in December 2001 at a panel discussion on the Bush presidency at the American Enterprise Institute, Johnson reflected back on his work:

> We are going to do this with them, not to them. And it takes one black ball. If we don't want them, it's not going to happen. If they don't want them, it's not going to happen. And there are lots of discussions, and it's harder that way. It takes longer. It's a little messy. But . . . it's just a better way of doing it. You end up with a better product, and it's people that they like having on their own team, we like having on their team and so forth. So, again, it's collaborative—we've approached it in a collaborative fashion.[17]

Overall Assessment

Despite the delay over Florida, Bush had quickly assembled a cabinet that was generally lauded. Most nominees reflected Bush's agenda, a signal that Bush was not prepared to back off the themes of his campaign. The selection of Ashcroft and Norton particularly pleased Bush's conservative political base. It was also a cabinet with a high degree of prior executive experience, with a number of them having served in prior Republican administrations. As the president-elect himself noted on January 2, "I'm not afraid to surround myself with strong and competent people."[18] Indeed, little noted at the time was the fact that Bush—often portrayed as prone to delegation—was an active participant and his face-to-face meetings with potential nominees were crucial to their final selection or rejection. Bush made the final call, just as it had been with his selection of Cheney as his running mate.

More generally, the selection process was one that fit Bush's needs. As James Bennet observed in a *New York Times Magazine* article on Bush that appeared shortly before inauguration day, "Cheney said that he and Bush spoke by telephone four or five times a day. Bush set no quota for recommendations for each post, and for some, like State there was only one. Bush aides insist that he used the same straightforward method for finding nominees in Washington as in Texas: starting with the qualities he wants in a particular officeholder, considering the department's needs and then taking recommendations."[19]

That a number of them had served in his father's administration was initially a source of some concern: "They are very conscious of 'your father's Oldsmobile,' one Republican official said. 'If this is not your father's Oldsmobile' and they're naming five people tomorrow, some of those people will have to be new."[20] On Sunday, December 24, appearing on ABC's *This Week* show, George Bush Sr. defended his son's cabinet choices: "If you are looking for a Republican who has experience in agriculture or in defense or whatever it is, then in all likelihood, that person probably would have served in the four years in one way or another in the Bush administration or certainly the Reagan administration." As the selection process continued, the concern lessened a bit, as observers noted not just that a number had served not only in the Reagan presidency, but also in the Ford administration. Several, too, were from outside the Washington Beltway: Martinez (HUD), Paige (Education), Governor Tommy Thompson (Health and Human Services), and Donald Evans (Commerce).

While the prior experience and expertise of some nominees might have indicated a cabinet more independent of the White House, the selection process countered that by a heavy emphasis on ensuring loyalty to Bush and his agenda. According to Representative Roy Blunt (R-MO), Bush's transition liaison to the House, "The key to understanding this cabinet is that whatever the different points of view, the people who were chosen agree with him on the issue they're being given responsibility for." Discipline too was stressed. As Bush himself told the press in announcing Ashcroft's appointment: "When he gives me his legal advice, you won't know about it unless I tell you."[21] Experience, loyalty, and discipline were central to the selection process—and themes Bush himself looked for in his one-on-one interviews with candidates.[22] Would they come to fruition once this administration was in office?

Organizing a White House Staff

The Bush transition's efforts to organize the White House were especially impressive in comparison to the Clinton experience eight years earlier. Here, the Bush transition actually beat the timetable set by their predecessor. Not only was transition work undertaken during the contest over the Florida crucial, but preelection decisions enabled the Bush transition to get an early start. Andrew Card's selection as chief of staff had been settled two weeks before election day.[23] In 1992, by contrast, Clinton's chief of staff, Mack McLarty, was appointed on December 12. Alberto Gonzales, the Bush White House counsel, and Karen Hughes, the head of its communications operations, were tapped on December 17, weeks before their Clinton counterparts. As Johnson would later recall, by the time of Gore's December 13 concession, "Andy Card had made, with the president's consent, almost all of the senior White House personnel decisions. It was decided who was going to go where."[24]

In so doing, the Bush transition followed one of the key lessons of prior transitions. Early staff appointments enable those selected not only to get a leg up on their own jobs, it also enables the transition to move on to other levels of staff positions. In Clinton's case, he and his advisers were essentially still stuck at the top layer of White House staff a few days before he was sworn into office. By contrast, the seemingly truncated Bush transition had already moved on to second- and, in some cases, third-level White House positions.

Two of the positions that Bush filled early—White House legal counsel (Al Gonzales on December 17) and the head of the White House personnel office (Clay Johnson on December 29)—were especially critical because they are so integrally involved in the appointment and vetting process for all presidential appointees. Swift appointments in these two areas, moreover, may have been an important lesson taken from the Bush Sr. 1988 transition. Both Boyden Gray, his White House legal counsel, and Chase Untermeyer, who directed personnel, were also early appointments—the day after his election in fact. Both contributed greatly to a smooth transition to power. Johnson's appointment to head the White House personnel office, moreover, followed a sequence of positions that his counterparts in the Reagan and Bush Sr. administrations had also held: in 1980, Pendleton James had been Reagan's chief preelection planner, then headed the transition's personnel operations, before becoming head of the White House personnel office. So too with Chase Untermeyer for Bush Sr. in 1988. For Johnson, the slight twist in 2000 was that he had a more robust mandate than James or Untermeyer (who were both essentially restricted to planning a personnel operation in the preelection period) and Johnson's title as transition director was broader in the postelection period, although he was a central figure in its appointments process.

The Bush camp also understood the political symbolism of the appointment process. Following the announcement of Card's selection as chief of staff, on December 17 Bush personally announced the appointment of Condoleezza Rice as NSC adviser, Gonzales as legal counsel, and Karen Hughes as "counselor" to the president.[25] Bush's first staff selections, besides Card, were two women (one of whom was an African American) and a Hispanic.

Although Rice's appointment came as no surprise, she was not given cabinet rank. As Bush noted in announcing her appointment: "I want Condi to come to every Cabinet meeting, but . . . I think it's best that she be an equal partner of the senior team in the White House. . . . I can assure you that she and I will be spending an inordinate amount of time with each other. I will be seeing her on a daily basis." Despite the lack of cabinet rank, Bush's words proved true: she would become a close adviser if not a confidant of the president, spending more time with him than any other member of his foreign policy team.[26]

Hughes's appointment to the White House staff was also expected, although her position as "counselor" to the president rather than just as another "assistant to the president" signaled both her stature within the Bush inner circle and a recognition of the importance of communicating the message of this White House. She was given responsibility for the White House press secretary, communications, and speech-writing offices—the first time those offices had been grouped together under a single White House aide.[27] But organizational control of the White House communications apparatus was not her only responsibility; she would also serve as an important Bush adviser on policy matters and legislative issues.

Over the next several weeks further appointments were announced and the organization and structure of the Bush White House began to take shape. With respect to his own staff in the chief of staff's office, Card decided to follow the Clinton model and have two deputy chiefs of staff. Initial media speculation focused on Joseph Allbaugh (Bush's campaign manager and, like Clay Johnson, a former gubernatorial chief of staff), who would be in charge of White House operations with Josh Bolten, Bush's chief domestic adviser, in charge of policy.[28] Although Allbaugh would end up as director of the Federal Emergency Management Agency (FEMA), the media reports otherwise proved correct. At a December 28 news briefing, press spokesman Ari Fleischer announced that Bush had named Bolten as assistant to the president and deputy chief of staff for policy. Bolten had served in the Bush Sr. administration as general counsel at the White House trade office, then as a deputy assistant for legislative affairs.[29] The other deputy chief of staff, with responsibility for White House operations, was Joseph Hagin, Bush's deputy campaign manager. It was Hagin's second stint in the White House as well. Hagin had been a young aide to Bush Sr. during the 1980 campaign, served in several positions on his vice-presidential staff, and, when Bush took office in 1989, served as his appointments secretary.[30] At the same press conference, Fleischer announced his own appointment as White House press secretary.[31]

Over the next days and weeks, other key White House positions were filled. On December 23, Mitchell E. Daniels was tapped to head the Office of Management and Budget (OMB). Daniels, too, drew on a wealth of Washington experience. He had started as an aide to then-mayor Richard Lugar of Indianapolis, served as Lugar's chief of staff when he went to the Senate, was executive director of the National Republican Party Senatorial Committee, and was then brought to the Reagan White House to serve as assistant to the president for intergovernmental affairs, where he had been Andrew Card's boss. He later served as director of the political affairs office from 1985 to 1987.[32]

On January 4, Bush named Nicholas Calio as his congressional liaison director. For Calio it was familiar territory: he had served as deputy assistant in the liaison shop and then as its head during the Bush Sr. presidency. The next day, the appointments of three members of Bush's "Texas mafia" were announced. Albert Hawkins, Bush's state budget director from 1995 to 1999, was named assistant to the president and secretary to the cabinet. Harriet Miers, managing partner of a large Dallas law firm and a former member of the Dallas city council, was picked for staff secretary. Margaret LaMontagne Spellings, an education expert and senior adviser to him while he was governor, was tapped as assistant to the president for domestic policy and director of the Domestic Policy Council (DPC).

The choice of Spellings to head the DPC staff raised two issues. First, she reported to deputy chief of staff Bolten, who was himself a close domestic adviser to Bush and on a larger range of issues. Second, the organization of the DPC remained unsettled. Another matter that remained unsettled was where to put Bush's third major domestic policy adviser, Stephen Goldsmith, the former mayor of Indianapolis. Although Goldsmith met with Bush on January 10, no announcement of an appointment was forthcoming. There was speculation that he would head "a governmental reform office in the White House that would incorporate an Office of Faith-Based actions, which Bush had promised to create, and the 'reinventing government' duties of Vice President Gore. But Bush aides oppose such a broad portfolio for Goldsmith."[33]

On Monday, January 8, another set of White House appointees was unveiled, now at the deputy assistant to the president level. Brad Blakeman, who held a similar position in the two Bush-Quayle campaigns, was named deputy assistant to the president for appointments and scheduling. Hector F. Irastorza Jr., another Reagan-Bush veteran, was named deputy assistant for management and administration.[34] Scott McClellan, who had been deputy communications director in the campaign, was tapped for deputy press secretary. Brian Montgomery, who worked in the Bush Sr. administration and in Bush's 1994 run for governor, was named director of advance operations. The next day still more positions were announced. Two rounded out Karen Hughes's staff. Dan Bartlett, a longtime gubernatorial aide and then the campaign issues director, was named deputy to Hughes, while Tucker Eskew, a campaign communications adviser and a former press secretary to Governor Carroll Campbell (R-SC), was named head of media affairs.[35] John Bridgeland, a former House aide (to Bush friend Representative Rob Portman [R-OH]) and the campaign's deputy policy director, was named Spellings's deputy at the DPC. The fourth position filled an important slot within Karl Rove's domain: Ken Mehlman's appointment as White House political director.[36] Card reportedly had decided to abolish the intergovernmental affairs office (one that he himself had worked in during the Reagan presidency) but in the end did not. Ruben Barrales, a former member of the San Mateo (CA) County Board of Supervisors, was tapped to fill the slot.[37]

In recommending staff appointments, Card was able to bring a pool of talent on board who had a variety of relevant experience and backgrounds. One, as Martha Joynt Kumar has noted, is knowledge of the president—past experience in working with him: "A president's rhythms are important to the information he gets, in what form, and its timing."[38] Prior association with the president is also likely to enhance a measure of loyalty. At the highest levels of the Bush presidency, Rove, Hughes, and Johnson fit this most closely. So too did other figures in the Bush White House: legal counsel Alberto Gonzales and secretary to the cabinet Albert Hawkins. In fact, eleven of the thirty-six staff members announced before inauguration day had worked for Bush in Austin.

Yet unlike Jimmy Carter's experience with his "Georgia mafia's" near total domination of the upper levels of his White House, a number of Bush associates brought other backgrounds to the table. Some 80 percent of top White House and administration personnel, according to a study done by the *National Journal,* had participated in some way in the Bush 2000 presidential campaign.[39] This "knowledge," as Kumar explains, "is clearly important as these veterans know the issues and the president, and during their time on the trail become close-knit."[40]

Bush also could draw on a pool of talent he had come to know who also had prior White House experience, whether under Reagan or Bush Sr. (and sometimes both): Card, Rice, Bolten, Hagin, Daniels, Calio, and Lawrence Lindsey, to name just a few. Calio, Jack Howard, his deputy in congressional liaison, and Hector Irastorza, director of White House management and administration, had even held the similar positions on the Bush Sr. staff. Many of them brought multiple categories of relevant experience. Card, NSC adviser Rice, domestic adviser Bolten, and economic adviser Lindsey, while not having served under Bush in Austin, had worked in the campaign, were well versed in a variety of policy areas, and held jobs in prior Republican administrations. That Bush's father had served both as president and vice president enabled Card to draw on a potential pool of talent who had not only administrative (especially White House) experience, but also close ties (and hence a measure of loyalty and personal connection) to the Bush family. Card's own past history is the best case in point. And the past performance—in terms of both substantive expertise and loyalty—of candidates for positions was often known by Card or others first hand.

It was also a White House staff that included eight women among its top eighteen members and a number of minority group members (Rice and Hawkins were African Americans; Gonzales, Irastorza, and Barrales were Hispanic). In their broader analysis of sixty-five top Executive Office of the President (EOP) positions, Kathryn Dunn Tenpas and Stephen Hess found that 28 percent were women and 11 percent were minorities; these figures compare to 29 percent women and 8 percent minorities among a comparable pool in the Clinton EOP, 5 percent women and 3 percent minorities for Reagan, and 14 percent women and 7 percent minorities for Bush Sr. Also notable in their study is the finding that 29 percent of George W. Bush's staff members came from the president's home state, compared to 10 percent for Clinton and 9 percent for Bush Sr.; only the 26 percent of the Reagan staff from California approached the Bush percentage.[41]

Bush was thus able to meld loyalty, personal connection, and adherence to his policy agenda with inside the Washington Beltway experience. The temptation that political outsiders face in assuming office—bringing novice loyalists from back home into the White House—was not a problem for Bush. An unusually high number of his loyalists had already worked in the White House before. According to one analysis, 38 percent had served in the Bush Sr. White House; according to another, of the thirty-six staff positions announced before inauguration day, eighteen (50 percent) had served under Bush Sr.[42]

Card, Rove, and Hughes: A Unique Division of Labor

What was unique about the Bush staff was its organization at the very top. Card brought a wealth of prior White House and cabinet experience and expertise. Karen Hughes's position signaled both her close ties to Bush and the efforts that were planned in crafting the public face of this presidency. But there was to be a third major player in the Bush White House—Bush's longtime political and campaign adviser Karl Rove—whose appointment was not announced until January 4. According to Rove, however, the decision had been made three weeks earlier but had been delayed until the cabinet was named: "We wanted to set the tone and make it clear he [Bush] wanted to bring in a lot of different faces."[43]

Rove's duties as "senior adviser" to the president were broadly political with special emphasis on developing better strategic efforts for policy initiatives. Rove was given authority over the political affairs office, public liaison, and a newly created Office of Strategic Initiatives, which would handle long-term planning. In organizational terms (much like Hughes's duties on the communications side), it was the first White House staff structure in which those political units were directed by a top-level aide other than the chief of staff.

That the Bush White House would have three central figures—Card, Hughes, and Rove—was not unique. In some ways it resembled the James Baker, Ed Meese, and Michael Deaver "troika" of the first Reagan administration; indeed, media reports quickly began to speculate about its operations with that past arrangement in mind. The other analogy was Bush's own gubernatorial "iron triangle" of Allbaugh, Hughes, and Rove, with the new arrangement now dubbed a "platinum triangle": "Rove will govern strategic and political decision, Hughes will create the public face of the White House, and Card will handle day-to-day operations."[44] In fact, in announcing the appointments of Rove to the White House and Allbaugh as head of FEMA on January 4, Bush himself used the triangle analogy: "Previously I named one of the legs of the triangle to a White House position. That was Karen Hughes. Today it is my honor to report that the remainder of the triangle has agreed to serve in my administration."[45]

As a White House staff structure, however, the tripartite arrangement was different from both Bush's own past practice and that of the Reagan troika. In the Reagan White House, Ed Meese controlled the cabinet councils and policy development, while James Baker was in charge of the remainder of the White House units, including political affairs, legislative liaison, speech writing, and communications. Deaver, moreover, was clearly subordinate to and closely allied with Baker, and while he played an important role in crafting the public face of the Reagan presidency, his formal responsibilities were limited to scheduling, appointments, travel, and liaison to First Lady Nancy Reagan. The Bush division of labor was clearly quite different.

But as with the Reagan White House, the arrangement could pose potential challenges. For the Reagan team, policy formulation (Meese) had been separated from administration, management, politics, and communications (Baker). One task was to see to their smooth integration, in developing a close working relationship among the principals and among their staffs. But that integration sometimes proved elusive. The other difficulty was that staff functions often cannot be neatly demarcated. Baker's duties, for example, were often inherently policy-related. To take but one example, his responsibility for congressional liaison, especially when he created the legislative strategy group, brought him directly into the bargaining and negotiation process with Congress, which can directly affect the particulars of policy outcomes.

For the Bush principals, while the division of labor was different (Card controlled policy in ways that Baker didn't), the challenge would remain difficult: three very central players with three very important functions. In an interview at the time of his appointment, Rove did acknowledge that "he and Hughes will yield to the chief of staff's authority. 'Andy Card will be the first among equals.'"[46] Yet although they technically reported through Card, Rove and Hughes clearly directed an important array of White House units dealing with two important functions: political strategy and communications. They also had a closer relationship and a longer personal history with George W. Bush than did Card.

The chief of staff still remained, however, the chief of staff in the new structure. As Clay Johnson would note, at a point almost a year into the Bush presidency, it was not a triumvirate or troika in the same sense that existed in the early Reagan White House. "Andy is the chief of staff, and if Karl and Karen and Clay and Al and so forth aren't working, aren't being orchestrated well, it's Andy who needs to step in and do something different. But I wouldn't describe it as a triumvirate."

Johnson also stressed that the arrangement was one familiar to Bush from his gubernatorial experience and was one that was particularly suited to Card's own temperament and demeanor:

> It all started with the kind of governor's office that [Bush] ran, where he wanted lots of access to—between him and his senior people. And Joe Allbaugh was not called and I was not called the chief of staff. We were called the executive assistant, on purpose. And that's the kind of person by nature Andy is, and so he was a perfect selection for this president. He may not have been the perfect selection for another Republican president, but he was a perfect selection, I believe, for this president.[47]

Nor were the three the only centers of power in the Bush administration. As we shall see, an unusually strong cabinet was selected and Vice President Cheney was a central player in an array of policy areas and in the White House's dealings with Congress. In fact, Cheney's own staff selections were also strong. Cheney had selected veteran Washington lawyer I. Lewis "Scooter" Libby as his chief of staff, and he had tapped Mary Matalin, a Bush Sr. campaign adviser and well-known media figure, for the position of "counselor" to the vice president.[48] Both also held the title "assistant to the president."

Moreover, within the White House there were other key players, a fact that the Bush camp quickly emphasized to defuse the troika analogy: "The White House power structure will be much broader than three people, Bush advisers are quick to note. Policy head Josh Bolten, a deputy chief of staff, has developed a close relationship with Bush and will have an important voice in administration's decision."[49]

The arrangement may also have been of positive benefit beyond bringing Rove and Hughes into the White House on terms suitable to them. The appointment of Rove as senior adviser to the president and Karen Hughes as counselor to the president may also have reflected some lessons learned from the Bush Sr. presidency, as well as a desire to find places in the administration for two longtime Bush aides. Both participants and observers of the Bush Sr. White House have noted that too much was delegated to the chief of staff alone and that its communications and political affairs units were poorly organized and utilized. Bush Sr.'s best source of political and strategic advice was campaign strategist Lee Atwater, but Atwater was made chair of the Republican National Committee (RNC) rather than given a White House position; his untimely death, moreover, created a strategic void. Those errors were not repeated.

Andrew Card, in particular, had long recognized these deficiencies in the Bush Sr. White House when he was serving as deputy chief of staff to John Sununu. In a September 1998 interview with me, Card noted that he himself had tried to organize a White House group to focus on a broader strategic mission and better public and media communications, coupled with a more focused day-to-day agenda, in order to "establish priorities and stay on the offensive." "We tried to make it a very inclusive group, and we would make recommendations up to [chief of staff John] Sununu. But it was hard to bring discipline to that process because there was no buy-in from the top. . . . I think the marketing and selling was deficient because the management didn't live up to its expectations."[50] Card not only clearly recognized the need for the functions Rove and Hughes would perform, but now, as George W. Bush's chief manager, was in the position to "buy in" and to "live up to expectations."

The arrangement that had been worked out also could potentially benefit from the internal discipline that had been a hallmark of Bush's governorship, his campaign, and now the transition. Where rival centers of power might have doomed such an arrangement in some other White House, its success— at least potentially—might be greater in this White House and under this president, who was attuned to organizational issues and management needs. Loyalty and teamwork were values embraced if not demanded by the boss, George W. Bush. "Bush insists that loyalty can flower in an institution known for distractions and back-stabbing," one transition adviser noted at the time.[51] In Karl Rove's view, Bush's own role in the appointment process was a key factor: "Bush has tended to surround himself with people he's taken the measure of."[52]

Keep the National Economic Council?

One area that apparently came under scrutiny during the transition concerned the economic policy apparatus of the Bush administration. Two issues stood out. The first was whether to retain the National Economic Council (NEC) in the form that had developed in the later years of the Clinton presidency (when it was more a White House staff operation), or to move to the NEC of the early Clinton presidency (when it was chaired by Robert Rubin, then a White House aide, but with more cabinet involvement), or to move to the model of the Reagan and Bush Sr. years, when their economic policy councils had been chaired by the treasury secretary but with extensive White House staff support. The second issue was whether the head of the Office of the U.S. Trade Representative (USTR)—part of the EOP—should be granted cabinet status and whether international economic issues were properly structured in the policy-making process.

On January 3, Bush came to closure at least on who would lead his White House economic policy team with the announcement of Lawrence Lindsey's appointment as his chief economic adviser. Lindsey had been Bush's chief economic adviser during the campaign and had organized and led the team of economic advisers who had developed Bush's tax cut and social security privatization proposals as well as his defense and education budget priorities. Lindsey had served on the staff of the White House's Council of Economic Advisers in the first Reagan administration and had been a special assistant in the policy development shop in the Bush Sr. White House before becoming a member of the Board of Governors of the Federal Reserve. Lindsey's appointment came as no surprise.[53]

In appointing Lindsey as assistant to the president for economic policy, the Bush team followed the Clinton pattern of two top aides, one for economic policy (Lindsey), the other for domestic policy. This is in contrast to the Bush Sr. administration, where one assistant to the president—Roger Porter—wore both hats. But the Bush team did not reach closure on how the policy process would be organized and whether a White House–led NEC, of the sort that had existed in Clinton years, would be retained. In the early Clinton presidency, when it was directed by Robert Rubin (then at the White House), the NEC had worked reasonably well by most accounts in bringing together both cabinet and White House staff members. Following Rubin's departure to become treasury secretary, the NEC became more a White House–centered operation and less a cabinet council than had been the case before. When asked about the fate of the NEC and whether Lindsey would head it, Bush told reporters, "We'll let you know." He added, "Not to diminish Mr. Lindsey."[54]

According to the *New York Times,* "Elimination of the [NEC] would probably leave Lawrence Lindsey, Mr. Bush's top economic adviser, with less bureaucratic sway over how cabinet departments conduct both domestic and foreign economic policy, a move consistent with what several top advisers describe as Mr. Bush's objective of creating a relatively small but powerful cabinet vested with extensive executive authority." One adviser said, "Bush is going back to the Eisenhower-type cabinet, where it's more like a board of directors. . . . He wants a small workable cabinet. In the Clinton years, you literally couldn't fit the cabinet around a table." In the view of press spokesperson Fleischer: "The focus is on collegiality of approach"[55]

The fate of the NEC as well as the issue of whether the USTR would be downgraded from cabinet status (a perk since 1976) may also have been caught up in a bit of turf-tussle with Bush's longtime friend Don Evans, who had been picked to head the Commerce Department. According to one account, two Bush advisers said Bush intended to give Evans a larger role in setting trade policy: "Enhancing Evans's role is one reason Mr. Bush is considering denying cabinet status to the trade representative." The issue also had a national security twist to it. According to the same report, NSC adviser-designate Rice (who was not given cabinet rank) was also pushing to downgrade the USTR: "Ms. Rice views economic policy abroad as part of her portfolio and would prefer that the trade representative not outrank her, these advisers said."[56]

Yet by Monday, January 8, the Bush camp had backed off the proposal. The downgrading of the USTR was criticized by incumbent trade representative Charlene Barshefsky as "an act of absolute folly." Another former Clinton trade representative, Mickey Kantor (who had also served as commerce secretary), also came to its defense, stating that it was "not one of the better ideas we've seen. This is the most successful trade agency in the world. Why change it?" The proposal also raised concerns among members of Congress and the business community. A spokesman for Representative Bill Thomas (R-CA), the new chairman of the House Ways and Means Committee, told reporters that Thomas had been assured by "high-level officials" that the position would not be downgraded.[57]

By January 10 the issue had been resolved. Robert Zoellick was named trade representative and given cabinet status. Zoellick had been undersecretary of state for economic affairs under James Baker, served as his executive secretary when Baker was at Treasury, then was deputy White House chief of staff when Baker was persuaded to take that position again in 1992.

But some organizational changes were made. On January 16, Fleischer announced that a new White House position would be added to coordinate economic policy with the NSC, since "international economic policy now has defense implications and economics implications." The position would be filled at the deputy assistant level, and Rice and Lindsey would jointly run the staff. Reports also indicated that the NEC would continue to exist and be run by Lindsey, but that the new international economic unit would have a separate staff. The position was eventually filled by Gary R. Edson. Edson too was a White House veteran. He had been chief of staff and general counsel to trade representative Carla Hills in the first Bush administration and before that was a senior aide to Kenneth W. Dam, a deputy defense secretary in the first Reagan administration. According to the *National Journal,* Edson "has the tricky role of trying to serve two masters. . . . His two-hatted job reflects an effort by the Bush White House to better coordinate international economic and security policy."[58]

Managing Early

The transition also was a time to instill a particular organizational culture that Bush valued. Part of it emerged from the shared experience of many of Bush's White House aides. James Barnes of the *National Journal* later observed that while "the Clinton White House was more of a coalition—with aides from all parts of the Democratic Party," the Bush White House was more cohesive: "Because so many people on the Bush White House staff worked together either on the campaign or, even before that, in Austin, they've not only demonstrated their fidelity to Bush, they've operated as a team and formed bonds with each other, which may diminish prospects for internecine warfare."[59] In an article that appeared in the *New York Times Magazine* a week before Bush's inauguration, reporter James Bennet noted, "One Bush adviser told me that he had been informed by Austin that he had been welcomed into the 'family'; then he called a couple of days later and asked me not to print his name, lest he be ejected."[60]

That sense of a "George W. Bush family" as well as the practice of its extension of loyalty and teamwork to newcomers was also a feature of the appointment selection process. As Clay Johnson later observed:

> There was a history of great loyalty to George W. Bush and great interest in working for him. That nucleus is half of the senior White House staff, that Austin group. So you start with that and then I think you also pick people—I saw this in the cabinet—there is a great deal of interest in effective teamwork and there are people you can select who understand what teamwork is and understand how to work and how to agree or disagree productively with each other and then there are other people for whom it has got to be their way, got to be their show. I saw a few people, one or two, who were lead candidates to be offered cabinet secretary positions who were not offered that because the feeling was that they were not going to be comfortable working in a team structure. So the same thing in the White House I suspect. I know that Andy picked people that he would be able to work effectively with and be able to work effectively on the George W. Bush team. You can

imagine [the possibility of] people that were more free agent types or solo performers; I think there is a minimum amount of that, if any, in this White House.[61]

Teamwork not only was a concern in the selection process, it also was something that the transition's leaders sought to put into immediate practice. With respect to the cabinet, according to Johnson, "The secretary-designates spent a lot of time in Washington during the last few weeks of the transition. We set aside offices for them in an area called 'Secretaries Row,' with the benefit being that they got to interact a little with one another before the administration began."[62] With respect to the staff, the final days of the transition even saw what Johnson termed "practicing to be in the White House," which Card had instigated: "The senior staff of the White House had begun to meet for the last ten days to two weeks of the transition, twice a day, to get in the habit of meeting with each other, communicating with each other, and to begin to talk about the president's schedule as if we were in the White House."[63] During the week of January 8, Card held a staff meeting of some 150 soon-to-be White House aides, delivering what came to be known as the "pin-drop speech":

> In a room usually reserved for freewheeling news conferences, Card summoned 150 subordinates for a sermon on the gravity of the task ahead. You are on the threshold of assuming the most coveted offices in the most powerful building on Earth, Card told his hushed audience. Beware, he said, of "White House-itis," an inflammation of the ego that flourishes within the complex's gates. In a town where nothing advertises status like a security pass, Card asked his staff to tuck their prestigious hangtags away when they leave the White House grounds. "Be among the most humble people in Washington." Card reminded them that they will serve in roles few others will, and that "few things you do in your lives you'll remember as vividly as the day you walk into the White House."[64]

From Campaign Promises to a Policy Agenda

In addition to putting together a presidential team and crafting decisionmaking processes, transitions are times when campaign themes are prioritized and translated into a legislative agenda. For Reagan in 1980 and Clinton in 1992, the period was especially crucial in developing their respective economic and fiscal proposals. For Carter in 1976, it was the time when his energy plan was developed, but it was also a period when priorities failed to be established, leading to a laundry list of legislative proposals once he was in office. For Bush Sr., the 1988 transition was a period when proposals dealing with failures in the savings and loan industry and Latin American debt were crafted. It also was the time when OMB director-designate Richard Darman developed a plan for dealing with the deficit that would involve muddling through in 1989, but potentially raising taxes in 1990—and the latter would have a significant effect on Bush's presidency and his electoral prospects for 1992. Crafting a policy agenda during the transition is especially crucial in order to take advantage of whatever "honeymoon" period a new president might enjoy in dealing with Congress.

George W. Bush and his associates used the transition to focus on a limited number of policy proposals that Bush had made during the 2000 campaign: tax cuts, education reform, faith-based initiatives, defense modernization, and social security reform. In so doing, Bush drew not just on the experience of his predecessors, but also on how he dealt with the Texas state legislature on becoming governor: stick with a limited number of proposals that had been the centerpiece of the campaign.

In Karl Rove's view, the Bush presidential agenda was clearly formed in the campaign, and, for Rove, the distinction between campaigning and governing was less clear-cut for Bush. "When he talked about a tax cut in the campaign, he meant it. When he talked about, went and gave three speeches on education reform, he meant it. . . . It was tax cuts, education, faith base, Medicare and Social Security reform, and defense modernization. He talked about five things during the campaign endlessly."[65]

Bush also, according to Rove, sought to flesh out his proposals by building a strong advisory network during the campaign: "So when he began thinking about running for president, he began to build a robust team of advisers on issues for exactly that reason . . . he wanted to use the process of campaigning and the development of public policy during the campaign as an integral part of his governance." Policy planning during the campaign "was an integral part of governance." Josh Bolten was hired (in December 1998) as a domestic policy adviser to Bush, well before a political director of the campaign had been brought on board.[66] Moreover, Bush reportedly told Bolten that three policy advisers were already at work: Condoleezza Rice for national security and foreign policy, Larry Lindsey for economics policy, and Indianapolis mayor Stephen Goldsmith for domestic issues. By the spring of 1999 the group had organized a wide range of experts who provided briefing papers to Bush. In the domestic area alone, Goldsmith had formed eighteen task forces, with 200 briefing papers forwarded to Austin and some fifty policy experts called down to brief Bush and his team. From this network of advice, Bush's domestic agenda was whittled down to his campaign themes. In foreign policy, Bush's agenda began in April 1998, well before he had made a final decision to run, with a visit to Stanford University's Hoover Institution organized by former secretary of state George Shultz. Several months later, Bush met with Rice at the family compound in Kennebunkport, Maine. According to Rice, "We spent three days asking each other a lot of questions about the world. I didn't just assume he had his father's views."[67] Rice then coordinated Bush's foreign policy advisory group, which included not only former secretaries of state Kissinger, Shultz, and Baker and NSC adviser (under both Ford and Bush Sr.) Brent Scowcroft, but also an advisory group dubbed (after the Roman god of the forge, whose statue rises above Rice's hometown of Birmingham, Alabama) the "Vulcans." The latter included Richard Armitage, Richard Perle, Paul Wolfowitz, Robert Zoellick, Stephen Hadley, Robert Blackwill, and Dov Zakheim.[68]

There also was a strong presumption, at least in Rove's view, that these campaign advisers would become players in a future Bush administration: "We recognized that these teams of people that we would have in the policy apparatus, you know, people like Rich Armitage, and Paul Wolfowitz, and Dick Cheney, and Don Rumsfeld, and Condi Rice, and Larry Lindsey [and] Don Evans. . . . [T]here was a high likelihood of them finding their way into government. . . . We recognized that this was a prelude to transition, but we never called it transition."[69]

Bush and his policy advisers also understood that more work on policy needed to be done after election day, especially in moving from a campaign agenda to concrete legislative proposals. Furthermore, it was during the transition, Rove recognized, that the Bush agenda needed to be tailored into a tighter strategic plan. Here the 1980 Reagan transition provided important lessons, particularly the work of David Gergen and Richard Wirthlin in developing a long-range strategic plan for the emerging Reagan presidency. According to one account, Rove was placed in charge of

> drawing up a detailed action plan for the first 180 days of the Bush Administration. Rove's task: to take items in the agenda Bush campaigned on, turn them into pieces of actual legislation, and then choreograph their roll-out for maximum political benefit. The best antidote to the public's lingering qualms about Bush's legitimacy, says an adviser, is to "show that we're very busy doing things that real people want. We have to get some things done— fast. . . . Rove has laid out a plan—in a series of memos and calendars—for the boss's first four weeks."[70]

According to Rove, the impetus for the effort came from Bush shortly after Gore's concession:

> The president-elect held a meeting and said: "I want to have a plan for how we begin the administration for at least the first six weeks, but I'd like to extend it as long as possible. . . . I saw what happened to my dad, who got elected and came in and then said, What do we do? . . . I saw what happened to Clinton who campaigned on a number of issues, and then came in and . . . got enmeshed in an entirely different set of issues. . . . I want a plan that will describe from the moment I say 'So help me God' what it is we're going to do, based on fulfilling the things we did in the campaign."

But Rove also acknowledged that the effort had begun earlier: "We had a lot of people who, after the election and during the thirty-six days from hell, were in Austin and were not fully occupied, and so we put them to work basically researching the first 100 days or the first year [to] see how they had done it, what was important, and what was the framing and the flow of it, what were the successes and failures."[71]

Rove himself was busy, digesting the material that had been prepared by his staff and learning the lessons of past presidential transitions. "It is important to strike the right note," Rove told his associates, and "time is precious."[72] Rove's work, in turn, would structure the roll-out of the Bush agenda over its early months, beginning with his education reform proposals during his first week in office, followed by his faith-based initiative program, a plan for providing prescription drugs for seniors, and then his tax reform proposal. As Rove later told Martha Joynt Kumar, "We did take a look at the seven [presidential transitions], essentially [from John F.] Kennedy forward. We actually looked at the first 180 days and tried to draw lessons not only about the things that happened in the first 180 days, but what were the things that allowed them to then move on to have a successful period after that."[73]

Like the successful legislative strategy group that James Baker developed as chief of staff under Reagan, Rove and Card also used the transition period to create a number of White House staff groups designed to further the Bush policy agenda. One was an Office of Strategic Initiatives, under Rove's direction, designed to emphasize long-range planning and provide input to meetings of senior White House aides. Other groups were created to deal with long-range scheduling, communications, and congressional liaison.[74]

Foreign and national security policy did not figure heavily into the roll-out of the Bush agenda. Bush received his first national security briefing (along with Condoleezza Rice), conducted by members of the outgoing administration, on December 6. The nomination of Colin Powell as secretary of state brought star power to the Bush team, as did Rice's appointment as NSC adviser. On January 8, Bush met with members of Congress in Austin for a closed-door discussion on defense issues; eight Republicans and six Democratic members attended.

The only other major foreign policy announcements came on January 2, when press spokesman Fleischer told reporters that Bush was critical of the treaty establishing a global court for war crimes that Clinton signed on December 31; it was a "flawed treaty" that would not be sent to the Senate in its "current form." Fleischer also announced that Bush would continue the "don't ask, don't tell" policy for gays in the military.

Building Bridges and Creating Support for a Policy Agenda

The transition is also a time when bridges can be built with Congress and a political coalition assembled. In 1976, as Washington newcomers, Carter and his Georgia associates had difficulty understanding and dealing with members of Congress, incoming House Speaker Tip O'Neill (D-MA) most notably. In 1992, Clinton's efforts were compromised by his handling of the issue of gays in the military. In 1980, by contrast, Reagan sought to win over Washington during his transition, not just meeting with congressional Democrats as well as Republicans, but also introducing himself to social Washington, which Carter had scorned.

George W. Bush's situation was unusually precarious: the battle over Florida might have poisoned the atmosphere for future bipartisan cooperation or even the lessening of partisan tensions. But Bush followed the Reagan game plan and even upped it a degree, holding an unprecedented number of meetings with both Democratic and Republican members of Congress. Many of them were targeted at members on the key committees that had jurisdiction over his policy initiatives.

Once again, Bush's gubernatorial experience was helpful: a Republican governor who had to deal with a Texas state legislature controlled by the Democrats. While his experiences with Texas Democrats, Karl Rove would later note, were "not exactly transferable . . . nonetheless he's used to dealing with this. But I do think it made him sensitive, particularly when it came to the drafting of the inaugural and his desire to set this different tone and his desire to invite . . . members of Congress down [to Texas] so that they could make a judgment about him firsthand, not through intermediaries." According to Rove, moreover, it was Bush's own political instincts and leadership style that led him to value his personal contact with legislators, especially of the opposition party: "We can't personalize everything," Bush told Rove, "but if people sort of see who I am, and I see who they are, and we have a chance to talk about these things, we'll have a better chance to have a civil dialogue."[75]

Even before Florida was fully settled, Bush sought to strike a civil tone with members of Congress of both parties and to lessen the partisan tenor of his political agenda. On Saturday, December 2, Bush and Cheney met at his ranch with Speaker of the House Dennis Hastert (R-IL) and Senate Majority Leader Trent Lott (R-MS). Meeting with reporters before the session, Bush ticked off the key points of his agenda, noting, "This isn't a Republican agenda. It's not a Democrat agenda. . . . As a matter of fact, this election, and the fact that it's been as close as it's been and as long drawn out as it is, requires a group of citizens that rise above partisanship and do what's right for the country, more so than ever in recent modern history."[76] Bush also told reporters he had contacted Senator John Breaux (D-LA) earlier in the week. Breaux, a moderate Democrat, was a potential swing vote in a closely divided Senate on a number of key issues for Bush, including his tax cut proposal, Medicare reform, and energy policy.

Bush's efforts at reaching out to members of Congress also dovetailed with his policy agenda in other ways. Education reform was one area where Bush began work early. On December 1, Bush spoke with a number of legislators on his education reform package. One of those contacted by Bush was Senator Jeffords (R-VT), who said that Bush told him "his primary goal is to work in the areas of primary and secondary education." Bush also contacted GOP House members Thomas Petri of Washington, Peter Hoekstra of Michigan, and Michael Castle of Delaware, all members of the House Education and Workforce Committee. According to Representative Petri, "He indicated he was calling a number of people who had been involved in education on the Hill. . . . He said he was hoping we could move forward in the education area early in the next Congress."[77] According to Representative Hoekstra, "[Bush] reiterated that education is going to continue to be a very high priority for him, and he wanted to make sure he builds relationships with people in Congress who have been active on the education issue." Hoekstra also noted that Bush wanted to reach out to all kinds of Republicans and Democrats: "I was very impressed with his approach. It's kind of like, hey, let's begin this on a personal level. Let's build a personal relationship here, recognizing that we've all got our own policy priorities."[78]

On December 14, the day after Gore's concession, Bush spoke with the Democratic leaders of Congress—Senate Minority Leader Tom Daschle (D-SD) and House Minority Leader Dick Gephardt (D-MO)—as well as the Reverend Jesse Jackson. The next day, Bush again met with Senator John Breaux, who reportedly turned down an offer to serve as secretary of energy; Karen Hughes described the meeting as part of an effort to hear from Democrats and reported that the two discussed a wide range of issues.[79]

On Sunday, December 17, Bush traveled to Washington for the traditional meeting of the president-elect with the incumbent president (as well as a brief meeting with Vice President Gore).[80] Bush used the trip to interview cabinet prospects, and he met with the entire GOP congressional leadership and then held a bipartisan meeting with Hastert, Lott, Daschle, and Gephardt. For Lott, "This is a time for a new beginning, a new atmosphere, a new tone"; for Gephardt, "We will be there coming fifty percent of the way, sometimes even a little further"; and for Daschle, it was "an opportunity to wipe the slate clean, to begin anew." Bush also used the trip as an opportunity to meet with Federal Reserve Chairman Alan Greenspan. Greenspan reportedly had reservations about some of Bush's proposed tax cuts (but several weeks later would endorse it in congressional testimony). According to David Broder, Bush's "determination to press for the agenda on which he campaigned was clear" and both Republicans and Democrats "found him in their private sessions to be self-assured, surprisingly direct, yet ready to listen to different views. . . . Bush hardly behaved like someone who was sneaking into the White House by the back door."[81]

Bush's efforts with members of Congress, especially on key committees, continued over the next several weeks. On December 21, Bush met with still another group of legislators to discuss his education initiatives. Although the bipartisan group did not wholly endorse Bush's proposals (Bush's voucher plan raised particular concern, as it would over the next year until it was finally dropped), it apparently was an unusually productive meeting, particularly in establishing personal relationships with some of the Democratic members. As Bush later told reporters, "It is safe to say we had an extraordinary meeting." Senator Zell Miller (D-GA) described it as a vigorous give-and-take, with Bush articulately responding to lawmakers' questions and points. According to Senator Miller, "I think it spoke volumes on how this new president is going to operate. It was a candid exchange."[82] Rove later recalled that this was "an extraordinary meeting":

> This is the famous meeting where George Miller (D-CA) got his name (from Bush), "Big Jorge," "Jorge Grande," and where there's just an unbelievable meeting about education, about accountability. . . . [I]t went on for hours, but I mean it was very, very focused and very powerful. And at the end of the meeting Zell Miller, who had said very little, . . . stood up, after this fabulous conversation about shared goals and the president-elect's vision, and said, "You know, I'm against vouchers. . . . I've been against choice. I've been against it forever. But if it's part of your plan, I'm for your plan, all of your plan." And this was a great signal that there could be some bipartisan agreement on education.

Bush also impressed Representative Miller of California—"Big Jorge"—a liberal Democrat who had been concerned about the racial impact of Bush's proposal. As Rove later recalled, at one point in the meeting, Bush said, "Disaggregate the data" (on test results and failing schools by racial and ethnic subgroups). He then turned to Miller: "I know how you've been calling for disaggregation of the data and I know how important that is." According to Rove, "You would have thought George Miller had been slapped with a wet towel, for [Bush], who he obviously had a low opinion of at the time, [to] say, 'Disaggregate the data,' [it] sort of shocked him."[83]

Cheney's efforts were also a part of Bush's overtures to Congress. In Clay Johnson's view, Cheney's role was crucial to the Bush legislative effort: "[Cheney] was able to reach out and engage all members of Congress very, very effectively to make the point that we understand how Congress works, we understand your reservations, we understand your anxieties, we're going to keep you informed. And it was a huge priority to stay plugged in with Republicans, primarily, but also the Democrats in Congress, and he led that effort."[84] As a former GOP House leader, Cheney's résumé had paid off again for Bush. Cheney's lobbying efforts began even before Florida was fully settled, most notably a December 6 meeting with the GOP congressional leadership. After Gore's concession, Cheney's efforts stepped up, including meetings with a number of Democrats, notably Gore's vice-presidential running mate, Senator Joseph Lieberman (D-CT), a potential source of support on education and national security issues, as well as Democratic leaders Senator Daschle and Representative Gephardt.[85]

Among Republican members of Congress, Cheney's efforts were directed at making sure that they were in tune with the Bush agenda, especially the Bush tax reform plan.[86] Deviations from the Bush plan were quickly corrected. Remarks made by House Speaker Hastert on December 14, for example, were interpreted to suggest that Hastert and other GOP congressional leaders opposed Bush's across-the-board plan and instead favored dealing with the so-called marriage penalty and reducing estate taxes (a bill dealing with both had passed Congress but was vetoed by President Clinton).[87] The next day Hastert's press secretary informed the media that there had been "some miscommunication," and Hastert issued a written statement supporting Bush's plan, noting the difference was only on legislative tactics.[88] Bush too continued to emphasize that the across-the-board plan was central to his agenda, but also acknowledged the realities of the legislative process. After his December 18 Washington meeting with Lott, Hastert, Daschle, and Gephardt, Bush told the press (with the four at his side), "I think the case is even more solid today than it was a year ago when I started campaigning on the issue. There is going to be a lot of discussion, a lot of head-knocking, kind of gentle arm-twisting. I'm sure they'll be twisting my arm and I might try to twist a few myself to reach what's right for America."[89]

From mid-December 2000 through January 2001, Bush also undertook a number of public relations efforts to emphasize his policy agenda. These included meetings with educators and school officials to sell them on his education reform and school voucher plan, with African American religious leaders to explain his faith-based initiatives program, and with business executives and Republican governors to sell his tax cut plan. Bush's efforts to use public appearances to sell his policy agenda and build support were not new—Clinton had his much publicized "economic summit" during the 1992 transition—but they did represent an expansion in scope, covering a range of policy issues. They fit, moreover, Charles O. Jones's notion that the transition process now involves not just a shift to "governing" but a continuation of campaigning.[90]

Bush's effort for his faith-based initiatives was emphasized on December 20, when he met with a group of religious leaders—with a large number of African American pastors in attendance—at Faith Baptist Church in Austin. On January 11, Bush convened an "education summit," which included both educators and business leaders. The Bush team even invited one critic of school vouchers to attend: Hugh Price, president of the National Urban League. Price later told reporters, "I thought much of what the president said was on point. . . . This is authentic with him. I saw accountability and early literacy as where he is going to place the greatest emphasis."[91] Several days later, Bush commemorated Martin Luther King Day by speaking at Kelso Elementary School, located in a predominantly black neighborhood of Houston. Bush was flanked by two African Americans, the school's principal and Roderick Paige, Houston's superintendent of schools and Bush's choice for education secretary. Bush spoke warm words in praise of King, but also used his remarks to emphasize his education agenda and pledge that "no child shall be left behind."

Starting on January 3, Bush began a two-day series of meetings with top business executives in Austin to promote his tax cut plan. Unlike Clinton's 1992 economic summit, which was broadcast on C-SPAN, this one was held in private. That same day, the Federal Reserve made a sharp cut in interest rates and Bush took the opportunity to use it as a call for his tax plan: "One of the messages Mr. Greenspan sent was that we need bold action, not only at the Fed, but . . . bold action in the halls of Congress to make sure the economy stays vibrant." On hearing of the rate change, the business leaders responded by raising their water glasses in a toast to Greenspan. In addition, Bush used the occasion to raise the possibility that a worsening economic situation might require a faster phase-in of the tax cut plan, as well as to signal that he was open to talks and suggestions.[92] Several days later, on January 6, Bush's tax cut plan, his education reform proposals, as well as a desire to shift power from Washington to the states were themes the president-elect emphasized in a meeting he convened at his ranch with nineteen GOP governors.

Warning Signs

Yet despite their best efforts, Bush and his advisers could not completely control the upcoming political agenda. By early January, it had become clear to them that the Clinton White House was issuing a number of last-minute executive orders and other regulatory measures that Bush would need to address. These included such controversial issues as banning logging and road-building operations in nearly 60 million acres of national forests, as well as new rules dealing with ergonomics in the workplace. According to press spokesman Fleischer, Bush planned to review "each and every" last-minute Clinton order.[93] As well, on January 4, Senator John McCain (R-AZ), Bush's recent rival for the GOP nomination, announced at a press conference that he would pursue, once again, his effort at campaign finance reform. Pledging an all-out battle, McCain also announced that Senator Thad Cochran (R-MS) would be supporting his effort, potentially providing him with sixty votes in the Senate to overcome any filibuster.[94] Nor would McCain delay consideration of his bill until later in the year, after the Senate had taken up the Bush agenda. Finally, despite Cheney's meetings with him, Senator Joseph Lieberman (D-CT) had raised strong objections to the voucher and school choice provisions in Bush's education reform plan. So too did Senator Jim Jeffords

(R-VT)—then chairman of the Senate committee handling education issues—who supported a less ambitious measure that he hoped would not raise partisan passions.[95]

*   *   *

By January 2, Bush had finished selection of his cabinet. That date placed him only about a week behind Clinton's schedule in 1992. More notable in fact, Bush was actually well ahead of Clinton in naming his White House staff. In 1992, Clinton's press secretary, White House legal counsel, congressional liaison, and domestic policy adviser were not announced until the last week before his inauguration. For both the cabinet and the White House staff, the transition planning undertaken before the Florida vote had been settled allowed the Bush transition to move quickly once the official transition was under way in mid-December. As Clay Johnson later noted, it was a process that involved "a lot of planning, a lot of focus, a lot of rigor and discipline."[96] It was an effort that was particularly notable for the attention not just to the normal job of getting an administration in place, but also to understanding how those pieces fit together organizationally and the management tasks that they set forth. The question that remained was whether the choices made, particularly in crafting channels of information and advice and a decisionmaking process, had been the right ones once this administration was in office.

The Bush team recognized the need to use the transition period as a time to move from campaign promises and proposals to a more concrete political agenda. Its efforts here resemble the work undertaken by the Reagan transition in 1980, especially in crafting a more limited set of legislative proposals that Congress could digest. Rove's work on strategy and tactics also mirrored activities of the Reagan effort. As Clay Johnson later noted, "On the agenda, a commitment to do a few things very well, that was mark of the transition."[97] Bush and his associates also used the remainder of this truncated transition in an attempt to build public and congressional support, efforts that were especially necessary given the divisiveness over the way he had acceded to the presidency. His legitimacy in office began to be established and closer bonds began to form with some congressional Democrats. Yet some warning signs were apparent. The qualms raised by Lieberman and, especially, Jeffords would prove significant down the road. Building bridges was no guarantee that all—or even a bare majority—would choose to cross.

Notes

1. The nomination of former senator John Tower (R-TX) for secretary of defense was rejected by the Senate on March 9, 1989. Representative Richard Cheney (R-WY) was quickly tapped to replace him on March 10.

2. The last appointment made, that of Zoe Baird for attorney general, quickly ran into controversy concerning her employment of an undocumented alien (and her husband) as household help and her failure to pay their social security taxes. Baird's replacement, Kimba Wood, had a similar problem. It was not until February 11, 1993, that Janet Reno's nomination to the post was made public.

3. In the interim the following nominations were announced: December 20, Paul O'Neill (Treasury), Donald Evans (Commerce), Mel Martinez (Housing and Urban Development), and Ann Veneman (Agriculture); December 22, John Ashcroft (Attorney General) and Donald Rumsfeld (Defense); December 29, Tommy Thompson (Health and Human Services), Roderick Paige (Education), Gale Norton (Interior), and Anthony Principi (Veterans Affairs); January 2, Spencer Abraham (Energy), Norman Mineta (Transportation), and Linda Chavez (Labor). On January 11, Chavez's replacement, Elaine Chao, was announced.

4. Frank Bruni, "Advisers to Bush Say He Would Use Appointments to Send a Message About Diversity," *New York Times,* December 1, 2000.

5. Frank Bruni, "Quietly but Confidently, Bush Pushes Ahead," *New York Times,* November 28, 2000.

6. Former New Jersey governor Christie Todd Whitman, Bush's choice to head the Environmental Protection Agency, was also given cabinet rank.

7. Mike Allen, "With Eye on Transition, Bush Confers with Powell," *Washington Post,* December 1, 2000.

8. Mike Allen, "Bush to Forge Ahead with Agenda," *Washington Post,* December 14, 2000.

9. According to one Bush adviser, "Cheney didn't want Powell's guy; Powell didn't want Cheney's guy." Richard A. Oppel Jr. and Frank Bruni, "Bush Adviser Gets National Security Post," *New York Times,* December 18, 2000. Rumsfeld had also been under serious consideration for appointment as director of the Central Intelligence Agency. Mann, *Rise of the Vulcans,* pp. 262–269. Mann also has an interesting account of the positions that Paul Wolfowitz and Richard Armitage were considered for; see Mann, *Rise of the Vulcans,* pp. 270–274.

10. Eric Schmitt and James Dao, "GOP Split Slows Bush's Selection for Defense Post," *New York Times,* December 22, 2000. Coats had good connections to the Bush transition: Cheney's congressional transition leader, David Gribbin, had been Coats's chief of staff, and Bush's top speech writer Michael Gerson had also worked on Coats's staff. But Coats may have carried too much baggage due to his skepticism on gender integration in the military and his vehement opposition to Clinton's plan for gays in the military; as well, he may not have been a good fit to lead the Pentagon restructuring that Bush hoped to pursue. Also see Mann, *Rise of the Vulcans,* p. 267.

11. Eric Schmitt and Elaine Sciolino, "To Run Pentagon, Bush Sought Proven Manager with Muscle," *New York Times,* January 1, 2001.

12. See, for example, Allissa Rubin, "Bush Faces Push from the Right," *Los Angeles Times,* December 8, 2000; David Johnston and Neil Lewis, "Religious Right Made Big Push to Put Ashcroft in Justice Dept.," *New York Times,* January 7, 2001.

13. Conservatives felt Racicot had not done enough to restrict abortions in Montana, nor had he pushed school choice hard enough; he had also supported adding sexual orientation to Montana's hate crimes legislation in the aftermath of the Matthew Shepard murder. See David Johnston and Neil Lewis, "Religious Right Made Big Push to Put Ashcroft in Justice Dept.," *New York Times,* January 7, 2001.

14. The nomination of Ashcroft was especially criticized for his opposition to abortion and his successful efforts to deny a federal judgeship to an African American member of the Missouri Supreme Court. Ashcroft's nomination was narrowly voted

out of the Senate Judiciary Committee (on which he had just served) by a vote of 10–8, and he was confirmed by the Senate on February 1 by a vote of 58–42. Norton was seen as a protégée of Reagan's controversial interior secretary James Watt and she was a supporter of opening up the Arctic National Wildlife Refuge for oil exploration. She was confirmed on January 30 by a vote of 75–24.

15. Mike Allen, "A Team Built on Conservative Discipline," *Washington Post,* January 3, 2001.

16. Eric Schmitt, "Cabinet Selection Over, Transition Now Focuses on Those Important No. 2's," *New York Times,* January 5, 2001.

17. Clay Johnson, panel discussion, "Bush Transition to the Presidency: Planning and Implementation," American Enterprise Institute, Washington, D.C., December 11, 2001.

18. Mike Allen, "A Team Built on Conservative Discipline," *Washington Post,* January 3, 2001.

19. James Bennet, "The Bush Years: CEO, USA," *New York Times Magazine,* January 14, 2001.

20. Frank Bruni, "Quietly but Confidently, Bush Pushes Ahead," *New York Times,* November 28, 2000. Also see Mike Allen, "Bush Turns to Veterans of Father's Team," *Washington Post,* November 29, 2000.

21. Mike Allen and Amy Goldstein, "A Cabinet Sworn to Loyalty," *Washington Post,* December 24, 2000.

22. Mike Allen and Dana Milbank, "Cabinet Chosen Quietly, Quickly," *Washington Post,* January 7, 2001.

23. Telephone interview with Clay Johnson, September 20, 2001.

24. Clay Johnson, panel discussion, "President Bush's First 100 Days," Kennedy School of Government, Harvard University, May 2, 2001.

25. Rice had been a political science professor at Stanford University and a staff member and Soviet expert at the NSC for two years in the Bush Sr. administration. She then returned to Stanford and was appointed its provost at the age of thirty-eight. She became acquainted with Bush during his father's presidency and became a close foreign policy adviser early on in his candidacy, heading an eight-member advisory team dubbed the "Vulcans." Gonzales was a partner at Vinson & Elkins, a leading Houston legal firm, then was Bush's first general counsel as governor in 1995. Bush appointed him secretary of state, then named him a member of the Texas Supreme Court (he had just won reelection in November 2000). Hughes had been a television reporter and had worked in public relations before becoming active in Texas GOP politics, later serving as a key media and communications adviser to Bush during his gubernatorial campaigns.

26. In late December, Stephen J. Hadley, a former assistant secretary of defense for international security policy in the Bush Sr. presidency, was tapped as deputy national security adviser under Rice. Hadley advised Bush during the campaign on foreign policy, was a partner in the D.C. law firm of Shea & Gardner, and a principal in Brent Scowcroft's international consulting firm.

27. Card had initially placed the public liaison office under Hughes's jurisdiction, but she felt that her communications duties might give the unit short shrift and that Rove would be a better choice to oversee that office. Hughes, *Ten Minutes from Normal,* p. 293. According to Hughes, it was also Card who had suggested "counselor to the president" for her title, "saying he modeled it on the role and title given Ed Meese in Ronald Reagan's administration." Hughes, *Ten Minutes from Normal,* p. 184.

28. Mike Allen and Thomas Ricks, "At Odds over the Economy," *Washington Post,* December 22, 2000.

29. From 1994 to 1999, Bolten had been executive director of legal and governmental affairs for Goldman Sachs in London. Before joining the Bush Sr. White House, Bolten had worked in the State Department's legal counsel's office, was the international trade counsel for the Senate Finance Committee from 1989 to 1989, and had served as executive assistant to the director of the Kissinger Commission on Central America.

30. From 1985 to 1988, Hagin was director of public affairs for Federated Department Stores and after the Bush Sr. presidency was an executive at Chiquita Brands.

31. Following college at Middlebury, Fleischer worked for the Republican National Committee, and then on the staffs of Representative Norman Lent (R-NY), Senator Peter Domenici (R-NM), and the House Ways and Means Committee. In the 2000 campaign, Fleischer initially worked in Elizabeth Dole's campaign, and when she dropped her bid he was asked to join the Bush effort.

32. Daniels then served as CEO of the Hudson Institute and since 1990 was a senior vice president at Eli Lilly and Co. He reportedly was not Bush's first choice for the job; Bush had offered it to Stanford University economist John Cogan, who turned it down. Michael Grunwald, "Washington's Loudest Voice for Frugality," *Washington Post,* January 20, 2003.

33. Mike Allen, "Matalin Appointed Counselor to Cheney, Assistant to Bush," *Washington Post,* January 6, 2001.

34. Irastorza had been deputy director of the Office of Management and Administration in the Bush Sr. White House and now headed that office under George W. Bush.

35. Eskew had interned in the Reagan White House's political affairs office when it was run by veteran strategists Lyn Nofziger and Ed Rollins; while there he worked with Lee Atwater, who introduced him to Governor Campbell. A third—albeit short-term—appointment to Hughes's staff was unveiled on January 10: Margaret Tutweiler, former State Department and Treasury press spokesman and a close aide to James Baker, agreed to join the White House communications team as consultant for ninety days.

36. Mehlman had ties to Rove going back to a 1996 congressional campaign. More recently, Mehlman had served as field director of the Bush campaign, with particular responsibilities for organizing the Bush efforts at the Iowa straw poll in 1999 and the states that held caucuses.

37. Dana Milbank, "Bush Names Rove Political Strategist," *Washington Post,* January 5, 2001. Barrales had also run a losing race for state controller of California in 1998, and he had become acquainted with Bush during the campaign and had kept in touch with him.

38. Kumar, "Recruiting and Organizing the White House Staff," p. 37.

39. James A. Barnes, "Bush's Insiders," *National Journal,* June 23, 2001, p. 1868.

40. Kumar, "Recruiting and Organizing the White House Staff," p. 38.

41. Kathryn Dunn Tenpas and Stephen Hess, "Organizing the Bush Presidency: Assessing Its Early Performance," in Gregg and Rozell, *Considering the Bush Presidency,* p. 39. Interestingly, there were little age differences among the four; all averaged either forty-four or forty-five years of age.

42. James A. Barnes, "Bush's Insiders," *National Journal,* June 23, 2001, p. 1869. Other accounts offer slightly different figures depending on when calculations were made and the pool of staff members included. According to Ryan Lizza of the *New Republic,* "W.'s White House is populated almost entirely by Bush family loyalists. While the Cabinet, selected in large part on symbolic and political criteria, may defy easy summation, W.'s White House breaks cleanly into two categories: close associ-

ates from Texas and Washington insiders who worked for his father. Of thirty-six staffers announced before the inaugural, eighteen [50 percent] previously served under George H.W. Bush . . . and eleven worked for W. in Texas. Of the remaining staffers, four come directly from the Bush campaign." Ryan Lizza, "Spokesmen," *New Republic,* January 29, 2001. For further analysis of the backgrounds of Bush White House appointees, see Kumar, "Recruiting and Organizing the White House Staff."

43. Dana Milbank, "Bush Names Rove Political Strategist," *Washington Post,* January 5, 2001.

44. Ibid.

45. Mike Allen, "Bush Appoints Allbaugh, Rove," *Washington Post,* January 4, 2001.

46. Dana Milbank, "Bush Names Rove Political Strategist," *Washington Post,* January 5, 2001.

47. Johnson, panel discussion, "Bush Transition to the Presidency."

48. Libby had been a deputy to undersecretary of defense Paul Wolfowitz in the Bush Sr. administration, where he earned the title "Wolfowitz's Wolfowitz." Matalin had also served as chief of staff to Lee Atwater when he was chair of the RNC. The announcement of her appointment also stated that she "will be responsible for providing advice to the vice president in a variety of areas, including communications, political strategy and coordination," a portfolio that embraced both Rove's and Hughes's territory, and perhaps made her a Cheney counterweight to them. Cheney also picked David Addington, former general counsel for the Defense Department, when Cheney was secretary of defense, as his legal counsel.

49. Dana Milbank, "Bush Names Rove Political Strategist," *Washington Post,* January 5, 2001.

50. Telephone interview with Andrew Card Jr., September 17, 1998.

51. Mike Allen, "A Team Built on Conservative Discipline," *Washington Post,* January 3, 2001.

52. James A. Barnes, "Bush's Insiders," *National Journal,* June 23, 2001, p. 1869.

53. The announcement came the same day that Bush presided over an economic conference in Austin to promote his tax cut plan, a proposal that Lindsey was instrumental in crafting. Also that day the Federal Reserve made a sharp cut in interest rates, followed by another the next day. On the first day, the Dow Jones industrials were up 248 points, a 2.3 percent gain, and the Nasdaq was up 324 points, 14.2 percent, its largest daily percentage gain to that date.

54. Joseph Kahn, "Contrarian of Boom Decade Put in Bush Inner Circle," *New York Times,* January 4, 2001.

55. Joseph Kahn and Frank Bruni, "Bush Seeking to Overhaul Policy Making," *New York Times,* January 6, 2001.

56. Ibid.

57. Steven Pearlstein, "Trade Representative to Keep Rank," *Washington Post,* January 9, 2001.

58. "As the traffic cop who coordinates policies toward Europe, China, and Japan, Edson must balance trade-policy concerns with traditional diplomatic issues. Edson also serves as the lead U.S. coordinator for the annual summits of the Group of Eight industrial nations." "The Decision Makers," *National Journal,* June 23, 2001, p. 1895.

59. James A. Barnes, "Bush's Insiders," *National Journal,* June 23, 2001, p. 1869.

60. James Bennet, "The Bush Years: CEO, USA," *New York Times Magazine,* January 14, 2001.

61. Telephone interview with Clay Johnson, September 20, 2001.

62. Clay Johnson, "The 2000-2001 Presidential Transition: Planning, Goals, and Reality," in Kumar and Sullivan, *The White House World*, pp. 316-317.

63. Ibid.

64. "Wide-Eyed Staffers Confront Awe at Taking White House," www.cnn.com, January 18, 2001.

65. Rove, "A Discussion with Karl Rove."

66. Ibid.

67. Howard Fineman, "Bush Goes Back to School," *Newsweek,* November 22, 1999.

68. Elaine Sciolino, "Bush's Foreign Policy Tutor," *New York Times,* June 16, 2000. Also see Mann, *Rise of the Vulcans*, pp. 250–255.

69. Rove, "A Discussion with Karl Rove."

70. James Carney and John F. Dickerson, "Rolling Back Clinton," *Time,* January 29, 2001.

71. Rove, "A Discussion with Karl Rove."

72. Dubose, Reid, and Cannon, *Boy Genius,* p. 189.

73. Kumar, "Communications Operations in the White House," p. 388.

74. Dana Milbank, "Serious Strategery," *Washington Post,* April 22, 2001.

75. Rove, "A Discussion with Karl Rove."

76. Frank Bruni and Eric Schmitt, "Bush, Acting Presidential, Meets with Leaders of Congress," *New York Times,* December 3, 2000. Bush and Cheney reportedly floated the idea of a Democrat for treasury secretary, but Speaker Hastert and Majority Leader Lott were strongly opposed to it. This report was later rejected by the Bush camp on Sunday, December 3, as erroneous. "There was no such discussion," spokesman Fleischer said. While the issue of a Democrat in the cabinet was discussed, "there was never a discussion that said certain cabinet agencies are off-limits to members of the other party." Richard W. Stevenson, "History Will View Gore 'in a Better Light' if He Quits Soon, Cheney Says," *New York Times,* December 4, 2000.

77. Frederika Schouten, "Jeffords: Bush Says Education Is Priority," *Burlington Free Press,* December 2, 2000.

78. Eric Schmitt and Frank Bruni, "As Gore Presses His Case, Bush Camp Molds Image of Administration Building," *New York Times,* November 30, 2000.

79. Allison Mitchell, "Bush and Cheney Starting to Enlist Democrat's Help," *New York Times,* December 15, 2000.

80. The meeting between the two competitors lasted sixteen minutes. Bush reportedly wanted to get to the airport before he was snowed in.

81. David Broder, "On First Look, Approach Earns Praise," *Washington Post,* December 20, 2000.

82. Richard Oppel and Diana Schemo, "Bush Warned Vouchers Might Hurt School Plans," *New York Times,* December 22, 2000.

83. Rove, "A Discussion with Karl Rove."

84. Clay Johnson, panel discussion, "Bush Transition to the Presidency."

85. The Lieberman-Cheney meeting took place on December 21. Helen Dewar, "Cheney, Lieberman Discuss Education, National Security," *Washington Post,* December 22, 2000. Also see Eric Schmitt, "Cheney to Play a Starring Role on Capitol Hill," *New York Times,* December 16, 2000.

86. At his December 13, 2000, meeting with GOP House leaders, Representative Christopher Cox (R-CA) noted that Cheney stressed "that President-elect Bush will want to follow through on the four main themes of his campaign—national security, social security, education and taxes—and that they're going to stick with that." Helen Dewar, "Cheney Woos Both Wings of Hill GOP," *Washington Post,* December 14,

2000. On January 8, 2001, Cheney met with three prominent moderate members of the House, Representatives Mike Castle (R-DE), Nancy Johnson (R-CT), and Fred Upton (R-MI), to discuss the legislative process and fiscal and education issues.

87. Lizette Alvarez, "House Leader Differs with Bush on Across-the-Board Tax Cuts," *New York Times,* December 15, 2000.

88. Lizette Alvarez, "Speaker Clarifies Stand on Bush's Tax Plan," *New York Times,* December 16, 2000.

89. Alison Mitchell, "President-Elect Offers a Message Aimed at Healing," *New York Times,* December 19, 2000.

90. Jones, *Passages to the Presidency,* pp. 188–197.

91. Dana Milbank, "Bush Taps Chao for Labor Position," *Washington Post,* January 12, 2001. Others attending included Pennsylvania education secretary Gene Hickock, Arizona schools superintendent Lisa Graham Keegan, Chicago public schools executive Paul Vallas, and business leaders from TRW, Texaco, Lockheed Martin, Pfizer, Bristol-Myers, and the Hartford Financial Group.

92. David Sanger, "Hailing Move by Greenspan, Bush Presses for His Tax Cut," *New York Times,* January 4, 2001; Mike Allen and Glenn Kessler, "Bush Says Tax Cut Open to Talks and a Speedup," *Washington Post,* January 5, 2001.

93. Douglas Jehl, "GOP to Press for Unraveling of Clinton Acts," *New York Times,* January 6, 2001.

94. According to McCain's calculations, nine GOP senators had supported some version of his bill in the past; those nine plus Cochran would give McCain the sixty votes needed to stop a filibuster.

95. Janet Hook, "School Issue May Be Lesson for Bush, *Los Angeles Times,* December 24, 2000.

96. Johnson, panel discussion, "President Bush's First 100 Days."

97. Ibid.

4

The Bush Team in Office

Although Bush and his associates had assembled a talented cabinet, the White House staff would emerge—as it does in most modern presidencies—as the administration's policymaking core and its political center of action. Decisions made during the transition ensured this: an experienced chief of staff, Andrew Card, who had been quietly planning Bush's White House staff even before election day, and the appointments of Karl Rove and Karen Hughes with unusually broad control over White House units dealing with, respectively, political strategy and media communications.

The Bush White House

Below the "Big Three" of Card, Rove, and Hughes, an unusually high number of Bush staff members had worked in prior White Houses (38 percent in the Bush Sr. White House, according to one estimate),[1] yet a significant number had also served under then-governor Bush in Austin and were involved in the campaign.[2] This yielded a staff that was more experienced, more collegial, and at the same time more disciplined than its recent predecessors. It was less prone to leaks and a public venting of its internal workings than the staffs of Carter, Reagan, and Clinton, as well as that of Bush Sr., which also embraced personal loyalty to the boss. In the view of former Reagan speech writer Peggy Noonan, Bush staffers "know who's boss. They are loyal to him, and they are loyal to each other. . . . His staff seems to have learned how to get along, how to thrash things through and hash things out and leave it in the room."[3] According to Mary Matalin, a senior aide to Cheney, "There's no turf-building, no turf-fighting."[4]

As legal counsel Alberto Gonzales observes, the shared experience of a number of them who had worked for Bush in the past was especially important: "Karl Rove, Karen Hughes, Clay Johnson, Margaret LaMontagne

[Spellings], Albert Hawkins—we were all senior members of the governor's staff in Austin. For three years, I provided them with legal advice as well. So we have long-standing relationships."[5] While some of them now occupied positions that might put them in potential conflict, that a number of them had worked together in the past or had worked in the Bush Sr. administration (or both) may have been useful in avoiding—or at least dampening—the kind of internecine quarrels that sometimes erupt and divide White House staffs into competing camps: the divisions, for example, in the Reagan administration between the California-based conservatives that coalesced around Ed Meese and the more moderate "pragmatists" led by Chief of Staff James Baker.

Furthermore, collegiality and discipline were both part of the operational codes of George W. Bush and Andrew Card. Both set expectations about civil behavior, timeliness, and even proper attire. According to former speech writer David Frum, nobody referred to the president as "Bush" or as "POTUS" (the acronym for "President of the United States"—which had been commonly used in the Clinton White House). Instead, "Bush was 'the president' on the phone, 'the president' in e-mails, 'the president' in meetings, 'the president' when kidding around in the halls."[6]

As for Bush, according to Alexis Simendinger of the *National Journal,* "[He] has surrounded himself inside the White House with a team he trusts and with people who know him best. His organization reflects, in part, the players he wanted around him."[7] As for Card, according to Mary Matalin, "Everyone's pretty coordinated, and I give a lot of credit to Andy [Card] for that."[8] Collegiality, discipline, and allegiance to the Bush agenda were central, moreover, to the selection and appointment process of top decisionmakers during the transition and after.

There were no media stories of organizational disarray and internal feuding of the sort that had become standard fare in the early months of the Clinton presidency. Nor did that apparently carry over into day-to-day life in the West Wing. In other White Houses, the prominence of key aides has often been a recipe for conflict and dissent; Bush's troika—Card, Rove, and Hughes—made that even more likely in this White House. Yet as David Frum notes in his book on the early Bush presidency, that rivalry and contention did not erupt. With respect to Rove and Hughes, for example, they brought different perspectives on American politics to the table, and sometimes differed on policy issues in his view, but "they worked together with perfect self-discipline."[9] In the view of Douglas Sosnick, a former Clinton aide: "I am impressed by how much this White House seems to be geared toward the president and his interests rather than self-promotion. If there's a mistake, staffers take the blame and insulate Bush from it. I am not sure I could always say that about the Clinton White House."[10]

Organizational Changes

As with every new presidency, internal organization varies somewhat from that of its predecessor. While some units of the Executive Office of the President are created statutorily and thus limit organizational alteration, others are the result of executive order and can be changed from administration to administration. Presidents especially have a free hand in organizing the internal operations of the White House Office, the unit within which many of the staff operations reside that we normally associate with the presidency and the West Wing.

The Bush experience was no exception. Card initially created fewer "assistant to the president" positions than had been the case in the Clinton administration. Some units, such as intergovernmental affairs and public liaison, had their heads downgraded to the "deputy assistant to the president" level. Initial salaries were also lower than they had been at the end of the Clinton presidency (and several staff members who had been working on Capitol Hill had to take a pay cut when they moved over to the White House). In so doing, Card was following a precept that had been practiced at the beginning of the Bush Sr. presidency. According to Card, in 1988 Bush Sr. "wanted fewer people in the hierarchy in the Bush White House than were in the Reagan White House. He also wanted to leave room for advancement. In government you cannot often give people a promotion that results in more money, so you give them a promotion that results in a better title."[11] The presence of Hughes as "counselor" to the president and Rove as "senior adviser" also meant that some of the units reporting to them need not be at the highest rank.

The most important change in White House organization was the creation of a number of groups that centered around Karl Rove's duties as a political and strategic adviser to the president. The effort here was in marked contrast to the relative absence of such groups in the Bush Sr. administration. In addition to the creation of the Office of Strategic Initiatives during the transition, other groups were formed. Perhaps the most important of these was the informal "strategery group," named after the *Saturday Night Live* parody of candidate Bush. It consisted of a dozen or so senior White House aides who met weekly in the Cordell Hull Room of the Old Executive Office Building next door to the White House. Regular attendees included Card, domestic adviser Margaret LaMontagne Spellings, economic adviser Lawrence Lindsey, National Security Council (NSC) adviser Condoleezza Rice, Card's deputy Joshua Bolten, Karen Hughes, Mary Matalin, and congressional lobbyist Nicholas Calio.

The aim was to institutionalize a broader planning effort within a White House environment that is often trapped within a day-to-day context. As Rove explained at the time:

> By involving what is a larger than normal group of people, we'll be pulling the best talents in the White House into planning. The object is to have a strategic framework developed by the Strategery meeting, which is brought down to each office by the participants. Everybody in the White House has a role in long-term planning and a seat at the table so they buy into the process.[12]

In the early months of the new administration, topics under discussion ranged from the 2003 budget to more political concerns such as Bush's reelection campaign and attracting Hispanic voters to the Republican Party (GOP).

Rove and Card also created a mid-level "conspiracy of deputies." The aim here was to provide ideas for the senior group. Still another group met daily at 10:00 A.M. to work on Bush's future schedule. Rove also conceived the "Echo Chamber" to deal with media reports of Bush's first 100 days in office. It devised a list of accomplishments that were presented to the media in preparation for that date—April 29, a Sunday—and it also set up an event with members of Congress and their families to mark the occasion.

Still other planning and strategy groups were also formed. In June, as Bush's energy proposal was coming under fire, top White House aides began to convene a daily strategy meeting to sell the plan. Rove also created two strategy and issue groups to think about the next phase of the Bush agenda, beyond what had been rolled out in its first few months:

> We did have a process, ironically enough, in place before September 11th, because there was a recognition that this agenda that Bush had talked about in his campaign and that he pursued in the first nine months or eight months of his administration were not adequate for 2002. Americans . . . don't vote retrospectively. . . . And so we were working before September 11th through a complicated process known by its acronym PIG and WIG, the Policy Issue Group and the Working Issue Group, to sort of provide thinking within the White House about what was next, what comes next on each of these big issues? What is it that the president ought to begin to lay out as big policy agenda items? . . . Now, that was sort of derailed by September 11th, but here was another process in place that is aiming to do this for 2002 and beyond.[13]

Other units of the White House complemented Rove's strategic efforts, but with different time frames and horizons. The press office reportedly operated on a twenty-four- to forty-eight-hour perspective, while Karen Hughes's communications group had a two- to three-week horizon. Rove focused on six to eight weeks, while his strategic initiatives effort looked forward three to six months if not more. The purpose, above all, was to control the political agenda. "Our ability to stay focused is how we stay in control of the agenda," according to Rove.[14]

Yet while creating better internal strategic and communications operations than had been present in the Bush Sr. White House, it is not clear that sufficient efforts were made to reach out beyond the Bush staff and involve participants from other power centers outside the White House. According to one report, "The operation runs the risk of becoming insular. Already Republicans on Capitol Hill complain that they have been left out of the strategic planning efforts, citing how the tax cut should be moved through Congress."[15]

Furthermore, in the view of former top aide John DiIulio, political and communications strategy sometimes swamped policy deliberation and analysis:

> In eight months, I heard many, many staff discussions, but not three meaningful, substantive policy discussions. There were no actual policy white papers on domestic issues. There were, truth be told, only a couple of people in the West Wing who worried at all about policy substance and analysis, and they were even more overworked than the stereotypical, non-stop twenty-hour-a-day White House staff. . . . [T]hey could stand to find ways of inserting more serious policy fiber into the West Wing diet. . . . [T]hey have been for whatever reasons, organized in ways that make it hard for policy-minded staff, including colleagues (even secretaries) of cabinet agencies, to get much West Wing traction, or even to get a non-trivial hearing.[16]

Other staff changes generated further controversy. In an early February interview, Card indicated that the White House race relations and AIDS offices would be phased out. It was the first public stumble in what had been a smooth transition. Card's comments generated immediate concern and, within hours, Press Secretary Ari Fleischer told reporters that Card had been mistaken. There would be entities within the White House dealing with those issues, according to Fleischer, but they might not be organized and staffed in the same way as they had been under the Clinton administration. According to the *New York Times,* "A few wondered whether Mr. Card's comments indicated that the White House had been moving in the direction he outlined, then simply hit the brakes as some administration officials fretted over the symbolism of that course and the reaction to it."[17] Yet another account noted that Card might not have been aware of ongoing discussions about the two offices, even though the option of closing them had been at least considered during the transition. Card's deputy, Josh Bolten, had been working on how the two offices would be organized in the new administration, but apparently had yet to share his latest proposal for the two offices with Card. According to one White House official, "Josh said, 'I feel bad. I wish I had told Andy.'"[18]

By early April, the White House had decided to keep the Office of National AIDS Policy and appointed Scott Evertz, a Republican and the first openly gay person to head the office since Clinton created it in 1994. The White House also decided to continue to focus on race issues by creating a Task Force on Uniting Americans, which would involve senior officials (principally the DPC [Domestic Policy Council] and the public liaison office) but would not be formally organized as a White House unit as had been the case under Clinton.

Another Clinton-era White House office fared less well when a decision was made to discontinue the Office for Women's Initiatives and Outreach, which Clinton had created in 1995. Feminist groups were outraged when rumors of the office's disbanding circulated in late March. More conservative groups welcomed the change, feeling that the Clinton office had promoted a more radical women's agenda. The White House position was that the public liaison unit would once again have responsibility in dealing with women's groups and issues, as had been the case before Clinton created the office.[19]

Card as Chief of Staff

During the transition, Card was instrumental in crafting a White House staff structure that seemed to meet Bush's needs as a decisionmaker, meshed with his experience as governor to an extent practicable, and took into account both Bush's and Card's assessments of the strengths and weaknesses of the Bush Sr. White House staff. Once in office, unlike some of his predecessors (Donald Regan and John Sununu most notably), Card was not prone to serve as a policy advocate or presidential counselor on policy issues. That did not mean that the office of chief of staff was devoid of involvement in the substance of policy. As we shall see below, in some ways it was structured to serve as a powerful focal point for policy initiative and review. But it was not Card himself who generally served as an advocate.

At the same time, however, Card did not shy away from providing management and direction to the White House staff. Although managing with a reportedly gentle hand and easy demeanor, Card was a central figure in ensuring that the discipline and collegiality that both he and President Bush valued was put into practice.

Card's daily schedule was not untypical of most recent chiefs of staff: a workday beginning shortly after 6:00 A.M. and ending by 9:00 or 10:00 P.M. The first meeting of his day occurred shortly after 7:00 A.M., with his deputy chiefs of staff Bolten and Hagin, plus Rove and Hughes. This was followed by a meeting of the senior staff at 7:30 A.M., usually consisting of eighteen members (eight of whom were women), a much smaller number than attended Clinton-era senior staff meetings (sometimes thirty) and closer in number to the smaller group that Sununu had convened during his tenure under Bush Sr. As a sign of Card's own allegiance to the discipline of this White House, the meeting promptly ended at 7:58 A.M. so that Card could attend the president's morning briefing at 8:00 A.M.

That discipline and allegiance to order extended, moreover, to the ethos that Card sought to instill among the staff. "I do like discipline," Card told one reporter in February, 2001. "People recognize the job they have to do."[20] Card also served as the "enforcer" of the president's schedule, a given duty for an effective chief of staff. And he was particularly concerned that this president not be overburdened by demands. "I call it the test of needs versus wants," according to Card. "If you *need* to see the president, you will see the president. But if you *want* to see the president, you won't."[21] Nor was Card shy about enforcing his decisions; "nice guy" reputation notwithstanding, his first duty as deputy chief of staff in the Bush Sr. administration had been kicking out Reagan aides who delayed leaving the White House.

At the same time, Card was not heavy handed; although his direct experience with the chief of staff's office had been under John Sununu, his own style was decidedly different. According to David Frum, the contrast between Card and Sununu was marked, and deliberately so: "Just as certain Christians govern their conduct by the shorthand WWJD ('What would Jesus do?'), Card seemed constantly to be asking WWJSD ('What would John Sununu do?')—so that he could then do precisely the opposite." Card liked to be called by his first name, never bellowed orders, lunched in the White House mess or in the cafeteria of the Old Executive Office Building, where more junior aides and secretaries were free to join him.[22]

Indeed, Card was a primary source of the collegiality that also was valued in this White House. According to Karl Rove, a lot of the credit for that

> has to go to Andy Card, who has the right kind of structures and the right kind of personality, and the right kind of operating that sort of takes a lot of the rough edges off. You could expect a lot of people to come and clash harshly against each other, but the way he runs the White House and the way he runs the president's business is enormously positive in minimizing the opportunities for that. I mean we still have very healthy dialog and very healthy debate. In fact the president encourages that, but the way that Andy structures that makes it an incredibly positive experience. People can walk into a meeting and walk out, having absolutely and utterly lost their point, and feel that they had their day in court in front of the president, and that the process treated them with fairness. And if you want a White House to operate, you've got to have that. That's absolutely vital to the success of the White House, that there is a comfort level in advancing a position, and an acceptance that the process will generate a good decision.[23]

But while Card's demeanor and tone were low-keyed, according to Frum, he "enforced [the administration's] code of unspotted loyalty."[24] Once the Bush staff was in office, Card continued the lectures he began before inauguration day on proper staff conduct and demeanor. According to Frum, Card began one with a story from his own experience in the Reagan White House, where staff members, going into a meeting, were asked whether they wanted to sit on the "Baker side" or the "Meese side." In the Bush White House, by contrast, "You are not Karl's people or Karen's people. You are the president's people." There would be no bickering, no self-aggrandizement. Staff members, he told them, are dispensable: "The average tenure of a chief of staff is about eighteen months. I will be here only so long as I help the president to do his job. And that's how long each of you will be here as well."[25]

Although Card was less enmeshed in details of policy issues and initiatives, his chief deputy, Josh Bolten, most decidedly was involved.[26] This was especially so because the DPC and the National Economic Council (NEC) reported through Bolten. Bolten, a Washington, D.C., native whose father was a Central Intelligence Agency officer, had worked for Goldman Sachs in the early 1990s, including a stint as chief of staff to its then-cochairman, Senator Jon Corzine (D-NJ). Perhaps more important for the task at hand, he was the Bush campaign's policy director and had served in the Bush Sr. White House congressional affairs staff. There Bolten got to know not only Nick Calio (who would return as head of the White House's congressional affairs office) but also Rob Portman, who was later elected to the House and was close to George W. Bush, serving as one of his informal contacts in Congress during the transition and thereafter.

According to Karl Rove, "You can't point to a lot of things and say this was the inspiration of Josh Bolten and Josh Bolten alone. But you could go to every piece of policy and see his fingerprints on the process. He's got a very agile mind where he's thinking through 'What would a president want to know?'"[27] Not only did Bolten coordinate the advice and information coming from the DPC and the NEC, but he also oversaw the forty-five minutes Bush spent daily for domestic and economic policy briefings when he was in Washington. He "is in charge of parcelling out those precious minutes, usually in the afternoons. He decides what is discussed, when it is to be discussed and who is to be invited." Not only did Bolten and those on the agenda attend, but so too did Card, Rove, and Calio, with Cheney, Fleischer, and communications director Dan Bartlett having standing invitations.[28]

Yet Bolten, still, was only deputy chief of staff, lacking his own domestic policy staff and perhaps without the resources or clout to bring policy deliberations to bear with the same impact as Hughes's communications efforts or Rove's strategic and political concerns. Card's definition of his job as a broker and manager rather than a policy advocate may have had a downside in this regard. In the view of former top-level staff member John DiIulio, it was one of the factors that may have pushed the Bush White House into taking politics and communications too seriously, at the expense of more robust policy analysis and a fuller political agenda:

> Maybe because the chief of staff, Andy Card, was more a pure staff process person than a staff leader or policy person. [It was one of the factors that] gave rise to what you might call Mayberry Machiavellis—staff, senior and junior, who consistently talked and acted as if the height of political sophis-

tication consisted in reducing every issue to its simplest, black-and-white terms for public consumption, then steering legislative initiatives or policy proposals as far right as possible.[29]

Hughes as "Counselor to the President"

One of the most important major changes from both the Clinton and Bush Sr. administrations was the communications operation headed by Karen Hughes in her capacity as counselor to the president. In past administrations, a number of her duties had been performed by the White House director of communications, a position dating back to the Nixon presidency. But Hughes's role would be more prominent, signaling both her close relationship with the president and the more central role that communications would play in this White House. Heading a staff of over forty, she was given broad duties overseeing White House press-corps relations, more general media communications, speech writing, and coordination of presidential events and appearances.

Although Hughes lacked prior Washington experience, she sought initially to compensate for the lack of it by enlisting the services of Margaret Tutweiler, a veteran Reagan and Bush Sr. staffer (and, importantly, a close aide to former secretary of state and White House chief of staff James Baker). Tutweiler served as a volunteer during the first three months of the new presidency to help Hughes adapt to the new role and develop the institutional memory needed for the job. According to Hughes, "There's a lot about Washington and how the White House operates that I don't know. When I have a question about something, I say, 'Margaret do you remember how this was done in the past?'"[30]

Yet Hughes's role was not confined to just getting the White House message out. She also served as an important adviser to Bush. In some ways, she was closest to Bush personally among all White House aides, having worked with him as governor and on the presidential campaign trail. She reportedly was even able to finish his sentences on occasion.[31] A few days after taking office, Bush reportedly told Hughes, "I want you in every meeting where major decisions are made." According to Chief of Staff Card, Bush often asks him, "Has Karen seen this?" or "What does Karen think?" According to Vice President Cheney, "I've been around a lot of White Houses, and it's a unique role when the president has total confidence in someone. Karen is the first woman I've seen in that role."[32] In the view of Mary Matalin, Cheney's chief political adviser, Bush "will expect you to have procured her opinion, or he'll get it himself."[33] According to David Frum, who worked under her in the speech-writing staff, Hughes's relationship with Bush was so close that she "was the only person in the White House who could criticize Bush. She would tell him that he had done a poor job at a speech practice or at a press conference, and he would react with none of the angry defensiveness that criticism from a less supportive person could provoke."[34]

Hughes recognized that effective communications, like Rove's concerns for political impact, needed to be factored early into the policy process and not be restricted to marketing and selling after the fact. Early in the administration, the White House needed to make a number of potentially unpopular decisions concerning environmental rules and regulations that had been put in place in the waning days of the Clinton administration. Hughes recognized the danger and convened strategy meetings that led to a number of events that sought to portray Bush as more sensitive to environmental concerns. Those same concerns led her to weigh in on the energy policy being developed by Cheney. According to David Frum, they "battled over the energy policy page by page."[35]

But Hughes was not always successful in her efforts. At a June 2001 meeting of senior aides, Nick Calio, the White House's congressional lobbyist, urged that the administration threaten to veto the patients' bill of rights legislation then under consideration before Congress in order to force a compromise that would be more acceptable. Hughes urged restraint, arguing, "Once we say veto, that's all anyone's going to hear. This will hurt us."[36] Hughes lost that fight and press coverage of Bush's veto threat was negative in tone. But Hughes did succeed in getting Bush to support an alternative House Republican plan that sought to provide a limited right for patients to sue health care providers in state courts, a position Bush had long opposed (Bush favored patients' rights that permitted civil litigation only in federal courts).

Hughes was part of the mechanism for ensuring the discipline and order so valued in this White House. She was quickly dubbed the "Enforcer" by White House aides, especially in light of her attempts to control negative comments to the press by members of the administration. Nor was it a new assignment. "In the governor's office, Hughes imposed a strict discipline aimed at controlling the message—a precursor of the White House press office. Calls to the governor's division directors and even some state agency heads were redirected to the press office. Leaks were rare," note James Moore and Wayne Slater in their book on Karl Rove.[37] It was a role she continued during the campaign, especially when press aide David Beckwith was dismissed for being too close to the media. According to Dana Milbank of the *Washington Post,* "In the West Wing, she has presided over a White House virtually free of damaging leaks and unwavering in its portrayal of Bush as 'firm' and 'resolute.'"[38] Hughes especially sought to keep the White House and administration on message by carefully coordinating and orchestrating events and the timing of major initiatives.

The Bush White House also took the role of speech writers more seriously than had been the case in his father's presidency. In fact, the job levels of the Bush Sr. speech writers had been downgraded at the outset of that administration, their pay was cut, and they even lost mess privileges in the White House. Not surprisingly, the changes led to negative stories about the communications operation's competency and commitment.

For George W. Bush, it was a different story entirely. Bush's chief speech writer, Michael Gerson, was personally selected by Bush for the job, and he was given an office in the much coveted West Wing rather than the Old Executive Office Building next door. Gerson also was a member of Card's 7:30 A.M. senior staff meeting, again another sign of his stature and that of his work. Gerson's staff was clearly conservative in outlook, but represented a range of conservative views: David Frum, formerly of the *Weekly Standard;* Matthew Scully, who had been on the staffs of the *National Review* and the *Washington Times;* and Peter Wehner, who had worked for William Bennett.

According to another White House aide, "Neither Bush was a naturally articulate man. The elder Bush responded to his inarticulateness by denigrating the importance of words. The son has responded by treating words with added respect."[39] Yet the speech writers did not have the final say. Karen Hughes was also heavily involved in speech writing, often altering Gerson's more lofty language so that it fit Bush's plainer rhetoric. Bush too was involved, often fine-tuning language and suggesting tighter organization. He even caught a mistake in one early speech that referred to Pope John Paul II as pontiff in 1976. Frum's book on Bush, *The Right Man,* is replete with instances where Bush interacted directly with his speech writers, often editing their rough drafts.

But Hughes's central and commanding role also had some downsides: Press Secretary Fleischer, who reported to Hughes, was reportedly sometimes out of the loop (although that may have been a ploy on his part to deflect further press queries).[40] Fleischer's staff had fewer than half as many members as the press office under Clinton (twenty-four), although the total communications operation was larger under Bush (forty-two to forty-four). According to Martha Joynt Kumar, "The difference is that communications operations are about persuasion, while the press office is about information. The Bush people want to develop a message and stay on it. They use the press office to deliver that message and not answer a lot of questions about it."[41]

More generally, according to at least one former top White House aide, communications strategy swamped policy analysis. As John DiIulio later recounted:

At the six-month senior staff retreat on July 9, 2001, an explicit discussion ensued concerning how to emulate more strongly the Clinton White House's press, communications, and rapid-response media relations—how better to wage, if you will, the permanent campaign that so defines the modern presidency. . . . I listened and was amazed. It wasn't more press, communica-

tions, media, legislative strategizing, and such they needed. . . . No, what
they needed, I thought then and still do now, was more policy-relevant information, discussion, and deliberation.[42]

Rove as "Senior Adviser" to the President

Just as Hughes's communications operation broke new organizational
grounds, so too did Karl Rove's control over White House units dealing with
political strategy, planning, and outreach. Moreover, like Hughes, Rove had a
longtime association with George W. Bush. Just as Hughes had been a highly
valued adviser during his governorship, so too was Rove. Not only had Rove
spotted Bush's political potential early on, but he became indispensable once
Bush became governor. According to one account, "A common refrain in the
governor's office was: 'Where's Karl on this?' or 'Has Karl signed off on
this?'"[43] By early 2003, two books on Rove's relationship with Bush had
already been published. One was titled *Bush's Brain,* and had the subtitle *How
Karl Rove Made George W. Bush Presidential.*[44] The other was titled *Boy
Genius* (after a nickname Bush bestowed on Rove), and it featured a picture
of Bush above the word "Boy" and Rove's picture above the word "Genius."
The subtitle of this work was *Karl Rove, the Brains Behind the Remarkable
Political Triumph of George W. Bush.*[45] As a sign of his power in the Bush
White House, Rove took over the second-floor West Wing office that had
been Hillary Clinton's.

Rove technically reported through Card: "I work for the president, and
my immediate superiors are Josh Bolten, the deputy chief of staff, and Andy
Card, the chief of staff." Asked if he really had to get Card's approval for his
activities, Rove replied: "If I am smart I do. Listen, I do what I'm told."[46] Yet
Rove's effective mandate was quite broad. According to Ed Gillespie, a GOP
campaign strategist who had worked with Rove and became the chairman of
the Republican National Committee in 2003, "Basically Karl Rove has carte
blanche to stick his nose into anything he deems appropriate or necessary."[47]
According to John DiIulio, "Karl is enormously powerful, maybe the single
most powerful person in the modern post-Hoover era ever to occupy a political adviser post near the Oval Office. . . . Fortunately, he is not just a largely
self-taught, hyper-political guy, but also a very well informed guy when it
comes to certain domestic issues."[48] In Rove's own mind, his mandate was
broad: "Anything involving baseball" was all that was off his domestic policy
table, he told reporters in 2002.[49]

The work of Rove and his staff emerged quickly in the opening weeks of
the Bush presidency. They developed a strategic plan for Bush's first six
weeks in office, including how the various pieces of Bush's policy agenda
would be sequentially "rolled out" for maximum political benefit. Their work
led to Bush's early meetings with members of Congress, Bush's attendance at

a retreat of House Democrats, and visits of Democratic "elder statesmen" to the White House on Bush's first full week in office. In the first week of the Bush presidency, Rove also brought political advisers from New Hampshire to the White House to plot strategy for Bush's 2004 race, and, over the next several months, a number of events were scheduled in which academic experts on the presidency were brought to the White House to share their expertise.

Rove also served as the White House contact with the GOP conservative base, which was often ignored in the Bush Sr. administration. Early in the administration, one of Rove's aides—either the political director or the head of the public liaison office—attended weekly meetings run by conservative activist Grover Norquist as well as weekly lunches of Paul Weyrich's Free Congress Foundation.[50] Rove himself held a weekly conference call with leaders of the religious right, and the public liaison office held a weekly conference call with a group of conservative Catholics. According to *New Republic*'s Ryan Lizza, "The White House has determined that religiously conservative evangelicals and Catholics are best dealt with as two completely different constituencies."[51] The overall aim was to solidify Bush's religious, churchgoing base.

But Rove was not simply the emissary of the Republican right. He also maintained an extensive network of regular contacts with a wider range of groups and individuals, estimated by one account to be in the vicinity of 150. They included members of Congress, Washington insiders, former Texas associates, state officials, and party leaders. Even some Democrats were part of the network, most notably Donna Brazile, Al Gore's campaign manager in 2000, with whom "Rove regularly trades tips. . . . [S]he tells Rove how Bush's proposals are faring among Democrats, while Rove makes sure her clients are included at White House events."[52]

Rove and Policy Initiatives

Rove's duties often directly involved him in the substance of the Bush policy process, not just framing a political strategy after the fact or acting as the contact point with a variety of political groups. In April 2001, Bush was forced to deal with a number of controversial environmental issues, many generated by President Clinton's executive orders and changes in regulations issued just before leaving office. Decisions were made to suspend new standards for arsenic levels in drinking water, reject the Kyoto global warming treaty, and alter Bush's own campaign pledge of reducing carbon dioxide levels. Rove and his advisers quickly sought to bolster's the president's environmental image by having the White House announce a number of other initiatives such as stricter rules on lead contaminants and support for Clinton's expansion of wetlands protection. Rove also was instrumental in having Bush back off—at least for the time being—on his plan to permit oil drilling in the Arctic National Wildlife Refuge. In Rove's view, Bush was enmeshed in too many political fights already. According to one White House source, "For Karl, it was a matter of priorities. Why fight all the battles at the same time?"[53]

Another controversial area where Rove had a hand was in Bush's decision about whether stem cells from fetal tissues should be permitted to be used in medical and other scientific research. It was a highly charged issue, especially to some Catholic voters and the hierarchy of the Catholic Church, and Rove made sure that the views of the latter were represented in the decision process. According to one account, "It was Rove who made certain that the president heard the views of anti-abortion groups, theologians, and conservative ethicists who favored a ban on the research."[54] But Rove's involvement raised the question of whether the issue was becoming overly politicized. An official connected with the National Conference of Catholic Bishops told reporters that Rove had consulted with the group because "Catholic voters are seen as such a swing vote in the elections."[55]

Yet in John DiIulio's view, Rove performed admirably: "Karl was at his political and policy best, I think, in steering the president's stem cell research decision."[56] Moreover, Rove did not dominate the debate on stem cell research. According to one report, Karen Hughes "favored liberalizing the rules."[57] And President Bush was personally and directly involved in the deliberations to a greater extent than in other policy areas, often informally contacting a range of experts as well as nonexperts in order to query their views. According to DiIulio, it was the

> president himself who really took this issue on board with an unusual depth of reading, reflection, and staff deliberation. . . . [T]his was one instance where the administration really took pains with both politics and policy, invited real substantive knowledge into the process, and so forth. It was almost as if it took the most highly charged political issue of its kind to force them to take policy-relevant knowledge seriously, to have genuine deliberation.[58]

In May 2001, Bush personally charged Rove with revving up the administration's faith-based initiatives, which were languishing in Congress. Bush had chatted with Michael Joyce, former president of the Bradley Foundation, who registered his concerns with the faltering effort. According to Fred Barnes of the *Weekly Standard,* "Bush was fearful the issue was languishing. He called Rove, instructed him to talk to Joyce, and told him to get the issue moving again."[59] Yet here, as we shall see, the administration was to suffer a major setback and its strategy may have contributed directly to the impasse that developed in the Senate.

Other areas where Rove weighed in included education policy, Bush's response to the campaign finance bill, the tax cut, patients' bill of rights, tariffs on steel imports, and the civil war in Sudan between Christians and Muslims (at the behest of American Christian evangelicals). Rove was in the loop on all of Bush major public addresses, and he chaired weekly lunches on communications strategy when Karen Hughes was absent.

Rove's influence on policy and politics also extended outside the White House. He played a direct role as liaison to (if not the effective head of) the Republican National Committee (RNC). He also personally sought to recruit candidates to run for the 2002 midterm elections, particularly Norm Coleman for a Minnesota senate seat (Coleman won) and Representative John Thune for a senate seat in South Dakota (Thune narrowly lost). Rove's efforts, however, were not always a success: he backed former Los Angeles mayor Richard Riordan for the GOP nomination in the California governor's race, but Riordan was given a substantial drubbing by political novice William Simon in the GOP primary.

Balancing Policy and Politics

Rove's efforts reflected an important understanding that political feasibility, impact, and success need to be factored into making policy decisions. The "best" policy choice is not always the "right" choice if it is politically unpalatable. Jimmy Carter's experiences are especially telling in this regard. According to adviser Peter Bourne, "Policy recommendations were forwarded independently to Carter and without assessment of their political implications."[60] Members of the Carter inner circle, most notably Hamilton Jordan, were reluctant to fill that vacuum. As a result, according to one aide, "The only place where politics and policy came together was in the person of Jimmy Carter," who himself had a visceral distrust of political calculation.[61] By contrast, the internal organization of the Bush White House ensured a more orderly process for policy and politics to come together. Furthermore, according to campaign strategist Mark McKinnon, Rove was suited to be both a policy and political adviser: "He's really got a policy heart beneath his political veneer. He knows more about policy than so-called policy wonks. Besides, all policy is political. And good policy is good politics."[62]

Yet Rove's success may also have come at a price. As the *Washington Post* noted in late March 2001, "There is a danger that the lack of competing views in the famously tight White House could cause Bush advisers to become stale and insular." As one Bush official said "with satisfaction," according to the *Washington Post*, "There isn't a lot of competition in the policy arena."[63]

Rove's role as a key political and policy adviser continued to raise controversy, particularly with a deliberative ratio that was perceived to favor politics over policy. By July 2001 the *New York Times* was reporting that White House decisions had become too political: "A frequent complaint among

Republicans is that Mr. Rove has overextended himself, and insufficiently concealed his tracks, so that many decisions coming from the White House have an overly political taint."[64]

Rove was a key participant (the "chair," according to one account) in an early June 2001 meeting that was apparently instrumental in Bush's subsequent decision to halt the Navy's controversial bombing program on the Puerto Rican island of Vieques. Here the administration encountered criticism from its right flank, with critics charging that the decision was too political (i.e., an attempt to win Hispanic support), was sprung suddenly, and failed to take into account the Navy's training needs. Press Secretary Fleischer later told the press that Rove was often centrally involved in meetings dealing with intergovernmental affairs and the decision had been "announced by the Secretary of the Navy, and the president concurs with it."[65]

Yet others questioned Rove's role. Senator James Inhofe (R-OK) felt that Rove had almost single-handedly made the decision and cut members like Inhofe out of deliberations. Inhofe reportedly insisted to the White House that Rove be pulled out of the decision process, and he reportedly had a telephone conversation with Rove that was, in Inhofe's words, "a little contentious": "He wasn't responsive—he didn't hear what I had to say. . . . It was Karl Rove who made the decision. It was politically motivated." For his part, Rove responded: "I respectfully disagree with the Senator."[66]

Another controversy came to light in July. As part of his efforts in the area of faith-based initiatives, Rove was reportedly involved with officials from the Salvation Army in their attempt to allow religious groups participating in those programs to be exempt from anti–gay discrimination legislation. Although the Office of Management and Budget (OMB) eventually decided that the change could not be made, when the story became public in July there were conflicting accounts of who had been contacted, how deeply involved Rove was in the matter, and whether the White House had misled the Salvation Army.[67]

By July, relations between the White House and the Republican National Committee had also begun to suffer. Earlier in the year, Rove had initially envisioned Governor James Gilmore III of Virginia in the more honorific position of "general chairman" of the RNC, but Gilmore prevailed and was given the normal title (and, presumably in his mind, the duties and power) of chairman of the RNC.[68] As months went on, he sought to exercise a more active role in the job than had apparently been envisioned by the White House. According to one report, there were "tensions with Mr. Bush's advisers. The advisers think they are running the political operation, and the strong-willed Mr. Gilmore thinks he is in charge."[69]

However, a Bush loyalist, Jack Oliver, had been installed to run the day-to-day operations of the RNC, and Oliver was close to Rove and had been finance chairman of the Bush campaign. In essence, he was Rove's surrogate in the RNC. Gilmore, however, was reported to be "chafing" over the extent of Oliver's mandate and stopped him from convening staff meetings without his permission, as well as limiting his authority to make hiring and budget decisions without Gilmore's consent.[70] On November 30, 2001, Gilmore tendered his resignation, and he was replaced by former governor Marc Racicot of Montana.[71] According to one GOP official, "I haven't seen anybody win in a clash with Karl Rove. The party is being run out of the White House and that is not Jim's [Gilmore] style."[72]

The White House's difficulties in balancing policy and politics (and Rove's prominent role in factoring in the latter) were especially compounded by prior GOP criticism of President Clinton's use of polls to guide his policy decisions. Although Democrats claimed that Clinton was less reliant on polls than news media accounts suggested, Republicans made much of the prominence of pollsters and political strategists in the Clinton inner circle. Then-candidate Bush had also denounced decisionmaking by polls rather than "principles," and he had promised an end to the "permanent campaign." Once in office, the tune changed a bit: according to Press Secretary Ari Fleischer, "Every White House weighs principle, policy, and politics. We've got it in the right order."[73]

Rove's prominence also served to make him a lightning rod for criticism of the Bush administration, especially once it came to light that Rove had not sold all of his shares in corporations that had sought White House contacts. As was the case for Vice President Cheney and others in the business-friendly Bush administration, personal holdings, friendships, and contacts served to arouse suspicion, especially as a number of corporate scandals began to emerge in the spring of 2001. The problem was compounded by Bush's own comments at the initial swearing-in ceremony of his White House staff, when he warned them of ethical improprieties: "This means avoiding even the appearance of problems."[74]

One charge that Rove faced concerned a March 12, 2001, meeting that Rove attended with executives from the Intel Corp. who were seeking approval of a merger of one of their suppliers with a Dutch firm. The problem was that Rove still owned at least $100,000 in Intel stock. The White House response was that Rove merely referred the Intel executives to others in the administration, did not know that the proposed merger would be discussed when he met with Intel executives, and played no part in the subsequent approval of the merger two months later. The White House also attempted to spin the incident as a simple bureaucratic error. Rove had wanted to sell the shares back in January but had been advised by transition lawyers to wait until a certificate of divestiture had been issued (specifying that the holdings did constitute a conflict of interest) in order to avoid capital gains taxes.[75]

The controversy over connections to business resurfaced in late fall with the collapse of Enron. Rove's name was again mentioned as some Democrats in Congress sought to discover whether there were any links between the energy company and members of the Bush administration. But an investigation of Rove's meetings and potential dealings with the large group of companies in which he held stock did not occur. Representative Dan Burton (R-IN), the chair of the House Government Reform Committee, refused to conduct an investigation. Nor was Senator Joe Lieberman (D-CT), chair of the Senate Governmental Affairs Committee, willing to take up the matter. The issue then disappeared.

For Rove, reports of his prominence in the inner circle of the Bush White House were overblown at times. On January 22, 2003, he told reporters, "I'm one voice among many around the senior staff table in the morning. This town can only operate successfully through myth, and one of the myths is that there has to be some Svengali-like person sitting in the White House."[76]

The Bush Cabinet

Despite the general praise given to Bush's cabinet nominations, the role of the cabinet, before September 11, 2001, generally followed the pattern of recent presidencies: a White House rather than cabinet-led policy process. Shortly after taking office Bush did initially reinstate regular monthly meetings with the cabinet, and he met regularly with key cabinet members such as Powell, Ashcroft, O'Neill, and Rumsfeld. Chief of Staff Card also convened weekly lunch meetings with individual cabinet members, and Albert Hawkins, the White House secretary to the cabinet, set up daily conference calls and a monthly meeting with departmental chiefs of staff. Each department also produced a weekly progress report for the White House.[77]

While the transition planners for the Bush White House staff had moved quickly to fill cabinet-level appointments, the process was much slower for subcabinet members. At a breakfast gathering at the Brookings Institution on March 29, 2001, White House personnel director Clay Johnson told the audience that about 230 people had been approved by Bush for the some 485 positions that the Brookings Institution's Presidential Appointee Initiative had been tracking. Johnson, moreover, hoped that all nominations would be confirmed by Congress's August recess, beating the timetables of the Reagan, Bush, and Clinton first-year efforts (it was a goal that would not be reached). Johnson also noted that some 30 percent of those approved so far were women and 20 to 25 percent were members of minority groups (and only about 55 percent were white males), numbers that were closer to the diversity levels of the Clinton presidency than to those of either Bush Sr. or Reagan. Moreover, according to Johnson, the figures were very close to those of Bush's gubernatorial appointments: 35 percent women and 52–53 percent "not white male."[78]

Yet in terms of appointees who had been confirmed or were otherwise in place, the Bush effort lagged behind its predecessors. By the end of the first 100 days of the new administration, in nine of fourteen cabinet departments, only the secretary had been confirmed by the Senate, according to Brookings's Presidential Appointee Initiative. The study further found that only 29 nominees had been confirmed by that date, compared to 42 at the same point in the Clinton presidency, and 72 under Reagan.[79] By the end of July, Bush (with 257 nominations and 175 confirmations) was slightly ahead of Clinton's pace (209 nominations and 170 confirmations) but behind Reagan's (282 nominations and 210 confirmations).[80] By the end of August, out of 500 positions, 227 Bush nominees had been confirmed, 55 awaited Senate confirmation, 41 had been announced but not sent to the Senate yet, and 144 positions remained unfilled.[81] When it completed its study of the appointment process in June 2003, the Brookings group found that it had taken, on average, 8.7 months for the Bush administration to move its appointees through Senate confirmation and into a position, compared to 8.3 months in the Clinton presidency and 5.2 under Reagan.[82]

Unlike earlier transitions, Bush and his associates had the advantage of an additional $1 million in federal transition funding to "orient" senior officials once the administration was under way. Clay Johnson, the White House personnel director, saw this as helpful in dealing with about half of the appointees who did not have prior Washington experience. It was, in his view, not an opportunity "to teach them all the ethics laws or not to scare them all to death about all the ethics laws," but an effort to achieve three broader goals. First, "Make them into a team, make sure they understand who else is on that team, and that they have an emotional attachment to their team leader, the president." Second, "We want to make sure that they understand what the playbook reads, what the president's, what the administration's goals, values, and expectations are." Finally, according to Johnson, "We want to try to give them as much benefit from hindsight and what has gone right and wrong in the past . . . give them the tools, like the president's management agenda, give them all the tools, including the lessons from history, so that they can get up the learning curve as quickly as possible, so they can be effective members of this Bush-Cheney team."[83]

But a White House Still Basically in Charge

Although at least one Bush transition adviser had spoken of the centrality of the cabinet in the president's policy deliberations ("Bush is going back to the Eisenhower-type cabinet, where it is a board of directors"),[84] most cabinet members with domestic and economic portfolios took a back seat to their White House counterparts. On the key Bush initiatives, the White House remained policy central. The White House, rather than the Department of Health and Human Services (HHS), took the lead on patients' bill of rights, welfare reform, stem cell research, Medicare changes, and prescription drug coverage for seniors. The White House, rather than the Pentagon, played the crucial role in ending the Navy's controversial bombings on the island of Vieques in Puerto Rico. Energy policy fell to a Cheney-led task force rather than an effort led by Energy Secretary Spencer Abraham.

The White House's education reform proposals, a centerpiece of the Bush agenda, offer an especially telling example of White House rather than cabinet involvement. The proposals were largely crafted by White House staffers Margaret LaMontagne Spellings and Sandy Kress rather than Education Secretary Paige and his department, and the White House remained central in getting a compromise passed by Congress. In the view of one House GOP staff member, "People realized that [Paige] was outside the process."[85] According to another congressional staffer, Paige was "bringing nothing. He's not part of the discussion. He's not the negotiator. He's not the guy things are cleared through . . . the president wants it for himself. It makes it difficult for the secretary to be anything other than an echo machine for the president." By August 2001, Paige was reported to be eager to be a more visible actor, despite reports of his irrelevance: "I've tried to deal with it in several ways. One was to try to debunk it, to say it's not true, but now I'm saying the hell with it, and going on and doing my job."[86]

Although touted as a CEO who would delegate much to his cabinet, a number of them former executives from the private sector, Bush—and his White House—largely retained control of key decisions and the deliberative processes leading to them. As Transportation Secretary Mineta, a cabinet veteran who served as commerce secretary under Clinton, noted: "I know that I am going to be checking with Andrew Card or somebody before I go off on a toot."[87]

Cabinet Missteps

Despite clear signs that power remained in the White House, several missteps occurred on the part of some cabinet members who sometimes felt they could make policy pronouncements without prior clearance or authorization. Environmental Protection Agency (EPA) administrator Christie Todd Whitman, in particular, was at the center of several controversies. During the transition, Whitman had apparently been promised a broad portfolio in environmental policy making. "I want you to be the environmental person," Bush reportedly told her. And at a March 2001 conference in Trieste, Whitman announced, based on a Bush campaign position paper, that the United States would consider changing its policy on carbon dioxide pollution (and adopting a position in accord with the Kyoto treaty). Whitman, however, did not clear her comments with the White House. A week later, the White House reversed its position and also called the Kyoto agreement "fatally flawed." Whitman tried to convince Bush of her position in a lengthy memo (which was subsequently leaked, one of the few occurrences in the early Bush administration, to Whitman's embarrassment). But her efforts failed. Her difficulties increased, moreover, following a decision on her part to postpone implementation of tighter regulations on the levels of arsenic permitted in the nation's water supply. She merely held for further review (until 2006) the new rule, but media accounts played up the administration's presumed insensitivity to levels of the poison in the water. The new rules would have been costly to some municipalities and water suppliers, and the issue could have been left to litigation rather than an administration decision. But Whitman made the call, apparently without informing the White House. According to Whitman, "It was a dumb decision on my part, really dumb. . . . Politically, I should have just let it go and allowed the courts to decide."[88]

The Department of Agriculture blindsided the White House by not informing it of changes in salmonella regulations in ground meat used in school lunch programs. Like arsenic levels in drinking water, the possibility of more salmonella in kids' hamburgers attracted negative media attention. Attorney General John Ashcroft also raised a public ruckus when he told the National Rifle Association in a two-page letter on May 17, 2001, that he "unequivocally" believed that the Constitution protected a person's right to own firearms. Ashcroft's position not only put him at odds with the federal court's standards over fifty years (a collective right rather than an individual one), but it also signaled a potential change in the Justice Department's position on the issue.[89]

Other cabinet members were sometimes at odds with the Bush agenda. HHS Secretary Tommy Thompson reportedly promoted his own candidate to head up the Food and Drug Administration before the White House had made a decision.[90] In early March 2001, Thompson told a Senate hearing that he was "troubled" by a federal law that prohibited stem cell research from destroyed embryos, a position at odds with Bush's. Later that week, Treasury Secretary O'Neill seemed to undermine the surplus projections that were (then) key to Bush's tax cut, when he acknowledged on a Sunday news show that he had used an unprintable word to describe them.[91]

In the weeks before September 11, 2001, there was rising speculation that Defense Secretary Donald Rumsfeld would be the first cabinet member to leave. That speculation immediately ceased in the aftermath of September 11. But Rumsfeld, prior to that, was increasingly frustrated with his efforts to modernize the military, and the military and members of Congress, in turn, were reported to be increasingly critical of Rumsfeld's often abrasive style.[92] Policy differences with Secretary of State Colin Powell also figured into the equation. In late July, while at a press briefing in Canberra, Australia, Rumsfeld was asked whether he agreed with Powell's more conciliatory policies toward China. Rumsfeld replied, albeit jokingly, that he did, "except for those few cases where Colin is still learning."[93]

Cabinet Councils

Domestic Policy Council

Not only was policymaking centered in the White House rather than the cabinet, but the organizational structure within the White House routed the work and recommendations of the Domestic Policy Council and the National Economic Council through the chief of staff's office, in the person of deputy chief of staff Josh Bolten. According to congressional affairs chief Calio, Bolten "got his hands in virtually everything at the White House. . . . All policy matter report to him eventually."[94]

This organizational arrangement and reporting line differed from both the early Reagan and Bush Sr. council setups. During Reagan's first term, while Ed Meese, in his role as "counselor" to the president, controlled the agendas, staffing, and inner workings of the cabinet councils, cabinet members chaired the councils' sessions (when the president was absent). In Reagan's second term, the White House's secretary to the cabinet was the conduit between the councils and the chief of staff (with cabinet members continuing to chair council meetings). This setup continued during the Bush Sr. administration. Under Clinton, the role of the White House directors of the DPC and (now) NEC were enhanced: they chaired meetings in the president's absence, not cabinet officers.

Given Bolten's central role, the arrangement in the George W. Bush administration not only tilted the process toward the White House and away from the cabinet (unlike under Reagan and Bush Sr.), but also placed a key White House aide between the directors of the DPC and NEC and the point of presidential decisionmaking. There are also indications that within the DPC, the deputy director (initially John Bridgeland) was an important figure, possibly given that Spellings's prior policy work had largely been confined to education policy during Bush's governorship.[95]

Yet some reports indicated that all was not well within the White House domestic operation. At least one former member, John DiIulio, perceived it weak on policy substance:

> On social policy and related issues, the lack of even basic policy knowledge, and the only casual interest in knowing more, was somewhat breathtaking— discussion by fairly senior people who meant Medicaid but were talking Medicare; near-instant shifts from discussing any actual policy pros and

cons to discussing political communications, media strategy, et cetera. Even quite junior staff would sometimes hear quite senior staff pooh-pooh any need to dig deeper for pertinent information on a given issue.

Reflecting on the need for a more robust record of domestic policy accomplishment, DiIulio specifically singled out the staff system for criticism: "In my view, they will not get there without some significant reforms to the policy-lite inter-personal dynamics of the place."[96] His observation is shared by David Frum, who notes that, with the exception of Karl Rove and OMB director Mitchell Daniels, "there was a dearth of really high-powered brains. One seldom heard an unexpected thought in the Bush White House or met someone who possessed unusual knowledge. . . . Conspicuous intelligence seemed actively unwelcome."[97]

National Economic Council

Domestic policy might have been able to withstand some of these perceived weaknesses in light of the strength of the Bush campaign agenda as a guide to its early policy efforts, as well as Rove's role both in the substance of policy as well as its strategic tailoring. But economic policy was a different matter, largely out of Rove's purview, and one where the economic well-being of the country looked decidedly less rosy than it had during the campaign. NEC director Lawrence Lindsey played a prominent inside role in Bush's efforts to make his 2001 tax cut the centerpiece of his early agenda and in getting it passed by Congress. But neither Lindsey nor Treasury Secretary O'Neill had the communicative skills to generate public confidence in Bush's handling of the economy as it continued to deteriorate through 2001 and 2002. Unemployment rose from 4.2 percent to 6 percent by the end of Bush's first two years in office, and the stock market lost almost $5 trillion in value (from $14.7 trillion to $9.9 trillion). The Standard and Poor's 500 Index had the greatest two-year decline under any modern president, dropping by 36 percent, a figure even larger than the 29 percent decline under Herbert Hoover's first two years in office. The $5.6 trillion in budget surpluses projected by the Congressional Budget Office for 2002 through 2011 had disappeared. By fiscal year 2003 the annual deficit had reached $375 billion—including $175 billion in surplus social security funds ($550 billion if you or I were doing the calculations). Short-term interest rates, controlled by Greenspan's Federal Reserve, had declined to 1.25 percent, and there was public speculation about the prospect of economic deflation.[98]

While a number of factors produced these economic consequences—an overvalued stock market in the late 1990s, the collapse of the dot.com and technology sectors, the effects of September 11, 2001, and concerns over terrorism—neither Lindsey nor O'Neill proved adept at building an administration defense. On December 6, 2002, both tendered their resignations as had been requested. The dismissals had been decided by President Bush on December 4 in a meeting that Card, Bolten, and Rove had reportedly attended.[99]

O'Neill, in particular, proved a maverick. He was less committed to Bush's tax cut agenda than others in the administration. And in late 2002 he publicly questioned the need for a further stimulus plan, a position that put him at odds with both Lindsey and White House political advisers. His public comments were especially notable: a House GOP stimulus plan was "show business," the Enron collapse showed that "companies come and go. It's . . . part of the genius of capitalism," currency trading was something he "probably could learn about in a couple of weeks," and "if you set aside Three Mile Island and Chernobyl, the safety record of nuclear [power] is really good."[100] According to one report, "Bush aides once jokingly compared O'Neill's news conferences to 'watching a child play with a loaded gun.'"[101] In the summer of 2002 his offhand comments about the Brazilian government sent its currency into a 13 percent decline and triggered a formal protest.[102] O'Neill also criticized Bush's decision to impose tariffs on steel imports at what he thought was a closed-door meeting, only to find them featured in a page-one story in the next day's *Washington Post*.[103] "Every time he got on TV, we would all say 'Don't talk,'" one Wall Street trader observed. According to one Treasury official, when his resignation was announced, "no one cheered and no one looked upset."[104]

While Lawrence Lindsey's allegiance to the president's tax cut plan was unquestioning and his public gaffes fewer, he too came to be perceived as a liability. Both his managerial skills and his ability to sell the president's program were called into question. According to one account, "People close to the White House said he [Lindsey] was not adept at coordinating the flow of policy, and he caused a furor when he predicted [ultimately more accurately than did others at the time], in an interview with the *Wall Street Journal*, that the cost of war with Iraq might reach $200 billion."[105] Nor did Lindsey's rocky relationship with O'Neill help him out. O'Neill reportedly was in the habit of interrupting Lindsey when the two met with Bush, and Lindsey, in turn, reportedly was critical of O'Neill.

Their difficulties cropped up early. Just days after the new administration was under way, Lindsey sent Card a memo, with a copy to O'Neill, complaining that the Treasury Department's tax analysis unit was unable to provide data needed for revenue forecasts. According to O'Neill's biographer Ron Suskind, O'Neill took the memo for something more:

> It was a statement of loyalty. Lindsey was saying he was a stalwart supporter of the president and that O'Neill was not. This was the breach O'Neill had feared: that the "honest broker" was an advocate. Hard-eyed analysis would

be painted as disloyalty. He was clearly being characterized as contrarian. He grabbed a printout of the memo and scribbled across the top, "Larry: This is bureaucratic chicken ———. You must have something better to do with your time than send me memos such as this one."[106]

O'Neill then sent the memo back to Lindsey, with copies to Card and OMB director Daniels.

In a White House noted for its discipline, O'Neill was apparently one of the few targets of embarrassing leaks to the press. According to one of O'Neill's top aides:

> It was amazing before. But then it got crazy. We would get calls every couple of days . . . [about] some out-of-context thing Paul had said at the weekly economics lunch or some meeting with Larry. It wasn't even subtle. From the first month of the administration, every reporter in town knew they could get some inside punch at O'Neill just by calling Lindsey's office.[107]

"There was no creative tension," according to one White House aide, "just tension." Both O'Neill and Lindsey lacked "the ability to conceive, the ability to execute and the ability to sell economic policy," observed another.[108] In contrast to the more tightly disciplined, White House–led domestic policy process, the broader sweep of the administration's economic deliberations led it to be more prone to error and dysfunction.

Rice as NSC Adviser

At the start of the Bush administration, one might have predicted that NSC adviser Condoleezza Rice and her staff would occupy a less central role in the policymaking process, unlike other parts of the White House staff. She had publicly announced that she would play a "neutral broker" role, rather than serving as a policy advocate in her own right. And she was serving in an administration in which she was surrounded by a number of foreign and national security policy heavyweights: former defense secretary and now vice president Cheney, past and present defense secretary Rumsfeld, and former NSC adviser, chairman of the Joints Chiefs of Staff, and now secretary of state Powell. Yet from the start of the Bush presidency, there was no one dominant figure, Powell notwithstanding, and the four would meet regularly for lunch to hash out their differences.

Rice also presided over a slimmer NSC staff, having cut its size (which had ballooned to more than 100 in Clinton's second term) by about a third. Plans for the change had been drawn up during the campaign and finalized during the transition, and they more closely resembled the NSC staff during Brent Scowcroft's tenure as NSC adviser under Bush Sr. than the more ambitious and expansive staff operation of the Clinton years.[109] The intent was to create a more strategically focused operation with a strong emphasis on defense strategy and an avoidance of replicating units elsewhere in the executive branch. According to Rice's deputy, Stephen Hadley, "There are a lot of things we don't do at the NSC staff because leaving them in the hands of a government agency is perfectly fine. We don't try and reproduce the State Department or the Defense Department. We try to get out of the way to let them handle the things they do. We don't want to reproduce the stovepipes that appear across the government."[110] Through the first eight months of the new administration, the organizational changes seemed benign, if not wise. But in the aftermath of September 11, particularly in the deliberations leading up to war with Iraq and its subsequent reconstruction, did it leave the NSC staff ill equipped to perform its role effectively, lacking the "stovepipes" that might have better questioned intelligence or being too prone to "get out of the way," as Hadley himself phrased it?

The reorganization plan also included a new unit on international economic policy to be shared with Lindsey's NEC. Although the latter was not placed completely under NSC control, it did strengthen the White House's hand and lessen that of the Treasury Department, which had been dominant in that area under past administrations. "It's a way to make sure the economic people don't run off with foreign policy and vice versa," Bush told the press when he unveiled the new unit during the transition.[111] Furthermore, under the reorganization plan, the State Department would run interagency meetings that focused on particular countries and regions, while the NSC staff would chair meetings dealing with "crosscutting issues." NSC legislative liaison and communications staff were also eliminated, and the press and speech-writing staffs were reduced in size.[112]

Yet the size of the NSC staff under Rice, while reduced, was still larger (approximately seventy) than that under many of her other predecessors. Furthermore, while some of the units that had been created in the Clinton years were formally slated for elimination, informally a number still persisted. As Ivo Daalder, a senior fellow at the Brookings Institution and a well-respected academic expert in foreign policy, noted at a panel discussion in April 2001, "Twelve weeks into this NSC [staff], you now have a legislative director, senior director in the NSC staff. You have a press spokesperson who in fact speaks publicly, and consistently. You have a speech-writing shop, and the numbers of people who are in these functions are slowly but surely increasingly."[113]

But Rice remained a central player. She chaired the meeting of the foreign policy principals, an assignment laid out in Bush's first National Security Presidential Directive on February 13, 2001. According to one account, she was not the most vocal of the group. "But when the meeting is over, Rice is the one who gets up and goes to a smaller meeting—in the Oval Office with the president."[114] Some rumors were floated before the directive was issued that Cheney had sought to lead the principals' meeting, but Rice's position prevailed.[115] In addition, her deputy, Stephen Hadley, was assigned by the same directive to chair the deputies committee of NSC members. And Hadley, like Rice, faced a room full of heavyweights: Deputy Secretary of State Richard Armitage and Deputy Secretary of Defense Paul Wolfowitz most notably. According to one participant, one of Hadley's tasks was "reining in some of the right-wing ideologues who can get the president in trouble. He's methodical. He runs meetings like an orchestra conductor. But when they are over, he's quietly tossed some pretty extreme ideas overboard." He also served, in Rice's words, as her "alter ego. I can sometimes jump from A to F. He backs me up to B and C, makes me think through implications."[116]

Most important, of the four principals, Rice enjoyed the closest personal relationship with President Bush. She was a longtime Bush family loyalist, having served in the Bush Sr. administration on the NSC staff of her mentor, Brent Scowcroft. She had been, in effect, George W. Bush's foreign policy "tutor" during the campaign. And she had a much stronger personal connection to him once he was in office. Not only was she more often at his side than the other principals on a day-to-day basis, but she frequently traveled with him to Camp David on the weekend, not only to discuss policy but also to relax, particularly sharing their mutual interest in professional sports.

In some policy areas, missile defense most notably, she became an important advocate; so too with the administration's position on the Kyoto treaty, handling North Korea, and relations with Russia (her academic specialty).[117] In other areas, she often found herself in alliance with the more hawkish members of the Bush team—Cheney and Rumsfeld—rather than Powell. Yet at the same time, up through September 11, she did not seek to undercut Powell's role or to engage—at least in public view—in the kind of bureaucratic battles that some of her predecessors have waged—usually successfully—against the secretary of state in asserting their control of the policymaking process. According to Powell, "It isn't threatening to me. She's not supposed to be in my corner. She's not supposed to be in Rumsfeld's corner. She's supposed to be in the president's corner, and she is, and she enjoys his confidence."[118]

She clearly became a public presence, both in press appearances and in public speeches. But while a publicly visible adviser, Rice adhered to the (usual) tight-lipped discipline that pervaded the Bush White House. According to one feature story on her in *Newsweek,* "Rice wants people to think of her as an enigma. She has often said that she is 'determined to leave this town' without anyone outside Bush's tight inner circle ever figuring out where she stands on major issues." And if she does on occasion advise the president, she never shares that, "not even with her closest aides." In meetings of the principals (especially when Bush is present), she asks "pointed questions" but "rarely takes an open stand." The other principals are often clear about her positions from private conversations. But in interactions with them she holds the reins more "lightly": "She wants the president's other advisers to believe that she doesn't play favorites or whisper in the president's ear. By seeming above the fray she preserves her ability to influence decisions, however subtly."[119]

Her style and demeanor also fit Bush's comfort level. According to one account, "When Bush doesn't know the issues, he falls back on personal relations. . . . That sweet spot is now occupied by Condi Rice. . . . [S]he's just down the hall whence it's easy to run into the Oval Office ten times a day. Bush wants his info whittled down to one-page memos, and she writes them; he likes one-person oral briefings, and she provides them." According to one White House aide, "A lot of this is personal chemistry. Condi and the President are very close. They're friends. He trusts her. That means a lot."[120] According to Rice herself, her extra time with Bush "gives us a chance to step back . . . and talk more about our broader objectives."[121] Rice also fit Bush's penchant for having issues laid out, albeit crisply and concisely. Rice's role was defined the way it was, according *Newsweek*'s Evan Thomas, "because that's the way the president wants it. Bush is suspicious of bureaucracy and does not want to be fed decisions that have been precooked. . . . He wants clear choices and original thinking." According to former treasury secretary O'Neill, "She doesn't drive to consensus. Rather she drives toward clarity. Then he [Bush] decides what the consensus is."[122]

As with the early organizational changes made in the NSC, Rice's role as NSC adviser appeared to mesh well with Bush's own preferences and workways and with the realities of a talented foreign policy team. Yet under the tougher times after September 11, would holding the reins "lightly" still work? Would seeming "to be above the fray" be effective? Would "driving toward clarity" be enough? Would President Bush, in turn, have the "clear choices and original thinking" that would enable *him* to really decide "what the consensus is"?

An Even More Influential Vice President

The role of the vice president as an influential voice, often with substantive policy-related assignments, has grown enormously. Although some earlier vice presidents (Nixon in foreign affairs under Eisenhower for example) were participants in their administration's inner deliberations, it was with Mondale under Carter, Bush Sr. under Reagan, and (especially) Gore under Clinton that the modern vice presidency emerged as important in its own right. Richard Cheney's vice presidency continued this development, and he became, arguably, a more central figure in the Bush presidency than Al Gore had been under Clinton.[123]

During the first eight months of the new administration, Cheney met every morning with Bush and then several other times depending on the day's business. Cheney regularly reviewed the president's daily schedule and then decided which meetings he would attend, in addition to his weekly lunch with the president. According to one account, "He asks his own questions of the staff, and shares intelligence he and his aides have gathered from Congress, but often offers his advice to the president in private. Even his closest aides are not privy to the contents of those discussions."[124] He met for a weekly lunch with the three other foreign policy "principals"—Rice, Powell, and Rumsfeld, as well as (before September 11) weekly meetings with Powell and Rumsfeld. In addition to his offices in the West Wing and the Old Executive Office Building, Cheney also used the vice president's offices near the Senate and, for the first time, an office that was given to him by Speaker Hastert just off the House floor.

Cheney assembled a skilled staff, including Mary Matalin as "counselor" to the vice president and I. Lewis ("Scooter") Libby, as his chief of staff ("Cheney's Cheney," according to a number of accounts). Both also held the title of "assistant to the president" (compared to one person with that title under Gore) and both attended Card's morning senior staff meeting. In fact, according to Libby, "I'm invited to attend any meeting Andy Card goes to and he's invited to any meeting I go to."[125] Although Cheney's staff was smaller than that of Vice President Gore's (some 50 to 60 compared to Gore's 85 to 110), in many ways it was more powerful and tightly woven into the White House's operation. Cheney's staff, for example, included his own congressional liaison team, headed by congressional veteran Nancy Dorn.[126] It was a unit, according to *Roll Call,* that "mirrors the structure and function of the White House legislative office." Recent vice presidents have had congressional lobbyists, but none as formally organized as Cheney's operation. According to Dorn, the two offices (Cheney's and the White House's) hold a single staff meeting, share offices, and coordinate their lobbying activities.[127] More generally, according to Karen Hughes, the White House and vice-presidential staffs "are very integrated, I view them as part of our team, and I think they view themselves as part of our team."[128] "Everybody in our shop is connected at the hip with one of theirs," in the view of Matalin.[129] And unlike some prior vice presidents who may have harbored presidential ambitions and been keen to carve out their policy agendas, Cheney "has no personal or political agenda other than advising the president," noted Matalin.[130]

Cheney's role in the Bush policy process ranged widely. In early 2001, Cheney led the appeals process for the administration's internal budget process. Bush and his advisers set overall spending limits and the OMB did much of the preliminary negotiations with individual departments. Cheney's group—which included Card, OMB director Daniels, economic adviser Lindsey, and Treasury Secretary O'Neill—handled the disputes. Unlike in other administrations, not a single request was appealed directly to the president.

Cheney's most important policy job for the new administration was chairing a task force—formally titled the "National Energy Policy Development Group"—that would propose a new comprehensive energy policy. Its proceedings were closely guarded. Cheney, according to reports, chaired nine meetings of the cabinet-level task force, generally lasting ninety minutes. Toward the end of meetings, aides were asked to leave the room, so that the other principals—EPA administrator Whitman, Energy Secretary Abraham, economic adviser Lindsey, and Cheney—"could settle differences privately without risk of the differences being leaked to the news media. In only a few cases did Bush have to resolve disputes among advisers, participants said."[131] Its recommendations bore the strong imprint of Cheney: a proposal that strongly emphasized production rather than conservation and urged a marked increase in natural gas and oil exploration, as well as more power plants, including nuclear ones. As we will see in Chapter 6, both the task force's findings and its deliberative process raised controversies for the administration.

*   *   *

Compared to some of his recent predecessors, Bush and his associates had assembled and organized a White House staff that exhibited few major mistakes over his first eight months in power. The Bush track record here is especially notable in contrast with the early Carter and Clinton presidencies, where staffing difficulties and disarray frequently manifested themselves early on. The division of labor between Card, Rove, and Hughes, moreover, met the president's needs and organizational expectations, yet it might have led, under other circumstances, to competition and infighting. In the disciplined environs of the Bush administration, that did not emerge. Indeed, its record here even bests that of the early Reagan years, where similar divisions at the top were created, but which often led over time to division and discord.

Yet there were some potential weak spots. Rove's operation brought political strategy and calculation to the top level of this White House, yet it did so in a publicly visible and perhaps at times a too determinative manner. The National Economic Council and the Domestic Policy Council appeared weaker organizationally than at their high points in other presidencies. This may have been an artifact of an early presidency, where much initial policy formulation follows from the fine-tuning and prioritization of campaign themes. But as John DiIulio noted, the quality of policy deliberation appeared less than optimal. Overall, it was a staff and cabinet council system in which much delegation was the order of the day. Both success and failure would turn on the efforts of those to whom much was delegated. The early Bush presidency proceeded, for the most part, smoothly. But over time, as actors become embedded in organizational routines and their views and actions often become reflective of organizational interests, the challenge ahead becomes whether delegation can continue to serve the president's interests and whether those channels of information and advice can fully serve his deliberative needs. Finally, the early Bush presidency was also largely domestic in its focus. Could it adjust to a context in which foreign affairs, particularly a war against terror, occupied the top of the president's agenda?

Notes

1. James A. Barnes, "Bush's Insiders," *National Journal,* June 23, 2001, p. 1869.

2. According to the *National Journal*'s estimate, over 80 percent of top White House decisionmakers "were either paid or volunteer workers during his presidential bid." This figure contrasted with 34 percent participation in the rest of the administration. James A. Barnes, "Bush's Insiders," *National Journal,* June 23, 2001, p. 1868.

3. Peggy Noonan, "A House Undivided," *Wall Street Journal,*" April 20, 2001.

4. Alexis Simendinger, "Stepping into Power," *National Journal,* January 27, 2001, p. 247.

5. Elisabeth Frater, "Al Gonzales: Drawing the Ethics Line," *National Journal,* February 17, 2001, p. 498.

6. Frum, *The Right Man,* p. 15.

7. Alexis Simendinger, "Stepping into Power," *National Journal,* January 27, 2001, p. 247.

8. Ibid.

9. Frum, *The Right Man,* p. 39.

10. Richard Berke, "Bush Is Providing Corporate Model for White House," *New York Times,* March 9, 2001.

11. Telephone interview with Andrew Card Jr., September 17, 1998.

12. Dana Milbank, "Serious Strategery," *Washington Post,* April 22, 2001.

13. Karl Rove, "A Discussion with Karl Rove," American Enterprise Institute, Washington, D.C., December 11, 2001.

14. Ibid.

15. Dana Milbank, "Serious Strategery," *Washington Post,* April 22, 2001.

16. John DiIulio to Ron Suskind, "Your Next Essay on the Bush Administration," October 24, 2002; Drudge Report, "Bush Aide's Letter to Esquire Reporter Revealed," www.drudgereport.com, December 2, 2002.

17. Frank Bruni, "White House Says Race and AIDS Efforts Will Be Adjusted, Not Abandoned," *New York Times,* February 8, 2001.

18. Mike Allen, "Bush Acts to Quell Flap on AIDS, Race," *Washington Post,* February 8, 2001.

19. Amy Goldstein and Mike Allen, "Women's Outreach Office Closed," *Washington Post,* March 29, 2001. A taped phone announcement on the office's line had the following recording: "As of January 19, 2001, this office no longer exists, and we will not be able to retrieve your calls. We apologize for the inconvenience." Bush also reactivated a science and technology council that had been created by his father in 1990. It was to be cochaired by Silicon Valley entrepreneur Floyd Kvamme and the White House science adviser. The move was announced at a meeting of 150 business leaders at the White House on March 28. Bush had held three meetings with technology executives since taking office, and the unit was designed to formalize contacts and liaison.

20. Dana Milbank, "A Loyalist Calls the White House to Order," *Washington Post,* February 20, 2001.

21. Maura Reynolds and Doyle McManus, "For Bush Burdens of Office Multiply," *Los Angeles Times,* January 26, 2003.

22. Frum, *The Right Man,* p. 21.

23. Rove, "A Discussion with Karl Rove."

24. Frum, *The Right Man,* p. 21.

25. Ibid., p. 23.

26. Card's other deputy was Joseph Hagin, who was in charge of staff operations and management. Like Card, Hagin had been a member of the Bush Sr. White House, where he was in charge of presidential scheduling.

27. Rove, "A Discussion with Karl Rove."

28. Elisabeth Bumiller, "An Invisible Aide Leaves Fingerprints," *New York Times,* January 6, 2003. Also see Ryan Lizza, "Bolten the Door," *New Republic,* August 20, 2001.

29. DiIulio to Suskind, "Your Next Essay on the Bush Administration"; Drudge Report, "Bush Aide's Letter to Esquire Reporter Revealed."

30. Richard Berke, "Bush Is Providing Corporate Model For White House," *New York Times,* March 11, 2001.

31. According to Moore and Slater, this also happened when Bush was caught short for words: "It was not uncommon for Hughes, whenever the governor found himself straining for a point, to step in and begin fielding the questions herself." Moore and Slater, *Bush's Brain,* p. 220.

32. Mike Allen, "Hughes Keeps White House in Line," *Washington Post,* March 19, 2001.

33. Dan Balz and Mike Allen, "Hughes to Leave White House," *Washington Post,* April 24, 2002.

34. Frum, *The Right Man,* p. 40.

35. Ibid., p. 63.

36. James Carney, "A Few Small Repairs," *Time,* July 9, 2001. Also see Frum, *The Right Man,* p. 73.

37. Moore and Slater, *Bush's Brain,* pp. 219–220.

38. Dana Milbank, "Shifts Predicted After Hughes's Exit," *Washington Post,* April 24, 2002.

39. Ryan Lizza, "Write Hand," *New Republic,* May 21, 2001.

40. "Ari Fleischer Out-of-the-Loop Watch," *New Republic,* December 31, 2001. Also see Ryan Lizza, "The White House Doesn't Need the Press," *New York Times Magazine,* December 9, 2001. It should be noted, however, that Fleischer was one of a handful of White House staffers who had walk-in rights to see the president when needed.

41. Ryan Lizza, "The White House Doesn't Need the Press," *New York Times Magazine,* December 9, 2001.

42. DiIulio to Suskind, "Your Next Essay on the Bush Administration"; Drudge Report, "Bush Aide's Letter to Esquire Reporter Revealed."

43. Moore and Slater, *Bush's Brain,* p. 220.

44. Moore and Slater, *Bush's Brain.*

45. Dubose, Reid, and Cannon, *Boy Genius.*

46. Richard Berke and Frank Bruni, "Architect of Bush Presidency Still Builds Bridges of Power," *New York Times,* February 18, 2001.

47. Ibid.

48. DiIulio to Suskind, "Your Next Essay on the Bush Administration"; Drudge Report, "Bush Aide's Letter to Esquire Reporter Revealed."

49. Dubose, Reid, and Cannon, *Boy Genius,* p. 194.

50. Fred Barnes, "Conservatives Love George W. Bush," *Weekly Standard,* March 5, 2001.

51. Ryan Lizza, "Salvation," *New Republic,* April 23, 2001.

52. Thomas Edsall and Dana Milbank, "White House's Roving Eye for Politics," *Washington Post,* March 10, 2003.

53. James Carney and John Dickerson, "The Busiest Man in the White House," *Time,* April 30, 2001.

54. Carl Cannon and Alexis Simendinger, "The Evolution of Karl Rove," *National Journal,* April 27, 2002, p. 1212.

55. John F. Harris, "Clintonesque Balancing of Issues, Polls," *Washington Post,* June 24, 2001.

56. DiIulio to Suskind, "Your Next Essay on the Bush Administration"; Drudge Report, "Bush Aide's Letter to Esquire Reporter Revealed."

57. Carl Cannon and Alexis Simendinger, "The Evolution of Karl Rove," *National Journal,* April 27, 2002, p. 1212.

58. DiIulio to Suskind, "Your Next Essay on the Bush Administration"; Drudge Report, "Bush Aide's Letter to Esquire Reporter Revealed."

59. Fred Barnes, "The Impresario," *Weekly Standard,* August 20, 2001.

60. Bourne, *Jimmy Carter,* p. 372.

61. Landon Butler, Miller Center Oral History, p. 36, Carter Presidential Library, Atlanta, Georgia. Butler was a deputy to Carter aide Hamilton Jordan. For further analysis of this problem in the Carter decisionmaking process, see Burke, *Presidential Transitions,* pp. 80–81.

62. Dubose, Reid, and Cannon, *Boy Genius,* p. 236.

63. Dana Milbank and Ellen Nakashima, "Bush Team Has 'Right' Credentials," *Washington Post,* March 25, 2001.

64. Richard Berke and Frank Bruni, "Crew of Listing Bush Ship Draws Republican Scowls," *New York Times,* July 2, 2001.

65. Randall Mikkelsen, "Bush Backs Rove Amid Ethics, Vieques Questions," *Washington Post,* June 19, 2001.

66. Richard Berke and Frank Bruni, "Crew of Listing Bush Ship Draws Republican Scowls," *New York Times,* July 2, 2001.

67. According to one report, the Salvation Army felt it had a firm commitment from the White House and proposed spending nearly $1 million to lobby for Bush's effort. Mike Allen and Dana Milbank, "Rove Heard Charity Plea on Gay Bias," *Washington Post,* July 12, 2001. Yet the matter had not been settled and was under review by the OMB. The deputy director of the White House Office of Faith-Based Initiatives apparently assured the Salvation Army that the administration would consider the change. Initially the White House indicated that senior officials were not involved in dealing with the issue. The White House also initially maintained that Rove was the first person contacted and merely referred them to the OMB and the White House Office of Faith-Based Initiatives. But, according to one report, other White House officials disputed this account: "Rove was intimately involved in courting the Salvation Army. . . . Literally nothing occurs around here without his blessing. He's the air traffic controller. He says, 'Here's your problem. Here's your answer.'" Mike Allen and Dana Milbank, "Rove Heard Charity Plea on Gay Bias," *Washington Post,* July 12, 2001. Subsequent reports also suggested that Rove was more deeply involved in the

issue. The OMB was nearly finished with its review of the issue when Rove called them in May. According to OMB general counsel Jay Lefkowitz, Rove "asked me to take a look at this issue, asked me whether I was aware of the issue and whether or not I could look at the issue again." Lefkowitz reported back to Rove two weeks later that the exemption would not work. Meanwhile the Salvation Army continued its lobbying efforts and was not informed of the decision until early July when the matter became public. Later White House statements also disputed the initial statement that Rove was the first person contacted. According to Press Secretary Ari Fleischer, "The faith-based office brought it to the OMB's attention." Fleischer also sought to minimize the White House's involvement in the issue: "If people had checked deeper, they would have seen that this did not even reach the senior staff level of the White House." He also suggested that it was "utter nonsense" to suggest Rove did anything wrong, as well as minimizing the incident: "So what—big deal. This is absurd. People contact and write the White House every day." Dana Milbank, "Story of Charity Plea Changes Again," *Washington Post,* July 13, 2001.

68. Dubose, Reid, and Cannon, *Boy Genius,* p. 211.

69. Richard Berke, "Tensions Touch GOP Chief's Tenure," *New York Times,* July 20, 2001.

70. The White House also felt that Gilmore "has not been suitably aggressive in pitching the president's agenda." Representative Thomas Davis (R-VA), chair of the National Republican Congressional Committee, observed, "The governor needs to understand that he's the president's guy. It's not his committee. He's the president's eyes and ears." Oliver, asked whether he reported to Gilmore or Rove, diplomatically replied, "It's sort of a seamless, frictionless cooperative partnership." It was also reported that Gilmore had only met with Bush once, in June, a meeting that Rove did not attend. Richard Berke, "Tensions Touch GOP Chief's Tenure," *New York Times,* July 20, 2001.

71. On June 16, 2003, the RNC announced that Racicot was stepping down as chairman in order to head up the Bush 2004 campaign. His replacement was Ed Gillespie, a veteran GOP strategist who had been a senior adviser to the Bush 2000 campaign.

72. Richard L. Berke, "G.O.P.'s National Chairman Resigning After Brief Term," *New York Times,* December 1, 2001.

73. John Harris, "Clintonesque Balancing of Issues, Polls," *Washington Post,* June 24, 2001.

74. Mike Allen, "Ethics of Key Bush Officials Targeted," *Washington Post,* June 16, 2001.

75. "Bush Aide with Intel Stock Met with Executives Pushing Merger," *New York Times,* June 14, 2001. Rove was eventually given the certificate on June 6 and sold the stocks on June 7 (had Rove sold the stock on January 20 rather than June 7, he would have gained more than $138,000). In the interim, he reportedly met with officials or representatives of at least six of the companies in which he held more that $100,000 worth of stock: Cisco, Enron, General Electric, Intel, Johnson & Johnson, and Pfizer. According to White House aide Dan Bartlett, the whole issue was a bureaucratic snafu: "This is a situation where the bureaucracy got the best of the process." Mike Allen, "Ethics of Key Bush Officials Targeted," *Washington Post,* June 16, 2001. But Rove's predicament did not escape congressional scrutiny. In mid-June, Representative Henry Waxman, the ranking Democrat on the House Committee on Government Reform, sent the White House a letter noting that ethics regulations prohibit officials from participating in matters in which there is a financial interest and where the matter would have a "direct and predictable effect" on that financial interest. According to Waxman, Rove

could have not participated or he could have sold the stock beforehand, neither of which he did. Rove also could have requested a waiver from the White House counsel's office, a matter that Waxman also raised. Ryan Lizza, "Go Away," *New Republic,* July 9, 2001. Waxman also requested that Representative Dan Burton (R-IN), chairman of the Government Reform Committee, hold a hearing on the Rove-Intel matter. "This is exactly the type of situation that you would have investigated had it occurred in the Clinton administration," Waxman wrote Burton, but Burton declined. On July 17, Waxman also called on the Justice Department to review Rove's contacts with executives and representatives of companies in which he held stock. However, Senate Majority Leader Tom Daschle told the press on June 17 that there would be no Senate investigation of Rove. Earlier, White House counsel Alberto Gonzales said he was satisfied that Rove "took care" to avoid ethical conflicts. Following Waxman's most recent July query, White House spokesman Dan Bartlett said that Waxman's letter was under review, adding, "We are confident that Karl followed all ethical guidelines and statutes in his role as senior adviser to the president." George Lardner, "Waxman Seeks Justice Query of Rove," *Washington Post,* July 18, 2001. The White House maintained that Rove's role in these meetings did not involve substantive discussions on policy matters and did not raise issues that required investigation outside the White House. But in the Clinton administration, NSC advisers Anthony Lake and Sandy Berger faced a similar difficulty. Both were forced to sell holdings of energy-related stocks and their cases were referred to the Justice Department. Lake was fined $5,000 and Berger $23,000. George Lardner, "Rove's First Step Toward Shedding Stock Took Five Months," *Washington Post,* July 26, 2001. On August 10, 2001, the White House legal counsel's office rejected the charges against Rove. Gonzales refused to compile information about any of Rove's contacts with the companies unless it was authorized by "a committee or House of Congress," not an individual request such as Waxman's. George Lardner, "White House Rejects Request for Rove Review," *Washington Post,* August 11, 2001.

76. Richard Stevenson, "Top Strategist Terms Bush a Populist About Taxes," *New York Times,* January 23, 2003.

77. Ellen Nakashima and Dana Milbank, "Bush Cabinet Takes Back Seat in Driving Policy," *Washington Post,* September 5, 2001.

78. Ellen Nakashima and Al Kamen, "Bush Picks as Diverse as Clinton's," *Washington Post,* March 30, 2001.

79. Press Release, "At 100-Day Mark, Presidential Appointments Process Again Bogs Down," Presidential Appointee Initiative, Brookings Institution, Washington D.C., www.appointee.brookings.org, April 20, 2001. Also see Mackenzie, "The Real Invisible Hand," pp. 27–31.

80. "Bush Is Ahead of Clinton Pace on Nominees," *New York Times,* August 6, 2001; and Al Kamen, "Senate Democrats Moving Right Along," *Washington Post,* July 23, 2001.

81. Presidential Appointee Initiative, Brookings Institution, Washington D.C., www.appointee.brookings.org, August 31, 2001. An additional thirty-three appointees were retained from the previous administration.

82. Christopher Lee, "Confirmations Fail to Reach Light's Speed," *Washington Post,* June 20, 2003.

83. Clay Johnson, panel discussion, "Bush Transition to the Presidency: Planning and Implementation," American Enterprise Institute, Washington, D.C., December 11, 2001.

84. Ryan Lizza, "Spokesmen," *New Republic,* January 29, 2001.

85. Noam Scheiber, "Rod Paige Learns the Hard Way," *New Republic,* July 2, 2001.

86. Diana Schemo, "Education Chief Seeks More Visible Role," *New York Times,* August 5, 2001.

87. Ellen Nakashima and Dana Milbank, "Bush Cabinet Takes Back Seat in Driving Policy," *Washington Post,* September 5, 2001.

88. Gregg Easterbrook, "Hostile Environment," *New York Times Magazine,* August 19, 2001.

89. Dan Eggen, "Ashcroft: Gun Ownership an Individual Right," *Washington Post,* May 24, 2001.

90. Robert Pear, "In Anthrax Case, Health Secretary Finds Unsteady Going," *New York Times,* October 25, 2001.

91. Dana Milbank, "In Bush Cabinet, It's Both Advise and Dissent," *Washington Post,* March 10, 2001.

92. Al Kamen, "Donny, We Hardly Knew Ye," *Washington Post,* September 7, 2001.

93. Robert Mann, "The Top-Drawer in the Cabinet," *New York Times,* August 5, 2001.

94. Ryan Lizza, "Bolten the Door," *New Republic,* August 20, 2001. Bolten had worked for Calio during the latter's first stint as congressional affairs director under Bush Sr.

95. Bridgeland had been Bolten's deputy issues director during the campaign as well as chief of staff to Representative Rob Portman (R-OH), an important Bush ally in the House. Bridgeland then moved to Bush's new national service office, "USA Freedom Corps," in late April 2002 and was replaced by Jay Lefkowitz. There is also some controversy over who in fact held the title of "director" of the DPC. Spellings was clearly higher than Bridgeland in the hierarchy of White House titles, holding the title of "assistant to the president." Yet different sources list either her or Bridgeland (and his successor Lefkowitz) as "director" of the DPC. See Timothy Noah, "Who Is Director of the Domestic Policy Council?" *Slate,* slate.msn.com, January 15, 2003.

96. DiIulio to Suskind, "Your Next Essay on the Bush Administration"; Drudge Report, "Bush Aide's Letter to Esquire Reporter Revealed."

97. Frum, *The Right Man,* p. 20.

98. These figures are taken from Allan Sloan, "Bush's Depressing Economy," *Newsweek,* February 10, 2003. Figures on deficit are from OMB projections in July 2003.

99. Lindsey took his dismissal graciously. Unlike O'Neill, Lindsey was seated in the front row when the nomination of a new treasury secretary, John Snow, was announced. O'Neill, however, was not present. O'Neill reportedly was surprised that his resignation had been requested, a job that fell to Cheney, who had been instrumental in securing his nomination for the job. After Cheney phoned O'Neill, the latter then tendered a four-line letter of resignation and immediately went home to Pittsburgh. O'Neill supporters claimed that he was not invited to the ceremony announcing his successor; the White House noted, however, that "he was informed of the ceremony and expressed no interest in attending." The request for his resignation apparently hit O'Neill hard. He had, according to reports, gone to Bush recently and asked the president if he still had his confidence, and Bush told him he did. However, as one "senior administration official" put it: "That's one way to interpret the conversations. Another way to interpret them is that he heard those portions of the conversations he wanted to hear." Nor was the way his dismissal was carried out suitable to him: "Mr. O'Neill's defenders point out that the president never called to say goodbye—or to explain why a goodbye was necessary. That was left to Vice President Dick Cheney." David Sanger, "Departure from Cabinet Niceties," *New York Times,* December 7, 2002.

100. "The Mint-Fresh Quotations of Paul O'Neill," *Washington Post,* December 7, 2002.

101. Dana Milbank, "With '04 in Mind, Bush Team Saw Economic, Political Peril," *Washington Post,* December 7, 2002.

102. Richard Wolfe, Michael Hirsh, and Tamara Lipper, "Bush Cleans House," *Newsweek,* December 16, 2002.

103. Owen Ullman, "Good Boy Don! Heel Tommy!" *Washingtonian,* June 2002.

104. Richard Wolfe, Michael Hirsh, and Tamara Lipper, "Bush Cleans House," *Newsweek,* December 16, 2002. Following his departure from the Treasury Department, O'Neill continued to come under criticism, now for the proposal for new tax-free savings accounts that were part of Bush's 2003 stimulus and tax cut plans. The accounts proved unpopular in some quarters in Congress, including with Speaker Hastert and Representative Rob Portman (R-OH), a key Bush ally and liaison with the GOP on the Hill. O'Neill was blamed for having developed the savings account plan in secret and freezing key Republican lawmakers out of the discussion. Jim VandeHei, "GOP Not Backing Savings Changes," *Washington Post,* February 7, 2003.

105. Edmund Andrews, "Bush, over Supply-Side Protests, Picks Wall Street Banker as Economic Adviser," *New York Times,* December 13, 2002.

106. Suskind, *The Price of Loyalty,* p. 69.

107. Ibid., p. 174.

108. John Dickerson and Karen Tumulty, "Take It Outside, Boys," *Time,* December 16, 2002.

109. The plans had begun in September 2000 when Rice asked Philip Zelikow of the University of Virginia (also a former colleague of Rice's at the Bush Sr. NSC staff) and Robert Blackwill, a former arms control expert at the State Department, to study NSC organization and draft plans "along Scowcroft's lines": "Edited by Rice and others, the memos were further refined when Rice's deputy Stephen Hadley came on board, and Zelikow and Blackwill became part of the transition and were free to roam the halls of the Clinton NSC operation." Karen DeYoung and Steven Mufson, "A Leaner and Less Visible NSC," *Washington Post,* February 10, 2001.

110. Dana Milbank, "Down to the Nuts and Bolts at NSC," *Washington Post,* July 25, 2001.

111. David Sanger, "Bush Plans to Stress Effects of Economics on Security," *New York Times,* January 16, 2001.

112. Karen DeYoung and Steven Mufson, "A Leaner and Less Visible NSC," *Washington Post,* February 10, 2001.

113. Ivo Daalder, panel discussion, "Assessing the Bush Foreign Policy Transition," American Enterprise Institute, Washington, D.C., April 18, 2001.

114. Martha Brant and Evan Thomas, "A Steely Southerner," *Newsweek,* August 6, 2001.

115. Jane Perlez, "Directive Says Rice, Bush Aide, Won't Be Upstaged by Cheney," *New York Times,* February 16, 2001.

116. David Sanger, "Missile Shield Point Man Does Not Shy From Tough Sell," *New York Times,* June 11, 2001.

117. In August 2001, for example, Rice not only was the first NSC adviser to undertake a diplomatic mission to Moscow, but also was the first top U.S. official, including Secretary of State Powell, to meet with President Vladimir Putin. Her aim was to impress upon him the U.S. case for missile defense and the need to abrogate the 1972 anti–ballistic missile treaty, decisions that the Russians eventually accepted.

118. Johanna McGeary, "Odd Man Out," *Time,* September 10, 2001.

119. Evan Thomas, "The Quiet Power of Condi Rice," *Newsweek,* December 16, 2002.

120. Johanna McGeary, "Odd Man Out," *Time,* September 10, 2001.

121. Massimo Calabresi, "The Charm of Face Time," *Time,* September 10, 2001.

122. Evan Thomas, "The Quiet Power of Condi Rice," *Newsweek,* December 16, 2002.

123. For more extensive discussion of Cheney's role as vice president, especially after September 11, see Paul Kengor, "Cheney and Vice Presidential Power," in Gregg and Rozell, *Considering the Bush Presidency,* pp. 160–176.

124. John F. Harris and Dan Balz, "First 100 Days Go By in a Blur," *Washington Post,* April 29, 2001.

125. Dana Milbank, "For Number Two, the Future Is Now," *Washington Post,* February 3, 2001.

126. Dorn was a former foreign policy adviser to Speaker Dennis Hastert, as well as a former staff member of the House Appropriations Committee, the Reagan legislative liaison office, and an assistant secretary of the U.S. Army when Cheney was defense secretary.

127. Susan Crabtree, "Cheney Gets Liaison Team," *Roll Call,* February 26, 2001.

128. Eric Schmitt, "Cheney Assembles Formidable Team," *New York Times,* February 3, 2001.

129. Dana Milbank, "For Number Two, the Future Is Now," *Washington Post,* February 3, 2001.

130. Eric Schmitt, "Cheney Assembles Formidable Team," *New York Times,* February 3, 2001.

131. Mike Allen and Dana Milbank, "Cheney's Role Offers Strengths and Liabilities," *Washington Post,* May 17, 2001.

5

George W. Bush:
Leadership and Decisionmaking

The organization of the White House staff, the impact of the cabinet, and other matters discussed in Chapter 4 are important in their own right, but they do not stand alone. They are there to serve the president in formulating policy decisions and seeing that they are carried out, as well as serving in other capacities that enhance the president's performance in office—lobbying Congress, building constituent support, and attempting to manage and communicate the president's message. But how they do so effectively will vary from one presidency to another; no one set template guarantees success.

It is conventional wisdom among most presidency watchers that staff systems must fit a president "like a suit of clothes." In some sense this is true: a White House filled with meetings and with adversaries vigorously arguing with each other were delights for Franklin Roosevelt and Bill Clinton, but they were deadly poison for Richard Nixon when they occurred early in his presidency. How presidents "process" information (to take but a piece of this issue) can often be markedly different. One test of a successful transition is how well the organizations, structures, and processes set up fit with the cognitive, emotional, and interpersonal needs of a new president.

But "fit" is not enough. Presidential predilections are not always effective, appropriate, or success-encouraging. Both Eisenhower and Nixon favored a more formal, hierarchical staff structure; this worked for Ike, but often was problematic for Nixon. Kennedy and Johnson favored looser, collegial, deliberative arrangements. They often served Kennedy well, but sometimes got Johnson into difficulty. Even within a particular administration, fine-tuning may occur: Kennedy's small, collegial group of advisers performed poorly during the deliberations over the Bay of Pigs invasion early in his presidency, but by the time of the Cuban missile crisis in October 1962, there were marked changes for the better. Like a suit of clothes, some tailoring may be required: What presidential weaknesses need to be compensated for? What strengths need to be accentuated?[1]

Bush as Decisionmaker

For George W. Bush, the staff arrangements and decision processes that had been established during the transition and early in this presidency reflected his style and preferences as a decisionmaker, often bore his own imprint, and in a number of aspects mirrored what had been present during his governorship. During the campaign, Bush summarized for reporters his decisionmaking and management style: "I'm the kind of person who trusts people. And I empower people. I am firm with people. On the other hand, I'm a decider. I do not agonize. I think, I listen, and I trust my instincts and I trust the advice I get. And I'm an accessible person."[2]

Delegation but Presidential Involvement

Bush's short summarization for reporters before he took office reflects a number of facets of how his decisionmaking and leadership would operate once he became president. First are his concerns to "empower" and "trust"—to delegate, in other words. The organization of the Bush White House, the responsibilities given Vice President Cheney, and the presence of able and experienced persons in the major cabinet departments, as well as in the White House, signaled that delegation would be a hallmark of this presidency. Bush was, after all, the first president who held an MBA degree, and "Bush as CEO" frequently appeared in news accounts of the internal workings of this administration. Bush valued order and process, as did those he selected for key positions. The Bush White House and Bush's own deliberative processes were in marked contrast to the ad hoc, ever-changing ways of the early Clinton presidency—once summed up by a White House aide as akin to a soccer game among ten-year-olds. Nor was Bush inclined to micromanage, as Carter had done. Unlike Carter, Bush understood the importance of staff work and the value of an advisory network for his deliberations.

The Reagan presidency is perhaps a more apt comparison. But here too there were important differences. While both delegated and had more orderly staff structures, Bush was a more active participant in setting the tone of his administration. As Andrew Card noted in March 2001, Bush's approach differed from the more hands-off approach of Reagan: "Reagan was used to, if you will, getting stage direction. But President Bush has been known as giving direction."[3] As Bush himself noted in his campaign biography, *A Charge to Keep,* "My job is to set the agenda and tone and framework, to lay out the principles by which we operate and make decisions, and then delegate much of the process to them." Fostering teamwork was especially critical. At one of his first staff meetings as governor, Bush told his aides "Always return each other's phone calls first." In his view, it was a practice that "would foster good communication and make sure my senior people would seek one another's advice and guidance. Many of them later told me it set the tone and was key to the team approach they developed."[4]

Bush's perceptions about establishing a clear agenda and communicating that agenda to his team are reinforced by comments made by his state budget director, Albert Hawkins (who later served as White House secretary to the cabinet), in a January 2000 panel discussion on a possible Bush presidency: "He has a clear focus on the agenda that he's established and wants to pursue as governor of Texas. . . . He really works from a Big Picture angle. One of the great pleasures of working with Governor Bush is that we get to understand very, very well what it is he's seeking. He sets the goal. We know what that goal is. We know that there are certain methods that would be compatible with achieving that goal and we move forward that way."[5]

Bush also was more active in the internal deliberations of his presidency. According to one press report at the end of Bush's first 100 days, "In meetings briefers never get through presentations; Bush interrupts without hesitation when he feels he has heard enough. On several occasions, he has casually issued edicts with little concern that he has undercut members of his cabinet. There is little doubt that it is Bush—his personality, his likes and dislikes, his political values—who is the animating force of this White House."[6]

Assistant Attorney General Eric Holder, a Clinton holdover who represented the Justice Department at cabinet meetings until John Ashcroft was sworn in as attorney general, found Bush "formidable." Holder recalled that Bush conducted the cabinet meeting off of an index card with just four or five items listed: "There was no question who was in charge. He has a light touch, but he takes up the space."[7] As David Frum observes in his book on the early Bush presidency, after his first major staff meeting with the president, "Bush had settled one thing in my mind: I could never again take seriously the theory that somebody else was running this administration—not Cheney, not Rove, not Card."[8]

In his speech-writing duties in the Bush White House, Frum quickly found that Bush was deeply engaged: "Bush was an exacting editor. . . . He hated repetition and redundancy," on one occasion striking the phrase "I've seen with my own eyes" and scrawling in the margin "DUH" with one of the heavy felt-tip pens he used. He also "insisted on strict linear logic," circling sentences, pointing to their correct position in a speech draft: "EDUCATION goes HERE. TAX RELIEF over HERE. And DEFENSE SPENDING should all go THERE." A sentence such as "We're increasing federal support for teacher training" would lead Bush to scrawl: "BY HOW MUCH?? FROM WHAT?? TO WHAT??"[9] Similarly, according to Karen Hughes, "Many a speechwriter has learned you do not just hand something to George W. Bush and expect him to read it. You had better be prepared to answer questions, crystallize the thoughts: 'What exactly does this mean? This doesn't get to the point. Say it more directly.'"[10]

Nor was engagement new to Bush. According to Texas state representative Steve Wolens, when (then-governor) Bush wanted "to make a decision, he [would] bring people of opposite sides in to argue the dickens out of an issue. . . . He [would] bring three or four or five key aides in there, and they argue with each other. Bush sits back and he listens, and then he starts picking a little bit, and will be sometimes a buzzard about chewing at an issue and making somebody go back and get some information, and he will ultimately make up his mind."[11]

In political scientist Donald Kettl's view, Bush's engagement had positive benefit. It allowed him "to keep focused on the task at hand. Bush watches the small things to sharpen his focus."[12] For Bush, it also brought other benefits: "One of my jobs is to be provocative, seriously to provoke people into—to force decisions, and to make sure in everybody's mind where we are headed."[13]

Personal Nuances

Yet there were also personal nuances to Bush's involvement. According to one report, "Bush is not disengaged, but there are clear signatures to the way he engages. His questions at meetings, say participants, usually focus on practicalities: What coalitions back a particular bill? Has someone or other been consulted? Bush's curiosity has an almost tactile quality to it." According to Senator Bill Frist (R-TN), "You can watch him click and register with individuals as they speak, and if he's not clicking he will quickly move on." At one meeting on healthcare, one person began "talking in very esoteric terms," according to Frist. Bush interrupted, asking, "What can we do in six months?" In Frist's view, "He'll turn a person off unless you make it practical."[14]

For former White House aide John DiIulio, Bush's more practical bent may have led him to tune-out more intellectually sophisticated analysis: "What Bush really dislikes are academic or other elites who, as I heard him phrase it on occasion, 'are' or 'come off' as 'smart without any heart,' who are 'down on average Americans' who 'just believe in this great country' and its 'great goodness.' Thus, compared to other presidencies since that of Franklin D. Roosevelt, the Bush administration is largely bereft of policy intellectuals."[15]

Nor was Bush's involvement total and all-consuming—this was George W. Bush, not Lyndon B. Johnson. Bush clearly was more engaged on issues that were a part of his agenda. But, where issues were of less importance to him, he tended to rely on the materials provided him. Even on some important issues, Bush appeared to spend less time on policy deliberations than had some of his predecessors. Two months into his presidency, for example, after his economic program had been presented to Congress, Chief of Staff Card estimated that Bush spent "in the neighborhood of five hours" in meetings on budget issues. By contrast, Bill Clinton, according Gene Sperling, one of his top economic advisers, spent twenty-five hours on budget meetings during his first two weeks in office and another fifty hours in informal gatherings with his aides.[16] As political scientist Hugh Heclo notes, "Bush learns quickly and becomes deeply informed about what he is interested in. But this sort of learning capacity turns into a liability when it comes to things that should interest him but do not."[17]

Nor was this pattern of selective engagement new to Bush. According to Albert Hawkins, Bush was "not totally hands off" as governor. He "does delegate and rely on the staff . . . but he checks back in. There's an expectation that significant decisions are brought back, he makes those decisions, he stays engaged but not at the detail level, and I think that's important for his leadership style. . . . He does not enmesh himself in needless details, particularly, you know, the kinds of things that I, as state budget director, have to deal with. . . . But he's very involved and very knowledgeable of the overall budget outlook, the key decisions that need to be made. He provides the direction to us."[18]

But did this pattern of delegation always serve Bush well? According to Fred I. Greenstein, "As governor, Bush was sweeping in his acts of delegation. A study of his Texas schedule found, for example, that when he was delivered a lengthy report on a tragedy in which a number of Texas A&M students were killed in a faultily constructed bonfire, he read neither the report nor its executive summary. Instead, he relied on his aides to highlight a few paragraphs of the report's conclusions." In capital punishment cases, he reduced the amount of time for his personal review from thirty minutes down to fifteen.[19]

More generally, as Greenstein has also noted, Bush lacks "intellectual curiosity."[20] In this, he is not unlike Reagan. And it had bearing on his presidency: when confronted with the unfamiliar or that on which he had not been fully briefed, Bush sometimes erred. An early example of this occurred when he was asked whether the United States would defend Taiwan from a Chinese attack and he replied that he would "do whatever it takes"—a marked departure from existing policy.[21] On another occasion early in his presidency, Bush told reporters that Saddam Hussein had to conform to the "no-fly zones" agreement he signed after the 1991 Gulf War; yet in fact the zones were not part of the agreement and had been established by the United States and Great Britain to protect Kurds in the north and Shiite Muslims in the south. In early February 2001, Bush attended a retreat for congressional Democrats. One of the questions he was asked concerned whether statisticians would be allowed to adjust census results, a controversial issue and one he had rejected during the campaign. Yet Bush told the group, "I haven't decided. I'll be briefed and we'll listen to the professionals." According to one House member who attended, Bush's answers lacked substance: "It wasn't as if there were one or two questions where he said, 'I'll look into it' or 'I'll get back to you' or 'I'm thinking about it'—he did that across the board."[22]

Bush and the Decisionmaking Environment

Organization but Within Defined Limits

A president's reliance on the work delegated to others could lead to overdependence on key advisers. More hierarchical staff systems are of positive benefit, but they can also isolate the president from the full range of information and advice needed to make decisions. Several features of the Bush staff system appear to mitigate this problem; others portend problems. One feature, moreover, stands out: Bush's own interest and involvement in organizational matters and his recognition of how they can affect his own performance in office. As Kettl has noted, Bush is a master at making "the organization fit your personality. Bush imposed his ways on the Oval Office, not the other way around."[23]

First, although Bush favored an organized structure whether within the White House staff or in his dealings with cabinet members, it was not a rigid structure. In many ways, the Bush staff and advisory system was a blend of two models—the more tightly organized, "hierarchical" model of the Eisenhower and Nixon presidencies, as well as the more collegial, "spokes-and-wheel" arrangements of recent Democratic presidencies. Although most recent presidencies have some facets of each—the models are "ideal types" defining a continuum—Bush is unique in having captured and incorporated key elements of each to such a significant degree.

Nor was it Bush's first go-around with this type of staff arrangement. As governor, he had a key assistant who functioned much as a chief of staff, but did not formally have that title. Instead Bush's chief aide was called "executive assistant," a position that Joseph Allbaugh and then Clay Johnson would hold. The gubernatorial staff, in turn, was much "flatter," with a number of aides having access to the governor through the executive assistant. As Bush notes in *A Charge to Keep,* "I wanted a flat organizational chart rather than the traditional chief-of-staff approach; I wanted the senior managers of different divisions in my office to report directly to me. . . . I like to get information from a lot of different people, plus I knew that high-powered people would be frustrated unless they had direct access to the boss."[24] According to Albert Hawkins, "As governor of Texas, he has used a fairly flat organization. There is a structure that allows senior staff direct access to the governor on a regular basis, any time we want it or need it, or any time he wants it or needs us. So, you know, there's not just this single focal point where everything goes through."[25]

In Austin, neither Allbaugh nor Johnson were "choke points" between the governor and his staff. A similar arrangement prevailed in the Bush White House. Although Card guarded access to Bush (his test of "needs versus wants," noted in Chapter 4), a number of aides—Rice, Rove, Hughes, Fleischer, and Vice President Cheney—could arrange for impromptu meetings with Bush through his personal secretary, Ashley Estes. As Bush told Bob Woodward in an interview, "I believe that a president must give people access. . . . It makes my job a heck of a lot easier to be able to have access to a lot of people."[26]

According to Thompson and Ware's study of Bush's leadership, "Bush's staff do understand when it's time to pull their boss in." As one staff member observes, "You set the table and insert him at key points in the process to get key things done, to make calls to certain people to tell them its time to get off the dime, time to hold hands and jump."[27] The downside, of course, is that it is the staff's job to "set the table" and decide when to "insert him"—the success of delegation and appropriate access turn on the skills and knowledge of those to whom much is delegated. And that proved to be no minor matter later in his presidency. The issue of whether delegation served him well would especially come to the fore in the controversy, following the Iraq war, over whether some of the intelligence evidence that had been used to make the case against Iraq had been properly vetted by others in the decisionmaking process.

Second, Bush himself was attentive to the organizational structure of his presidency. Unlike Reagan, Bush recognized the importance of how his White House was organized, how particular roles were defined, and who was selected to fill those positions. In some regard, this may be a useful antidote to the pitfalls of delegation: skill and knowledge were much on Bush's mind in selecting key members of his administration, and how their jobs were defined was of more than passing interest to him.

As a governor becoming president, Bush faced a particularly difficult challenge. Presidents need advisers and aides whom they trust, who are loyal, and who share their agenda and vision. Persons who fit that description often come from their statehouse experience. But presidents also need team members who have Washington Beltway insider knowledge and experience. Selection of the latter yields expertise but not necessarily trust and loyalty. Carter opted for the former, but his staff, many of whom had been brought up from Georgia, were often maladept. Other presidents have turned to the latter, only to find tensions developing between longtime associates and newcomers (e.g., Edwin Meese and James Baker in the early Reagan years.)

Like Reagan, Bush sought both: Texas loyalists such as Rove, Hughes, and Gonzales, but others such as Card, Daniels, and Rice who had prior White House experience. Bush's own persistent demand on loyalty, discipline, and teamwork may have been one important force in melding them together. But so too was Bush's unique position as the son of a former president. As noted in earlier chapters, those new to the Bush team may not have served him in Austin, but they were often drawn from his father's own administration—experience plus "loyalty once removed."

The experience of his father's presidency was important in a second regard, and it was a direct experience that his other gubernatorial predecessors (Carter, Reagan, and Clinton) did not share. Bush personally knew about how presidencies internally operate. In *A Charge to Keep,* for example, Bush notes that he didn't want a strong gatekeeper as chief of staff: "I had seen that problem in my dad's administration. Key members of his staff felt stifled because they had to go through a filter to get information to the president."[28]

At the same time, Bush recognized that a stronger chief of staff, albeit not a gatekeeper or a Sununu-like figure, was required in the White House to bring order to a much larger staff system. As Karl Rove later reflected:

> I do think the president, from the start, understood the importance of having a strong chief of staff. He wanted to have the right person in that job, but he understood the importance of having a strong chief of staff. The definition of a strong chief of staff is somebody who can make all the moving parts of this White House run in as an efficient way as possible, knowing that your object is to have parts of the White House run by significant players. . . . I mean we are talking about relatively significant people with relatively significant means of operating. And so to have a chief of staff who could orchestrate that all in a manner that is collegial.[29]

Bush also put his imprint on how the roles of his other top advisers would be defined. During the first week of his presidency, for example, Karen Hughes recalls that she asked him about his expectations of her role as an adviser above and beyond her duties in running the communications operation, "'What exactly do you want me to do?' His answer was short, the job huge: 'Go to meetings where major decisions are made. Make sure they're thinking about it the way I would; let me know what you think.'"[30]

More generally, according to Rove, Bush had "an amazing talent to understand the wire diagram. . . . He has a clarity about how he wants it structured and he has a pretty precise understanding of what he wants in particular slots."[31]

Bush also was aware of the organizational culture of previous White Houses and sought to make his White House a more livable working environment. Unlike some of his predecessors, Bush was not inclined to work late into the evening, usually ending his day at 6:00 P.M., with breaks for exercise, jogging, or personal time. It is a schedule that Bush also sought to have his staff follow. According to Karen Hughes, "The president has made it clear that you will be evaluated on your results, not whether the light is on at 10 or 11."[32]

Openness?

Bush also brought his practice of encouraging open deliberation and personal questioning and engagement to his dealings with staff members. John DiIulio recalled one example, on the occasion of a staff retreat on July 9, 2001, six months into the new administration, when concerns were raised about the operations of the staff's weekly message meetings: "The staff, like the president, was buttoned-down, but he often functioned more like an academic department chairman than a CEO, inviting brief but free-ranging discussions and hearing diverse views. He was subtle about letting staff know what he knew or suspected, and not infrequently seemed purposely to create circumstances that would test their honesty as well as their diplomacy."[33]

Bush's desire for internal openness within a formally organized and structured system is reflected in an interesting bit of organizational design that took place during the transition. At one point, Card consulted with Bush about senior staff and Card was concerned that Bush wanted too many deputy chiefs of staff. Card spoke to Clay Johnson about it and Johnson later recalled: "Andy's first reaction was the president wants to have multiple deputy chiefs of staff. [Card] said it's really not a very good idea. My thinking was, 'Then go back to him. He's not the one that gets locked in.'" According to Johnson, Bush "encourages people to push. He is interested in good ideas and to give people confidence to have a dialogue with him, to have that exchange of ideas and difference of opinion."[34]

But for at least one member of the Bush administration, Treasury Secretary O'Neill, meetings with Bush often proved to be unproductive and disappointing. At his first private meeting with Bush on January 24, 2001, O'Neill had hoped for a robust discussion of economic issues based on a lengthy memo he had sent to the president. According to Ron Suskind, O'Neill's biographer, "There were a dozen questions that O'Neill had expected Bush to ask. He was ready with answers." O'Neill raised some issues, "Bush didn't ask anything." O'Neill continued with other issues. "The president said nothing. No change in expression. Next subject." As O'Neill later recalled, "I wondered from the first, if the president didn't know the questions to ask, or did he know and just not want to know the answers? Or did his strategy somehow involve never showing what he thought. . . . It was strange."[35] An important cabinet meeting in March 2001, O'Neill later recalled, "was like many of the meetings I would go to over the course of two years. The only way I can describe it is that, well, the president is like a blind man in a roomful of deaf people. There is no discernible connection."[36]

For Rove, "very healthy dialogue and very healthy debate" were indeed things Bush encouraged.[37] But healthy debate depends on the willingness of participants to contribute to that debate, and in the view of at least one former member of the Bush inner circle, that willingness was sometimes dampened. According to John DiIulio, Bush's former faith-based initiatives adviser, who provided a controversial interview to a reporter doing a profile piece on Karl Rove, Rove's own perceived power within the Bush White House sometimes made others fearful of crossing him: "Some staff members, senior and junior, are awed by Karl's real or perceived powers. They self-censor lots for fear of upsetting him, and, in turn, few of the president's top people routinely tell the president what they really think if they think that Karl will be brought up short in the bargain."[38]

As for counterweights, especially policy substance, to Rove's heavy emphasis on political strategy and calculation, there was little in DiIulio's view: "I believe that the best may well be yet to come from the Bush administration. But, in my view, they will not get there without some significant reforms to the policy-lite inter-personal and organizational dynamics of the place."[39]

DiIulio's perceptions may be idiosyncratic. But they do raise potential problems for a president and a decisionmaker who favors the give-and-take of meetings and places a great deal of "faith and trust" in his staff.[40] As Bruce Buchanan, a professor of political science at the University of Texas and a longtime Bush watcher, has observed, Bush is "not a policy wonk, so he has to rely on people who are." But that reliance also has a downside to it: "Bush's biggest weakness is that he may not be in a position to discern the credibility of the options his advisers lay out for him."[41] Similarly, in the view of Donald Kettl, the success of the Bush decisionmaking process "depends critically on his staffers' skill in boiling complex issues down to their essence. If they miss important facts, they risk blinding Bush to things he ought to know. . . . The process, then, risks making the president especially vulnerable to what he and his staff don't know—or don't know to ask." Moreover, in Kettl's view, decisionmaking pathologies such as "groupthink" can arise: "a staff as disciplined as Bush's can develop 'groupthink' over time, and not know what they don't know." And Bush's predilection to focus only on certain policy areas of immediate importance to him may exacerbate rather then remedy any decisionmaking deficiencies: "No matter how intense Bush's attention to a subject might be, his instincts for the jugular of some issues might not be as sharp as for others."[42]

After leaving office, former treasury secretary O'Neill was especially critical of the performance of Bush and his advisers on some of these issues. According to his biographer, O'Neill felt that there wasn't "an honest broker in sight." Bush "was caught in an echo chamber of his own making, cut off from everyone other than a circle around him that's tiny and getting smaller and in concert on everything." Bush lacked "disinterested perspectives about what's real and what the hell he might do about it."[43] Not only was Bush surrounded by ideologues, according to O'Neill, he was captive to a flawed if not broken decisionmaking process. According to one report, "Each time O'Neill tried to gather data, sift facts and insert them into the system for debate, he would find discussion sheared off before it could get going."[44]

Some academic observers have also detected similar problems in the internal dynamics of Bush's decisionmaking and in his interaction with his advisers. Much like O'Neill, Colin Campbell has noted both a high degree of "unrestrained ideological entrepreneurship" and a flawed deliberative process. This has occurred, according to Campbell, "both because the president seems detached from open discourse about the crucial issues he faces and because the administration, more generally, seems to include a surfeit of doctrinaire players." The administration, moreover, "invests very little structure or effort in ensuring that policy initiatives receive intense collegial scrutiny."[45] For Gary Mucciaroni and Paul Quirk, "Much as the Clinton White House was dominated by liberal ideologues in 1993 and 1994, the configuration of Bush's domestic team created the hazard that his agenda, or parts of it, would be hijacked by the right. . . . Judging from their decisions, Bush and his advisers did not deliberate carefully about the actual consequences of their policies. And they succumbed to several of the threats to effective presidential deliberation."[46]

Loyalty and Discipline

As noted in earlier chapters, loyalty and discipline were hallmarks of the 2000 transition and the Bush White House, and they were often enforced by Bush's top aides. But Bush, too, was an important source of them; his preelection day comments to reporters—"I am the kind of person who trusts people" but "I am firm with people"—provide early testimony. Both during the transition and after, he took care to ensure that appointees reflected both his personal agenda and his expectations about their place as part of the Bush team. In this regard, Bush is in particularly sharp departure from all of his immediate predecessors from Carter through Clinton in being willing to exercise discipline, making sure that internal conflict does not develop, and discouraging his subordinates from pursuing their own personal and policy agendas. As he told reporters before election day, "I look for humility in people. I also want to make sure that the people are there for a cause as opposed to themselves."[47] And Bush's efforts paid off. As David Gergen, a veteran of both Republican and Democratic White Houses, would later note, "You have to give him high marks for organization and discipline. This is the smartest political team we've seen in a long time."[48] So too for Press Secretary Ari Fleischer, who also notes that Bush led by example: "Because he is disciplined and always on time, it forces down through the system. Everybody else has to be disciplined to get their work done and do it on time. No excuses."[49]

Bush's touch was often gentle. On one occasion in March 2001, economic adviser Lindsey thought he had arrived on time for the videotaping of an address by Bush to a banking convention, only to find that the taping had begun sooner. Afterward Bush gently chided him: "Lawrence, we're the on-time administration." On another occasion, several aides arrived late for a policy briefing led by Josh Bolten. At one point, Bush piped up: "Josh, seems you might have lost control of your meeting."[50] Bush, moreover, sought to lead by example in encouraging his aides to be on time. According to one White House aide, Bush often told his staff, "It is important that the president be on time. When I am on time, that shows people I respect them, and that shows discipline."[51] Many of Bush's aides have also commented on Bush's use of humor in keeping rein on his staff. According to Mitchell Daniels, director of the Office of Management and Budget (OMB), "He keeps people in their place in a friendly way." Condoleezza Rice, nicknamed "mother hen" by Bush, observes that "he will kid people, tease people."[52]

Bush used other interpersonal skills to create the staff culture that he wanted. In the view of speech writer David Frum, "Bush knew how to create the loyalty he demanded." One friend of Frum's on the staff fell behind on a project, and Bush called the whole team into the Oval Office to let him know about his displeasure. At the end of the meeting, Bush asked Frum's friend—the lowest-ranking member of the group—to stay behind. "Stay back for a second! I have one more thing to say to you," Bush said. Once they were alone, Bush told him, "I want you to know that I don't blame you for what happened. I know the fault lies elsewhere." Bush then inquired about the staff member's children by name. According to Frum, "When he emerged from the Oval Office, my friend would have charged a machine gun for George W. Bush."[53]

Early in the administration, Chief of Staff Card provided reporters with a list of some of the rules the president expected staff members to follow:

- Men and women must wear proper business attire. "I have not seen the president in the Oval Office without a suit and tie on."
- Briefing papers should be short. "He doesn't like memos that state the obvious. If he gets talking points that say, 'Welcome to the White House, I'm pleased to have you here,' he'll say, 'Oh, you think the president doesn't know enough to say 'Welcome to the White House?'"
- Punctuality is expected. "The president begins meetings and ends meetings on time."
- Staff members are expected to be cordial and return phone calls promptly. "I remind everyone that we are just staffers and no more important than anyone working at HHS [Health and Human Services] or HUD or the Department of Transportation—or the people opening the mail. If you like to get your calls returned, return other people's calls."

- Overwork takes it toll. "The president leaves the office by 6:30 usually and expects his staff to spend time with their families—and enjoy their weekends. He knows how to get that all-important battery recharged."[54]

Another important element in the internal dynamic of the Bush presidency, especially within the White House, has been its tight control of communications, especially how its members dealt with the press. Unauthorized leaks have been few and far between. This occurred, as we saw in Chapter 4, due to the efforts of key subordinates such as Card and Hughes. But it was a discipline that came from the very top. According to Peggy Noonan, a veteran of the Reagan and Bush Sr. White Houses (both of which were prone to internecine disputes that were played out by leaks to the press): "Dubya learned to hate leaks. And to hate leakers. And boy do his people know." Bush's emphasis on loyalty, in turn, reinforced this aspect of discipline: "Part of the reason for the leaking in the Reagan-Bush era, especially the Reagan era, was that both White Houses were riven by a left-right split, by philosophical and ideological divisions." And these are divisions that existed to a far lesser extent in the Bush White House. As Mary Matalin observes, "Because we have a common agenda we're not trying to advance any position but the president's. So we don't use the vehicle of leaks to advance our own agenda."[55] In Karen Hughes's view, "Unlike what I read and heard about infighting among previous White House staffs, ours was remarkably collegial. We weren't split into various factions or camps; we were all part of a team assembled to serve the president, and the team included the vice president and his staff, too."[56]

For Kettl, the initial care taken in making appointments during the transition had a significant impact on what transpired later: "The administration's reaction to aides who openly oppose a Bush position or wander off message is not really the point. The key lesson lies in the preemptory steps Bush takes to prevent this from happening in the first place. Discipline was first asserted by building the team, encouraging loyalty, and reinforcing that trait through close interactions."[57]

One innovation the White House undertook was the establishment of a website (www.results.gov) aimed at new and current appointees throughout the administration and funded by money left over from the transition. Organized by Clay Johnson and secretary to the cabinet Albert Hawkins and launched over the summer of 2002, the site was especially aimed at appointees who did not have direct contact with the president. Not only did the site include information about senior White House staff, the president's management agenda, ethics rules, and advice on dealing with members of Congress, but its purpose was also to encourage team building and a personal identification with the president. According to one account, Johnson envisioned "the web site as an extension of the president's personality and a way for appointees to rally around their leader." In a video welcome on the site, moreover, President Bush states, "We have to work together and learn from each other. This site will help us do that." Other messages by Bush are also linked to the site, as well as videos by Card on ethics rules, Gonzales on records management, and an address to members of the subcabinet by former secretary of state George Shultz. For Johnson, another goal of the site was to avoid "Potomac fever"— a delusion of bureaucratic grandeur—and the site includes advice on its symptoms and how to avoid them. Johnson also designed the site to overcome other features of an in-bred bureaucracy; users, in his view, should feel "like you are talking to a person—not your department talking to another department."[58]

But the Bush administration's emphasis on loyalty was not without its critics. In the view of former treasury secretary O'Neill, "Loyalty to a person and whatever they say or do, that's the opposite of real loyalty, which is loyalty based on inquiry, and telling someone what you really think and feel— your best estimation of the truth instead of what they want to hear."[59]

Willingness to Make a Decision

Another element of the Bush style is a willingness to be decisive ("I am a decider. I do not agonize."). Here the contrasts with Clinton are clear: while Clinton would often "walk around a problem" and postpone action, Bush was inclined to do the opposite. As Clay Johnson told reporters during the 2000 campaign, Bush "doesn't linger over decisions and doesn't second guess— 'That's the decision; let's get on with it. Next topic.' He's a very high-energy, frenetic type of person."[60]

Bush had no reservations, for example, about reversing Colin Powell's assertion early in his presidency that the administration would continue the Clinton policy of diplomacy toward North Korea, and Bush did so at a meeting at which Powell was present. Nor did Bush have any difficulty reversing some of the early environmental policy decisions that Environmental Protection Agency administrator Christie Todd Whitman had announced. According to one aide, "I have never seen the president the least bit concerned about being boxed in by a cabinet member. He assumes that he is in charge."[61]

So too with the Bush staff. For example, on the weekend after September 11, 2001, while at Camp David, Bush sat down with National Security Council adviser Condoleezza Rice and told her: "Here's what I want to do" about a war against terrorism, while she took copious notes. The next day, Bush summoned Karen Hughes to the Oval Office and told her he wanted the draft of a speech he planned to give Congress on his desk by that evening. Hughes balked, Bush then set a firm deadline: by 7:00 P.M.[62]

Given Bush's penchant for delegation, the possibility could have loomed that he would not have been able to make a decision when his advisers were divided in their counsel. Yet this does not seem to have occurred. For example, when the McCain-Feingold campaign finance reform bill passed, opinion was divided. Some advisers wanted Bush to veto it because it did not track closely enough with his own principles; others wanted him to sign it, fearing the political repercussions of being on the wrong side of a popular issue. According to one administration official, Bush agreed to sign it: "He felt there was enough in the McCain bill that was different from the current system to support it."[63]

Bush also made the call on the controversial issue of whether stem cells from human embryos should be used in medical and other scientific research. His final decision—that research could be undertaken on existing, dead embryos but not on new ones—ran counter to the advice in favor of a more liberal position that he had received from Cheney, Card, and others within the administration, as well as from Senators Orrin Hatch (R-UT) and Bill Frist (R-TN) and former first lady Nancy Reagan.[64] Nor did it sit well with those who completely opposed stem cell research, such as National Conference of Catholic Bishops. As we shall see in the next chapter, a number of Bush's most important decisions after September 11 would be made despite conflicting counsel within his inner circle.

At the same time, Bush does not appear to have been captive to his advisers when their counsel bordered on the near-unanimous. According to OMB director Daniels, "He can listen to a roomful of consensus and say no. He's often roughest when things seem too neat and pre-packaged. He will ask a person who hasn't spoken up. You better be ready with a point of view."[65]

Leadership and Vision

In his campaigns for both governor and president, Bush developed an ambitious but focused agenda. And those agendas, in turn, structured what he pursued once in office, whether in Austin or at the White House. It was, moreover, a lesson he learned from his father's presidency—Bush Sr.'s struggle with the "vision thing" and the failure to develop a more robust domestic agenda that hurt him in 1992.

Nor was George W. Bush daunted by the circumstances of his electoral victory. As David Frum observed firsthand, "Bush seemed utterly unperturbed by the weakness of his political position. He sketched a vision of a political future in which a win on taxes led to a win on education, which led to wins on missile defense and Social Security—a series of maneuvers as stately and smooth as the solution to a chess puzzle in the Sunday paper."[66] Dealt the worst electoral hand of any modern president (not only a contested election but a Senate split fifty-fifty), Bush managed quickly to control the political agenda. Gore's targeted tax cuts, for example, were quickly forgotten; the issue was how much of an across-the-board tax cut Congress would agree upon. While not getting all he wanted, as we shall see in the next chapter, he clearly got more than half the proverbial loaf (much of the rest would come in 2003). Bush recognized the need to spend whatever political capital he had or could acquire. "It doesn't matter whether you won by one point, two points, even ten points; it's important to move as quickly as you can in order to spend whatever capital you have as quickly as possible. You spend capital on what you campaigned on . . . and you earn capital by doing that," he told reporters at the end of his first 100 days as president.[67] It was another lesson drawn from his father's presidency: "Dad never spent the capital he earned from the success of Desert Storm. . . . I learned that you must spend political capital when you earn it, or it withers and dies."[68]

Bush was willing to take on political controversy. During the 2000 campaign, for example, concern was raised whether Bush should include social security privatization among his key proposals. According to Ari Fleischer, there was considerable worry about touching the "third rail" of American politics. But when he raised it with Bush, "The governor just looked at me and cut me off. He said, 'I am going to do this. This is what leadership is all about.'"[69] At the same time, Bush was a political realist. Once he was president, Bush recognized that the time was not ripe for social security reform. And as we shall see, as some of his proposals encountered congressional resistance—school vouchers, for example—he was willing to compromise in order to achieve some of his gains. On his faith-based initiatives proposal, he was willing to turn to other tools of presidential power—executive orders— to achieve what could not be done through legislation.

In fact, Bush's use of executive orders and other nonlegislative prerogatives of the presidency marked a noticeable attempt to expand the powers of the office. Claims of executive privilege were invoked to prevent revelation of the individuals and groups that Cheney's task force on energy had met with and to block congressional testimony of Tom Ridge during the period when he was heading the White House Office of Homeland Security. The White House even asserted executive privilege to block the opening of presidential records at the Reagan and Bush Sr. presidential libraries. Bush also gained congressional assent to "fast track" trade negotiation authority, permitting him to negotiate trade agreements with lessened congressional interference. That authority, first given to President Nixon, had lapsed in 1994, despite President Clinton's attempts to get it renewed.[70]

In his dealings with Congress, Bush was often willing to set the agenda, but let the House and Senate do their work. According to one staff member, "We pick fights that are winnable. We don't fight for the sake of fighting." Moreover, as Richard Cohen of the *National Journal* observes, "Put another way, Bush has focused on the terms of engagement and has left the details to Congress. In several respects that's a distinct contrast to other presidents—

most recently Clinton, who delighted in the fact that he and this top aides frequently had a seat at the negotiating table to craft the legislative fine print."[71]

Yet at the same time, Bush was hardly a passive observer of the legislative process. During the transition and early days of the administration (as we have already seen and shall see in more detail in the next chapter), Bush sought to charm key members of the House and Senate, often giving them a variety of nicknames and engaging in personal camaraderie in meetings. Coupled with a willingness to compromise, that strategy often proved successful, as with education reform and his tax cut proposal. It was, moreover, something else carried over from his governorship. According to Texas state representative Steven Wolens, a Democrat, "It is clear that Bush is a charmer. He has got an awesome social skill, of being able to do a pat on the back, or a squeeze of the arm, or a shake of the hand . . . he does bring people in. I mean he really does, and I can only speak, not from campaign rhetoric, but from my experience in dealing with him over six years."[72]

But, as president, Bush's relationships with Congress were not always smooth. The Republican-controlled House generally stuck loyally to the Bush agenda. But on some occasions, they went beyond its bounds and in a highly partisan fashion—for example, provisions passed in House legislation on faith-based initiatives that were unlikely to attract the support of Senate Democrats and even moderate Republicans. Nor did Bush successfully deal with the defection of Senator James Jeffords from the Republican Party, and it had marked impact on the success of the Bush agenda once the Senate was under Democratic control. Moreover, while successful at agenda control and willing to spend his political capital to achieve key components of it, at least according to one analysis, Bush may not have taken full advantage of opportunities to achieve a deal. According to DiIulio, "Faith initiatives got and remained on the president's policy agenda without concerted effort to draft proposals that could pass and, once passed, effect administrative and funding changes in keeping with the president's public positions on the issue." In fact, DiIulio observes, the pattern was repeated in other agenda items: "Several also were supported by the administration, but without accompanying legislative or administrative exertions."[73]

Bush was also more willing than his father to build support for his program, whether in meetings with members of Congress or at public events and other trips. He engaged in far more political travel during his first two months as president than had any of his recent predecessors: twenty-five states (and thirty days of travel), compared to seventeen states for Bush Sr. and twelve for Clinton.[74] The failure to "market and sell" the Bush Sr. agenda, as Andrew Card once put it, was not lost on George W. Bush.

At the same time, the early Bush presidency received less coverage on the evening news according to a study undertaken by the Center for Media and

Public Affairs. Evening news stories on the major networks during the first fifty days of Bush's presidency totaled seven hours and forty-two minutes, compared to Clinton's fifteen hours and two minutes in 1993.[75] Bush also avoided full-dress press conferences of the sort his predecessors held in the East Room of the White House. From inauguration day through November 2002, Bush held seven White House press conferences: five in the press briefing room, one in an auditorium in the Old Executive Office Building, and only one in the East Room, on October 11, 2001, shortly after the start of the war in Afghanistan. By contrast, according to data collected by Martha Joynt Kumar, Clinton had held seventy press conferences, while Bush Sr. had held more than sixty, at equivalent points in their presidencies.[76] Communications efforts in the Bush presidency would come not directly from the president's interactions with the press, but through image management and efforts to control the media message undertaken by Karen Hughes's operation and Karl Rove's political calculations.

The final piece of Bush's leadership comes from a "lesson" that Bush says he learned from his father's presidency: "I learned that it is difficult to protect incumbency. . . . I remembered all too well my dad's 1992 campaign. I knew how quickly a constituency can forget success. Politics is not about the past or rewarding office holders for a job well done. Voter's want to know a candidate's view for the future."[77]

Yet Bush's awareness of the need for a vision of the future may be limited in its realization by an ability to effectively construct and communicate that vision, Bush's "compassionate conservatism" notwithstanding. Hugh Heclo has termed this problem Bush's inability "to teach" the nation as part of his leadership: "It is dangerous to stop with decisive leadership and not take much interest in looking around the corner to teach Americans about the larger and longer-term realities of their situation. . . . Bush clearly understands the need for persuading the people to his point of view, but it is also possible to sell people on things without broadening their horizons."[78] Richard Brookhiser calls it the "phantom framework." According to him, "A leader is most effective when his policy framework is evident to others (Reagan is the most recent example). Then they know what to expect of him; they better understand what he is saying as he says it." The difference with Reagan is most notable, according to Brookhiser, on their common signature issue of cutting taxes: "Reagan was messianic about tax cuts, campaigning for them, identifying himself with them. Bush cut taxes—but he has not laid out a systematic, ideological case for what he is up to or how far he intends to go."[79]

*　　*　　*

The transition had served to craft an organizational structure and a deliberative process that fit Bush's needs. Through his first seven and a half months in office it served him reasonably well. Slip-ups and mistakes were few. Bush, moreover, achieved some success in moving his campaign agenda forward in those early months. The attacks of September 11, 2001, and their aftermath required grappling with a different and much more difficult set of issues. The challenge before him would be in ensuring that those structures and processes worked effectively, in continuing to craft a domestic, economic, and foreign policy agenda, and in convincingly communicating their merits to Congress and the American public.

Notes

1. For a more extended analysis of how modern presidents have dealt with the institutional resources of the presidency, how they have organized it, and how their managerial and deliberative styles affected their presidencies, see Burke, *The Institutional Presidency.*

2. Dan Balz and Terry Neal, "For Bush, Questions, Clues, and Contradiction," *Washington Post,* October 22, 2000.

3. Richard Berke, "Bush Is Providing Corporate Model for White House," *New York Times,* March 11, 2001.

4. Bush, *A Charge to Keep,* pp. 100, 104.

5. Albert Hawkins, panel discussion, "How Would George W. Bush Govern?" American Enterprise Institute, Washington, D.C., January 13, 2000.

6. John F. Harris and Dan Balz, "First 100 Days Go By in a Blur," *Washington Post,* April 29, 2001.

7. Mike Allen, "Bush on Stage: Deft or Just Lacking Depth?" *Washington Post,* February 19, 2001.

8. Frum, *The Right Man,* p. 29.

9. Ibid., p. 48.

10. Hughes, *Ten Minutes from Normal,* p. 81.

11. Representative Steven Wolens, panel discussion, "How Would George W. Bush Govern?" American Enterprise Institute, Washington, D.C., January 13, 2000.

12. Kettl, *Team Bush,* p. 36.

13. Woodward, *Bush at War,* p. 144.

14. John F. Harris and Dan Balz, "First 100 Days Go By in a Blur," *Washington Post,* April 29, 2001.

15. John J. DiIulio Jr., "A View from Within," in Greenstein, *The George W. Bush Presidency,* p. 248.

16. Richard Berke, "Bush Is Providing Corporate Model for White House," *New York Times,* March 11, 2001.

17. Hugh Heclo, "The Political Ethos of George W. Bush," in Greenstein, *The George Bush Presidency,* p. 46.

18. Hawkins, panel discussion, "How Would George W. Bush Govern?"

19. Greenstein, *The Presidential Difference,* p. 196.

20. Ibid., p. 209.

21. Ibid. p. 199.

22. Mike Allen, "Bush on Stage: Deft or Just Lacking Depth?" *Washington Post,* February 19, 2001.

23. Kettl, *Team Bush,* p. 36.

24. Bush, *A Charge to Keep,* p. 97.

25. Hawkins, panel discussion, "How Would George W. Bush Govern?"

26. Woodward, *Bush at War,* p. 255.

27. Thompson and Ware, *The Leadership Genius of George W. Bush,* p. 115; John Dickerson, Matthew Cooper, and Douglas Waller, "Bush's Two Sides," *Time,* August 6, 2001.

28. Bush, *A Charge to Keep,* p. 97.

29. Karl Rove, "A Discussion with Karl Rove," American Enterprise Institute, Washington, D.C., December 11, 2001.

30. Hughes, *Ten Minutes from Normal,* p. 204.

31. Kumar, "Communications Operations in the White House," p. 369.

32. John D. Solomon, "A Trickle-Down Theory for a Shorter Workday," *New York Times,* April 1, 2001.

33. DiIulio Jr., "A View from Within," p. 250.

34. Kumar, "Recruiting and Organizing the White House Staff," p. 37.

35. Suskind, *The Price of Loyalty,* pp. 57-58.

36. Suskind, *The Price of Loyalty,* p. 149. O'Neill's difficulties may also have stemmed from the fact that the Bush tax cut plan was pretty much set in stone and not subject to the alterations of a treasury secretary who had reservations about it. In addition, the Bush administration might also have wished to reduce the prominence of the Treasury Department—which had grown in power during the Clinton years under Treasury Secretaries Lloyd Bentsen, Robert Rubin, and Larry Summers. According to one account, the Bush White House was determined "to formulate economic policy with little input from Treasury." This was evident even as early as the transition, according to Gary Gensler, a Clinton-era Treasury Department undersecretary who worked with incoming Bush officials: "There was quite a feeling amongst the transition group that—we heard indirectly and directly—they thought some of the ascendancy of Treasury during the Clinton days needed to be adjusted." Noam Scheiber, "Buried Treasury," *New Republic,* August 11, 2003.

37. Rove, "A Discussion with Karl Rove."

38. Ron Suskind, "Why Are These Men Laughing?" *Esquire,* January 2003.

39. John DiIulio to Ron Suskind, "Your Next Essay on the Bush Administration," October 24, 2002; Drudge Report, "Bush Aide's Letter to Esquire Reporter Revealed," www.drudgereport.com, December 2, 2002.

40. Bush, *A Charge to Keep,* p. 103.

41. James Carney, "Why Bush Doesn't Like Homework," *Time,* November 15, 1999.

42. Kettl, *Team Bush,* p. 150.

43. Suskind, *The Price of Loyalty,* pp. 126, 293.

44. John Dickerson, "Confessions of a White House Insider," *Time,* January 19, 2004.

45. Colin Campbell, "Unrestrained Ideological Entrepreneurship in the Bush II Advisory System," in Campbell and Rockman, *The George W. Bush Presidency,* p. 97.

46. Gary Mucciaroni and Paul Quirk, "Deliberations of a 'Compassionate Conservative': George W. Bush's Domestic Presidency," in Campbell and Rockman, *The George W. Bush Presidency,* pp. 162, 182.

47. Dan Balz and Terry Neal, "For Bush, Questions, Clues, and Contradiction," *Washington Post,* October 22, 2000.

48. Maura Reynolds and Doyle McManus, "For Bush Burdens of Office Multiply," *Los Angeles Times,* January 26, 2003.

49. Ibid.

50. Richard Berke, "Bush Is Providing Corporate Model for White House," *New York Times,* March 11, 2001.

51. Richard Brookhiser, "The Mind of George W. Bush," *Atlantic Monthly,* April 2003.

52. Ibid.

53. Frum, *The Right Man,* pp. 28–29.

54. Richard Berke, "Bush Is Providing Corporate Model for White House," *New York Times,* March 11, 2001.

55. Peggy Noonan, "Loose Lips, Pink Slips," *Wall Street Journal,* January 18, 2002.

56. Hughes, *Ten Minutes from Normal,* p. 204.

57. Kettl, *Team Bush,* p. 106.

58. Stephen Barr, "DubyaDubyaDubya.theRules," *Washington Post,* October 18, 2002.

59. John Dickerson, "Confessions of a White House Insider," *Time,* January 19, 2004.

60. "What to Expect in Bush White House," www.msnbc.com, October, 27, 2000.

61. John F. Harris and Dan Balz, "First 100 Days Go By in a Blur," *Washington Post,* April 29, 2001.

62. Howard Kurtz, "What Bush Said and When He Said It," *Washington Post,* October 1, 2001. The staff finished the draft by 8:00 P.M. The next morning, Bush ran into Karen Hughes and asked her how the work was progressing. She told him she was on her way to a message meeting and would focus on it when she returned. As she later recounted: "He leaned over and smiled, his blue eyes twinkling only about three inches from my face, and spoke in slow, exaggerated tones: 'And you think a message meeting is more important than my speech to a historic joint session of Congress when our nation is at war?' Not anymore I didn't. The president had just clearly focused my priorities for me." Hughes, *Ten Minutes from Normal,* p. 257.

63. John F. Harris and Dan Balz, "First 100 Days Go By in a Blur," *Washington Post,* April 29, 2001.

64. Frum, *The Right Man,* p. 107. Also see Hughes, *Ten Minutes from Normal,* pp. 227–229.

65. Richard Brookhiser, "The Mind of George W. Bush," *Atlantic Monthly,* April 2003.

66. Frum, *The Right Man,* p. 29.

67. John F. Harris and Dan Balz, "First 100 Days Go By in a Blur," *Washington Post,* April 29, 2001.

68. Bush, *A Charge to Keep,* pp. 186–186.

69. Dan Balz and Terry Neal, "For Bush, Questions, Clues, and Contradiction," *Washington Post,* October 22, 2000.

70. Trade promotion authority permits Congress to veto any agreements en bloc, but not to tinker with particular details of an agreement.

71. Richard E. Cohen, "Checking and Balancing," *National Journal,* April 20, 2002, p. 1135.

72. Representative Steven Wolens, panel discussion, "How Would George W. Bush Govern?" American Enterprise Institute, Washington, D.C., January 13, 2000.

73. DiIulio Jr., "A View from Within," p. 256.

74. Richard Berke, "Bush Shapes His Presidency with Sharp Eye on Father's," *New York Times,* March 27, 2001.

75. Howard Kurtz, "The Quiet American," *Washington Post,* April 9, 2001.

76. Elisabeth Bumiller, "Bush Dodges the Pomp in Dealing with the Press," *New York Times,* November 11, 2002.

77. Bush, *A Charge to Keep,* pp. 186, 218.

78. Heclo, "The Political Ethos of George W. Bush," p. 48.

79. Richard Brookhiser, "The Mind of George W. Bush," *Atlantic Monthly,* April 2003.

6

Advancing the Bush Policy Agenda

Successful transitions can set the stage for a fruitful unfolding of a new president's policy agenda. Likewise, transition failures can hinder that agenda, causing the new president to "hit the ground stumbling." Aspects of transitions, moreover, can affect the agendas of new administrations in several ways. First, transitions are, as we have seen, times when decisionmaking processes begin to be crafted, offices and units are organized, and positions filled. But an administration in place, particularly within the White House, can also clearly benefit its policy efforts. Congressional liaison, political affairs, communications, and other staff units can powerfully advance the president's policy message. A chief of staff can foster order and discipline. All units in the White House, plus an orderly process of information and advice from the cabinet and other sources, can help a new administration deal with issues and crises that may not have been anticipated. The early Carter and Clinton administrations offer powerful lessons on how failure to organize properly can thwart the early efforts of a new presidency. Some of the actions taken during the Carter transition, for example, led to strained relations with Congress, especially its leadership.[1] In Clinton's case, according to aide Bruce Reed, "We made a lot of concessions [with Democratic congressional leaders during the transition] in the name of unity that didn't turn out well."[2]

A successful transition can also help a new administration in other ways, particularly by signaling the presence of managerial and political know-how, that are taken by observers as signs of skill and competence. The latter, in turn, can contribute to perceptions of presidential ability if not political clout. Here, too, the Carter and Clinton transitions are instructive, again by way of negative lesson. Both were plagued by numerous reports of infighting during the transition and in the early days of their administrations. By contrast, little of this surfaced for George W. Bush, and his transition was even lauded by *New York Times* reporter Richard Berke as "the most orderly and politically nimble White House transition in at least twenty years."[3]

The early Bush presidency also was affected by the actions that President Clinton undertook in his waning days in office. Here, it was the outgoing president's transition that proved consequential. Some of these actions—particularly environmental regulations that were promulgated—would later pose difficulties. But other actions would cast Bush in a more favorable light. Among these, most notably, were a number of questionable pardons that Clinton had issued, as well as issues dealing with Clinton's immunity agreement with the special prosecutor's office (he would lose his law license for five years and pay a fine), questions about the costs of Clinton's proposed postpresidential office in New York City, and questions relating to gifts the Clintons had received for their new residence in Washington, D.C. As this news emerged during the early weeks of Bush's presidency, it acted as a lightning rod for media criticism—of the old rather than the new president. As R. W. Apple Jr. of the *New York Times* put it: "It's a silly question, maybe, but one worth asking: What shape would President Bush be in if Bill Clinton had just skipped the last week of his presidency and left town quietly, without pardoning the fugitive commodities trader Marc Rich, without a carload of gifts and without casting a covetous eye on a plutocratic suite of offices in a Manhattan highrise?" In Apple's view, the question is "worth asking because the answer is so consequential: Mr. Bush would have had less of a free ride than he has in fact had. And he would probably not have taken command of his job so quickly."[4]

As we have already seen, successful transitions can be an important incubator of policy proposals, translating campaign promises into a finer-tuned set of concrete proposals. Successful transition efforts in this regard enable a president to move key proposals up to Capitol Hill, thereby taking advantage of whatever "honeymoon period" may exist with Congress. As Paul Light has noted in his analysis of presidential agendas, administrations "need to move it or lose it."[5] Successful transitions can also serve to prioritize proposals. As the Carter experience of 1977 suggests, a lengthy laundry list of policy proposals can prove deadly, often hampering passage of bills more central to the president's agenda.

Finally, transitions are important in assessing the overall strategic situation a president faces. Should the White House pursue a more ambitious policy agenda as Reagan did in 1981 or a more limited one as Bush Sr. did in 1989? What degree of partisanship, moreover, should be injected into the legislative fight? Is it a time to rally the partisan base and build outward? Or should a more bipartisan tone and cooperation with the political opposition figure more centrally in crafting policy proposals and devising political strategy?

As it had with the transition, the election potentially placed Bush in a precarious position with respect to what he would ask from Congress. He could obviously claim no electoral mandate, a dubious proposition for most modern presidents (save perhaps for Roosevelt in 1932, Johnson in 1964, and more arguably, Reagan in 1980). Indeed, Bush's situation was even more precarious.

Having lost the popular vote and only narrowly won the electoral college by the slimmest of margins, Bush faced the worst electoral circumstances of any recent president. Again, the closest historical approximations were Rutherford Hayes in 1876 and Benjamin Harrison in 1888—who lost the popular vote to Grover Cleveland.[6] Neither the subsequent Hayes nor Harrison administrations bode well as historical exemplars of successful presidencies.

On the positive side, Bush was the first Republican president since Eisenhower to have his party control both the House and the Senate. But unlike Ike in 1953 (who also faced an evenly divided Senate but whose party had just recaptured control of both the House and Senate), Bush was contemplating an ambitious policy agenda. In 2000, moreover, the Republican Party (GOP) had lost seats in both the House (four) and the Senate (four), with the latter evenly divided fifty-fifty (Vice President Cheney's ability to cast a tie-breaking vote would enable the GOP to organize the Senate, at least through May 2001).

Yet what is interesting and significant about the agenda of this presidency is that Bush and his associates not only resisted the post–December 13, 2000, call of some Democrats that he establish a coalition government in light of the election outcome, but instead quickly devised a set of legislative proposals based on Bush's chief campaign themes, prioritized them, and made the decision to pursue a fairly ambitious policy agenda. The contested election and the close balance of power in Congress seemingly dealt them a weak hand. Yet they overcame the limitations of that political environment and sought to seize the political initiative.

The administration's initial mode of dealing with Congress would also be complex: a rhetoric of bipartisanship and a Bush "charm offensive" with key legislators. But this would be coupled to different strategies for building a majority in each chamber: more partisanship and discipline with the House, but greater willingness to cooperate and compromise with the Senate. Moreover, Bush picked his legislative fights selectively. As Karen Hughes noted, "You won't find him issuing proclamations on every subject and proudly so, because he wants to reserve his capital, to use it where it helps implement his agenda."[7]

The Bush White House basically stuck to the terrain of its political agenda, but was willing to settle for less as legislative circumstances demanded. There were also some strategic differences based on the issue. Bush would be more amenable to compromise when the votes were clearly not there (as would be the case when he dropped his voucher plan on education reform in light of fairly substantial congressional opposition). Yet on tax reform, while Bush would compromise somewhat, he waited until the legislative action drifted closer to his position before striking a deal.

The politics of the Bush agenda would lead to victory on Bush's most important proposal, his tax cut plan. It would yield eventual compromise on his proposals for education reform. But there would be delay until 2003 on prescription drug benefits for seniors, and his faith-based initiatives would largely be achieved by executive order rather than legislation. Social security privatization was put on the back burner. Bush's political situation would also worsen—again with no recent historical parallels—with Senator James Jeffords's decision to abandon the GOP and join, as an independent, with the Democrats in June 2001 in reorganizing the Senate under Democratic control.[8]

Nor was the agenda always Bush's—despite the efforts of the White House. A shortage of electrical power in California led to the development of a comprehensive energy policy proposal under Vice President Cheney's direction, last-minute executive orders issued by President Clinton (particularly ones dealing with the environment) called for a response, a campaign finance reform bill that Bush opposed finally broke through the legislative logjam, and Bush himself would have to deal with the moral and political complexities of stem cell research.

Rolling Out a Policy Agenda

A Quick Agenda

In the days following his inauguration, Bush moved quickly to send a number of key proposals to Capitol Hill or took other, related actions to further his political agenda. It was not a Carter-era laundry list, nor was it the rather lean domestic agenda of his father's early days in the White House. The most important related to the "Big Six" as they were dubbed by the White House: tax cuts, education reform, changes in Medicare, faith-based initiatives, strengthening the military, and social security reform. Each was a central theme in the campaign, and Bush was prepared to move forward. On January 24, 2001, it was his education reform plan that took center stage. On January 29, faith-based initiatives were the focus; that same day, Bush also proposed legislation to deal with prescription drug costs for the elderly. On February 6, while not proposing specific legislation, Bush set out, in a letter to congressional leaders, a number of criteria for legislation on a patients' bill of rights that the White House could support. On February 10, in his Saturday radio address, the military was the chief topic and Bush announced that he would seek a $1.4 billion appropriation to improve military pay and living standards, plus another $1 billion to retain skilled personnel. In his early weeks as president he also reiterated his commitment to build a missile defense shield. Bush chose not to give a State of the Union address to Congress, but on February 27, Bush gave the second major speech recent presidents have chosen to deliver—an economic address before a joint session of Congress—and tax reform was at its core. During the speech, Bush also announced that he would create a bipartisan commission to provide recommendations for social security reform; it was the one major piece of the Bush agenda where action would be delayed for the time being.

Building Support

Most of these initiatives were also orchestrated with appearances and imagery designed to enhance public support for the president's proposals. Bush's first working week as president focused on his education initiatives. Among the events that were scheduled were a Monday afternoon "reading roundtable" that both the president and First Lady Laura Bush attended with twenty principals, education professors, and teachers; a Tuesday meeting with Democratic lawmakers to discuss education; and a Thursday visit to a District of Columbia elementary school to promote his plan. The next few days it was faith-based initiatives: a dinner at the home of the Roman Catholic Archbishop of Washington, church attendance on Sunday, January 28, 2001, at the predominantly African American Lincoln Park United Methodist Church, the announcement the next day of his new Office of Faith-Based and Community Initiatives, and a meeting on Wednesday, January 31, with the congressional black caucus.

With respect to foreign affairs, Bush sought to emphasize ties with the country's closest neighbors and its traditional ally. On February 5, the first visit of a foreign dignitary occurred: Canadian prime minister Jean Chretien. This was followed by Bush's own trip to Mexico to meet with its new president, Vincente Fox. Finally, British prime minister Tony Blair visited the White House on February 23.[9]

Bush's plans for the military and for defense also entered the picture. In the week following his early February announcement on improving military pay, Bush took three one-day trips to military installations: to visit active duty soldiers at Fort Stewart, Georgia, a high-tech command center in Norfolk, Virginia, and reservists at a West Virginia National Guard base.

Bush's most extensive efforts to build support occurred with his tax reform plan, an effort that begin with his February 2 Saturday radio address, then a meeting on February 5 with a group of citizens who would personally benefit from the tax cuts. On February 20 a more extensive public relations effort was undertaken to stress both the tax cut and education initiatives with a three-day tour through the Midwest. Following his February 27 economic address to Congress, Bush went on another three-day swing—to Nebraska, Iowa, Arkansas, and Georgia—to tout his plan. This was followed the next week by a trip to Illinois, North and South Dakota, Louisiana, and Florida. The states Bush selected were not random: many of them were states where Bush had won, but also were ones represented by Democratic senators who might be persuaded to support Bush's proposals.

Bush did not confine his efforts to "going public," but continued what was now dubbed his "charm offensive" with individual members of Congress, from both parties, an effort that had begun during the transition. On January 22, his first working day as president, Bush met with several Democrat elder states- man including Robert Strauss, former senators Paul Simon and John Glenn, and Jody Powell, press secretary in the Carter White House and a prominent Washington lobbyist. Senator Trent Lott called them the "old bulls" and dubbed the meeting a "smart move." That same day Bush also convened a luncheon meeting with GOP congressional leaders. He used the opportunity to "personally explain the issues and what I'm attempting to do." They should expect, he told them, "a strong education reform package, a tax relief package, a Medicare and Social Security reform package, and a package to help pay the folks in the military more money."[10] Over the next four days, Bush met with Democratic lawmakers to discuss his education proposals. This was followed a day later by another meeting with a bipartisan group of legislators to discuss election reform, and then another meeting with fourteen members of the House and Senate—four of them Democrats—on education reform.

All told, from the transition through his first week as president, Bush met with ninety lawmakers, twenty-nine of whom were Democrats. According to White House figures, this compares to fourteen members of Congress for Clinton and seven for Bush Sr. George W. Bush also met with seventeen gov- ernors from both parties (in late February he hosted a White House dinner and met with a number of them again at their annual meeting). During the week of January 29, Bush met with members of the congressional black caucus and, over the weekend of February 2, attended a GOP House and Senate retreat in Williamsburg, Virginia, met with Democratic senators at the Library of Con- gress, and then attended a retreat of Democratic House members in Pennsyl- vania. The meeting with the House Democrats was described as "tough," although Bush was given a standing ovation at the end. Not counting the House retreat, Bush had now met with 153 members of Congress, of whom 75 were Democrats and 73 were Republicans.

Yet in his early days as president, while building an agenda, reaching out for public support, and building bridges to Congress, Bush did not completely dodge controversy. On his first working day as president, he issued an execu- tive memorandum reinstating restrictions on abortions and abortion counsel- ing as part of U.S. foreign aid packages. He also issued an executive order that sought to block access to materials at the Reagan presidential library (includ- ing those from his father's vice presidency) that were ready to be made pub- lic now that the twelve-year period, set by federal law, from the end of the Reagan presidency had passed. Both signaled an unusually high reliance on executive orders and directives to accomplish presidential goals in nonleg- islative ways that would persist in this presidency.

By early April as the 100-days benchmark approached, Bush was gener- ally lauded for his performance in office to date.[11] Commentators generally noted (some with surprise) that Bush had stuck to his conservative political agenda, but had sought to build bridges to congressional Democrats and had avoided more strident rhetorical partisanship. As Kenneth Duberstein, a former chief of staff under Reagan, observed at the time, "He puts on a kind, gentle face, but he also stays on message, keeps faith with his agenda."[12] Yet there were also signs that his charm offensive with Congress was waning: on April 30, to mark his first 100 days as president, Bush invited all members of Congress to a White House reception and luncheon. One hundred ninety-three attended, but only fifty of them were Democrats.[13]

The "public presidency" of George Bush also differed from that of his predecessor. While Bush had undertaken a number of speaking events around the country (visiting far more states than his recent predecessors),[14] there was only one major address—his economic one to a joint session of Congress—and there were no formal East Room press conferences.[15] Coverage in the national media also was less than in the Clinton presidency. According to a study by the Project for Excellence in Journalism, there were 41 percent fewer stories about Bush over the first two months of his presidency than had been the case under Clinton eight years earlier. The drop-off in one outlet, *Newsweek* magazine, was 59 percent.[16] Yet the media response may have fit with the communications strategy of this presidency, one different from its predecessor's attempt to capitalize on nearly every political opportunity. In the view of Karen Hughes, it was a function of a different kind of "strategic thinking": "One of the hallmarks of President Bush's administration is he focuses on really big, substantive, important things, as opposed to a little initiative here and a little initiative there."[17]

Overall, Bush was clearly still a "work in progress," as David Gergen, a veteran of several White Houses, noted at the 100-day mark.[18] According to David Broder, it was still a presidency "without clear definition. . . . Nothing has gone seriously wrong; few achievements are in the books; and we don't yet feel that we know him."[19]

The Early Bush Agenda
and the Legislative Process

Although none of the major pieces of legislation had been enacted by the 100-day benchmark, most of the major White House proposals had been unveiled. Two, in particular, were moving forward. Bush's tax cut plan was moving through Congress, and the White House was working closely with Democrats on his education reform proposals. In both areas, Bush had quickly recognized the need to compromise. His proposal to give parents vouchers to send their children from ailing public schools to private schools had essentially been abandoned. His proposed $1.6 trillion dollar tax cut had been ratcheted down to $1.3 trillion.

The Bush Tax Reform Plan

A version of Bush's tax reform plan was initially introduced into the Senate on January 22, 2001, Bush's first full working day as president, by Senators Phil Gramm (R-TX) and Zell Miller (D-GA). The two jumped the gun a bit, since the White House intended to focus on the tax plan the next week and were then in the process of rolling out the Bush education plan at that point. Yet the joint effort by Gramm and Miller indicated that Bush could draw some Democratic support for his proposal. In fact, Miller's participation was an artifact of Bush's efforts during the transition. According to one account:

> What Miller and Gramm didn't announce was that their matchmaker had been Bush. . . . Miller had quietly offered his support to Bush a month earlier. "I'm going to be with you on a lot of things," Miller told him after a meeting on education in Austin. "I'm going to be with you on the tax cut." Bush got the word to Gramm, who hatched the collaboration idea with Miller on a Banking Committee trip to Mexico two weeks later.[20]

Democratic congressional leaders immediately criticized the proposal, and two moderate GOP senators, James Jeffords of Vermont and Lincoln Chafee of Rhode Island, publicly balked at the size of the Bush tax cut. Yet the agenda had been captured by Bush: his $1.6 trillion ten-year plan versus the Democrats' new counterproposal of $750 billion. Gone were the targeted cuts that Al Gore had proposed during the campaign—the issue now became the size of the across-the-board cut. Bush also resisted pressure from the right to increase the size of the tax cut and resisted calls from the business community to include corporate as well as income tax cuts in the proposal. On the latter, Cheney, Card, and Rove were central figures: they were "arm-twisting," according to one report, so that business groups would support income tax cuts but not push for corporate tax reductions. "The message is 'Get with the program,'" one business lobbyist observed at the time.[21]

Bush's timing of his tax cut proposal, moving it to Congress early and placing it at the top of his agenda, was also critical. Not only did it signal Bush's commitment, but it also avoided problems that might have occurred later on. First, unbeknownst at the time, the loss of Republican control of the Senate in June would certainly have put the White House in a weaker strategic position and would have likely led to a tax cut closer to the Democrats' proposed figures. Second, the worsening economy and decline in overall tax revenues (and their effects on projected budget surpluses) might have doomed the Bush proposal if it had been delayed until the end of summer. Bush's efforts in both the Senate and House were bolstered by the support, albeit qualified, of Federal Reserve Chairman Alan Greenspan, who appeared before congressional committees in support of the tax cut, but with some caution. Had legislation been delayed, Greenspan might not have given even qualified support to the plan. And third, had the White House delayed until the summer in presenting its plan or if the legislative process had been delayed into the fall (as had been the case in 1981 with the Reagan tax cuts), there might have been no Bush tax cut in the aftermath of September 11, 2001, as the costs of fighting a war against terrorists and expenditures for homeland security would now have to be factored in.

Throughout March, Bush continued to travel across the country urging public support for his plan. His appearances were again largely targeted at states with a strong GOP base but with Democratic or moderate Republican members of the Senate: Iowa, Arkansas, Georgia, North and South Dakota, Louisiana, Florida, Maine, New Jersey, Montana, and Missouri. The Republican-controlled House moved quickly on the Bush plan. By April 4, seventy-five days into the new administration, the House passed the major pieces of Bush's tax program.[22]

The legislative process took longer in the Senate. On March 21, an agreement was reached that Bush's proposal would be expanded to include a $60 billion tax cut for the current fiscal year, which the Democrats had been proposing (it was later raised to $85 then $100 billion, and would eventually take the form of set rebates to individuals who had paid taxes for the previous year).[23] More important, an alternative plan was brokered by Senator John Breaux (D-LA): it would give the administration a $1.24 trillion cut rather than the $750 billion the Democrats had initially offered. It was a proposal that the White House would eventually accept. A coalition of the GOP members of the Senate plus several moderate Democrats held, and the Senate eventually approved the compromise agreement on May 23 by a vote of 62–38, with twelve Democrats joining all forty-nine GOP members, plus Senator Jeffords of Vermont, who had just left the GOP. On June 7, Bush signed the bill into law.[24]

By most accounts, the effort was a major success for the White House. While not achieving all the tax reduction amounts that had been initially proposed, the legislative game was defined by Bush's rather than the Democrats' agenda: its centerpiece was an across-the-board reduction, the final size of the reductions was closer to Bush's request than to the Democrats' initial proposal, and the targeted, piecemeal tax plan that Al Gore had run on in the campaign was long forgotten.

Bush's success had been predicated on a strategy of fast action in a unified Republican House, followed by compromise and individualized attempts to pick up the support of several Senate Democrats. It was not a bipartisan strategy aiming to build stronger support at the outset with the Democrats (although a surprisingly large number of Democrats joined on in the end). Nor perhaps could it be. Yet as a strategy, it was not necessarily a sure path to success in other policy areas. In education reform, greater compromise prevailed almost from the outset. On Bush's faith-based initiatives effort, the White

House followed the tax cut strategy, but at a price. The House stayed firm, indeed too firm, and an early effort to build a more bipartisan consensus on some of the more controversial provisions of the plan was lost. Here the eventual outcome, at least legislatively, was even further from Bush's original plan.

Education Reform

Bush's second major initiative was education reform, fulfilling a campaign pledge to make education his top domestic priority. It was an area of policy, moreover, where Bush had particularly shown enthusiasm during the campaign and one where he pointed with pride to his record in Texas, particularly the increased performance of minority students. On January 24, 2001, the White House unveiled the plan, which included increased federal funding for schools, mandatory testing of students in grades three through eight, and the provision of vouchers for parents to place students, who were in public schools that failed performance standards, in other public or private (including religious) schools. The plan sought greater accountability in school performance, but at the same time more flexibility in how schools might use federal funds.[25] In his February budget proposal to Congress, Bush also proposed increasing education funding by $4.6 billion, a significant increase, but well short of the $10 billion in additional funds that some Democrats were advocating.

The voucher proposal drew immediate opposition to the plan, and the Bush administration itself sent early signals that perhaps it might compromise. On the Sunday following inauguration day, Chief of Staff Card seemed to indicate that the White House might not be fully committed to vouchers. So too did Roderick Page during his confirmation hearings as education secretary. Bush's own remarks at the unveiling of his proposal also signaled to some Democrats that Bush no longer regarded vouchers as the cornerstone of his proposal. "That's the flavor we get, that's the mood," Senator Joseph Lieberman (D-CT)—who had prepared his own education bill—told reporters. "That's the moment of decision the president is going to come to, whether the voucher component of the bill is worth sacrificing all the rest that we can accomplish."[26] Lieberman's words would prove prophetic.

Throughout the debate, Bush and his chief White House aides on education—Sandy Kress and Margaret LaMontagne Spellings—sought to work closely with both Democrats (particularly Senator Edward Kennedy and his House counterpart Representative George Miller of California) and Republicans in forging a compromise bill. But while the White House was able to salvage some of its proposals, vouchers proved too controversial. The White House may also have made a strategic mistake in not working more appreciatively with Senator Jim Jeffords of Vermont while he was still a Republican and serving as chairman of the Senate Health, Education, Labor, and Pensions Committee. In his book on why he defected from the GOP, Jeffords makes little mention of the Bush education bill, save that he was steering its passage on the floor of the Senate in his capacity as chair of the Senate education committee and that he wanted more federal funding of mandated special-education programs.[27]

Although Bush lobbied hard for the proposal and made a number of public appearances to build support for the program (his first appearance outside the White House was at a D.C. public school), both the House and Senate education committees quickly eliminated the voucher plan in the legislation they reported to their respective floors.[28] On May 23 the House passed its education bill, whose title—"No Child Left Behind"—echoed Bush's campaign rhetoric, 384–45. On June 14 the Senate approved its modified bill by a margin of 91–8.

Although both the House and Senate versions contained provisions for mandatory testing, they differed significantly over how testing would be undertaken and performance measured. The two bills also differed in the amounts of federal funds authorized and in provisions for how states and school districts might have some flexibility in using those funds. Had the GOP continued to control the Senate, the conference committee of the two bodies might have reached a quick resolution. Yet political time worked against the president now that the Democrats prevailed in the Senate. Despite White House prodding, the bill stalled in conference committee. On September 6, the White House unveiled a public relations effort, to take place the next week, that would try to speed action on the bill.[29] One of the events scheduled was an appearance by the president at a Sarasota, Florida, school the morning of September 11, and it was at this appearance that the president was informed of the terrorist attack on the World Trade Center.

Education Reform: After September 11

The conference committee took five months to complete its work, essentially writing a new bill of its own. Bush's relationship with Senator Kennedy was especially important. Although Bush had failed to invite him to a meeting with Senate leaders on education during the December transition, he called Kennedy, who was vacationing in the Caribbean, to press his proposal. In addition to frequent meetings with him, Bush also invited members of the Kennedy family to a White House screening of *Thirteen Days,* a movie that had just been released about the Cuban missile crisis, and he renamed the Justice Department building in Washington after Robert F. Kennedy. Kennedy stood firm in his opposition to Bush's school voucher plan, but he also compromised with the White House on less funding for the bill. In addition to Kennedy, the other key negotiators on the bill were Senator Judd Gregg (R-NH) and Representatives

John Boehner (R-OH) and George Miller (D-CA). According to reports, they had met at least nine times since September with White House aides Spellings and Kress.

On December 13, 2001, the House passed the bill 381–41; on December 18 the bill passed the Senate 87–10. It contained most of the reforms that Bush had requested, but without a voucher program for nonpublic schools.[30] It authorized federal funding of $26.5 billion for fiscal year 2002, $4 billion more than the White House wanted. But the bill provided some $6 billion less than Kennedy and other Senate Democrats had proposed in the initial Senate bill, and a higher appropriation had been one of their chief motivations for prolonging a compromise. Advocates for more federal funding of special education failed, however, to add an additional $2.5 billion to the bill to cover 40 percent of the costs of those programs. This led Senator Jeffords (I-VT), once chair of the education committee and initial floor leader of the bill, to vote against it. Ironically, the Democrats could not deliver funds for the one program that played a central part in Jeffords's defection from the GOP.

The White House quickly claimed a major victory, even though the public-to-private voucher proposal was long gone. According to one report, Bush's "victory lap . . . followed a pattern Bush established as governor of Texas: He would push hard in negotiations, take the best deal he could get, claim victory and share the credit."[31] On January 8, 2002, Bush signed the bill and made several appearances around the country with some of its key sponsors and negotiators: Massachusetts (Senator Kennedy), New Hampshire (Senator Gregg), and Ohio (Representative Boehner).

Following passage of the bill, Bush used a number of public appearances to both tout the proposal and emphasize his bipartisan efforts with Kennedy. Kennedy, however, was increasingly critical of the funding for education in subsequent Bush budget proposals.[32] Nor was the public much attentive to the plan. In a March 2001 *Washington Post* poll, only 44 percent knew that Bush had recently signed into law an education reform bill, 16 percent said he had not, while 40 percent did not know.[33] But Bush's drive for education reform did not end with the bill, and he continued to stress the need for a voucher plan that would enable students to transfer out of failing public schools and into private ones if parents so chose.[34]

Bush's efforts had succeeded in making the GOP competitive with Democrats on the education issue, but by the fall of 2003 there was a fourteen-point drop (from January 2002) in the public's perception of the GOP's advantage on education, as well as a fourteen-point gap between the GOP and the Democrats (36 percent to 50 percent). The White House and the Republicans also faced a potential backfire on the issue: the number of schools that had scored as failing under the new system was large in some states (almost 50 percent in electorally important states such as Florida, West Virginia, Missouri, and Tennessee), nor was there sufficient funding either by the federal government or by financially strapped state governments to remedy deficiencies.[35]

Faith-Based Initiatives

The third major agenda item was Bush's so-called faith-based initiative program, the most controversial part of which would have allowed religious groups to potentially participate in over $50 billion of federal service delivery programs. The "charitable choice" provision of the 1996 welfare reform law first allowed such groups to compete for federal funds for job-training programs, but it did not allow groups to directly proselytize.[36] The Bush proposal sought to expand the number of eligible federal programs and to get around the thorny issue of separation of church and state by continuing the prohibition on direct proselytizing. According to one White House official, the proposal "would divide religious and social service activities, although both could be offered as part of the same program. . . . [A] church-based program could alternate between religious and social service components; the government would fund only the service component, which could have religious values but no overt proselytizing."[37] The Bush proposal also sought to reduce regulatory barriers to faith-based groups and to provide charitable tax deductions for those tax filers who do not itemize their tax deductions.[38]

On January 29, 2001, Bush, surrounded by Christian, Muslim, and Jewish clerics, unveiled a new White House Office of Faith-Based and Community Initiatives (OFBCI) and announced that he had selected John DiIulio to head the effort. DiIulio, a Democrat, a Catholic, and a political science professor, had undertaken research on the issue and had worked with a number of African American ministers involved in faith-based programs.[39] That same day, by executive order, Bush also established centers in five departments—Education, Health and Human Services, Housing and Urban Development, Justice, and Labor—that would analyze barriers in departmental programs that blocked participation of faith-based and community organizations.

Work on the OFBCI had begun during the later half of the transition under the direction of a two-person team.[40] However, as Kathryn Dunn Tenpas has noted, the effort to bring it quickly to fruition may have the hurt the effort: "While it may have been reasonable to begin planning during the transition period and open the office well into the first year, Karl Rove and other senior staff members had decided that the second week after inauguration would be devoted to promoting faith-based programs." Moreover, there was difficulty in finding someone to head the effort—negotiations had begun not with DiIulio but with Stephen Goldsmith, the former mayor of Indianapolis. And by the time of its inception, few White House positions were available. According to Tenpas, "Staffing the OFBCI and obtaining a sufficient budget was an afterthought. . . . Ultimately, the OFBCI was granted a director and three commissioned staffers because the personnel office had reached the maximum allotment; it was a far cry from the twenty-five staff members some had initially hoped for. Understaffed, underfunded and without a firm grasp of their responsibilities, the White House OFBCI forged ahead in what would soon become very rough waters."[41] Nor, according to Tenpas, did DiIulio receive sufficient support from other parts of the White House staff once legislation hit Congress: "At DiIulio's first hearing on Capitol Hill, no one from the legislative affairs office was in attendance. . . . DiIulio was not briefed nor did he work in concert with other key components of the White House organization (i.e., the offices of communications, public liaison, political affairs)."[42]

In addition to its transition and organizational difficulties, the substance of the program was not an easy sell. The part of the proposal dealing with the participation of faith-based groups in social service programs (charitable choice) proved controversial. A number of lawsuits were pending in federal court that sought to challenge the 1996 law.[43] Concerns were raised both from those who feared erosion of the separation of church and state and from religious leaders—largely Christian fundamentalists and evangelicals—about government involvement, regulation, and scrutiny of religion-based programs. Some religious leaders were even alarmed by which religious groups might be able to participate: a group from the Anti-Defamation League, for example, met with DiIulio on February 12, 2001, to receive assurances that Louis Farrakhan's Nation of Islam would not be an eligible group,[44] while Pat Robertson warned on his *700 Club* television program on February 20 that the Unification Church, Hare Krishnas, and the Church of Scientology "could all become financial beneficiaries," opening up "a real Pandora's box."[45] Unlike with his other major agenda items, Bush's conservative base was not holding firm.

In early March, the White House decided to delay sending up proposed legislation in order to quell critics and fine-tune some of its provisions. DiIulio made a number of public addresses before religious groups in which he sought to explain that, under federal statutes and court rulings, religious groups would be required to separate their service-providing and religious efforts. But the reception was less than warm and even one of Bush's long-time advisers on the issue, Marvin Olasky, was critical of the proposal, noting that a number of the faith-based programs Bush had lauded during the campaign would not be eligible for funding.[46]

DiIulio sometimes clashed with religious conservatives. In one incident, when religious groups became concerned that the initiative might lead to governmental scrutiny of their efforts, DiIulio labeled them "predominantly white, ex-urban, evangelical and national para-church leaders," adding that they "should be careful not to presume to speak for any persons other than themselves and their own churches."[47] He also warned religious groups that any overtly religious programs would likely not receive government funding. "Bible-thumping doesn't cut it folks," he told a group of Jewish religious leaders on February 26, 2001. DiIulio was also reportedly incensed that his own deputy, Don Eberly, and Karl Rove had considered a request from the Salvation Army for the OMB to issue regulations that would have permitted it to discriminate against homosexuals in exchange for the group's support for the bill.[48]

In some sense, DiIulio's vision of faith-based initiatives differed from those (such as Olasky) who had introduced Bush to the idea during the campaign. For the conservative religious groups it was a means of providing religion-based service delivery. For DiIulio the central objective was more to get religious groups—particularly those in the inner city—eligible for federal funding, even if it meant separating out some of the religious components and abiding by some federal regulations. Religion for the Christian fundamentalists and evangelicals, funding for DiIulio.

The legislative strategy followed by the White House may also have hurt its prospects. DiIulio had favored building a broad consensus for the initiative in Congress, one that might require more time. Yet Karl Rove favored a more partisan approach and an effort that would achieve quicker results. Here the lessons of Bush tax cut strategy may have been ill advised. But Rove prevailed, and it led to an almost straight party line vote in the House in July 2001. But the bill that the House passed, although generally in accord with Bush's proposal, contained details that raised controversies lurking deeper in this policy area.[49] Unlike what occurred with the tax cut, the House's action may have scared off those who might yet be willing to reach a compromise in the Senate. The House bill especially contained a controversial amendment that would have allowed groups to ignore state and local antidiscrimination laws against gays and lesbians as well as to hire only members of their own faith.[50] In order to assure passage of the bill, one of its chief cosponsors, Representative J. C. Watts (R-OK), assured GOP moderates that he would address their concerns once the bill reached a conference committee with the Senate. The legislation passed 233–198 on July 19.

The Senate was a different matter.[51] Once the Democrats took over control of the Senate, the prospects for the bill became even more uncertain, despite both lobbying efforts by the White House as well as a number of personal appearances by the president to rally public support.[52] Concessions were made, but passage stalled through the remainder of the summer.[53]

On August 17, 2001, the White House announced that DiIulio was stepping down as head of the OFBCI. DiIulio noted that he was simply fulfilling his pledge to serve only six months in the White House.[54] Yet DiIulio would later express dissatisfaction with how the White House had decided to proceed with its faith-based proposal. Instead of the more partisan approach that Rove had devised for winning House approval and the support of the religious right, a more bipartisan effort should have been made at the outset, especially by emphasizing the kindred charitable choice provisions in the 1996 welfare reform act:

> Had they done that, six months later they would have had a strongly bipartisan copycat bill to extend that [1996] law. But, overgeneralizing the lessons from the politics of the tax cut bill, they winked at the most far-right House Republicans who, in turn, drafted a so-called faith bill. [That] was as anybody could tell, an absolute political non-starter. It could pass the House only on a virtual party-vote, and it could never pass the Senate, even before Jeffords switched.

Moreover, according to DiIulio, the House bill "reflected neither the president's previous rhetoric on the idea, nor any of the actual empirical evidence that recommended [faith-based initiatives]. I said so, wrote memos, and so on for the first six weeks."[55] Efforts to get the initiative back on track following the president's July meeting with Senators Lieberman and Rick Santorum (R-PA) foundered: "My staff and I worked closely with the two senators' staff on this effort throughout the summer. But rather than draft a fresh bipartisan bill unburdened by the more controversial features of the House bill, some senior [White House] staff wanted to back off charitable choice legislation altogether in favor of a 'communities of character' initiative."[56]

Faith-Based Initiatives: After September 11

Following September 11, 2001, the White House took a more conciliatory stand on the proposal and largely abandoned the more controversial charitable choice parts of the bill that had passed the House.[57] By the summer of 2002, almost a year later, a compromise measure passed the Democratic-controlled Senate Finance Committee. It was coauthored by Senator Lieberman and even had the support of Senator Hillary Clinton (D-NY). The bill again had no charitable choice provision. But the proposed Charity Aid, Recovery, and Empowerment (CARE) Act included provisions to provide tax deduction benefits that would help both religious and nonreligious charities.[58]

Yet what Bush had failed to gain through Congress he sought to achieve through executive order. Although the bill remained stalled in Congress, on December 12, 2002, Bush announced a series of regulatory changes that the White House felt did not require congressional action. One executive order put in place the charitable choice provisions that Bush had initially sought from Congress. The order required religious groups to separate proselytizing activities from service delivery, and it forbade service providers from discriminating against recipients based on religious grounds. But it did allow religious groups to hire employees on the basis of religious beliefs even though they were now in a contractual relationship with the federal government. The issue of potential discriminatory hiring had been a source of congressional concern, and Bush sought to skirt the issue through his executive order. Some Democrats criticized the new rule, saying it violated long-standing federal nondiscrimination provisions; others argued that the rule change was permissible because it was in accord with existing laws and Supreme Court rulings exempting religious groups from some aspects of nondiscrimination legislation. But Bush's order did not exempt religious groups from state and local civil rights legislation, which had been part of the House bill and had been a continuing source of controversy.[59]

The executive orders, while apparently clearing the way for parts of Bush's faith-based initiatives program, did not (and could not) include the provisions for increasing charitable giving, including tax deductions, that were part of the bills still before Congress. The latter, however, were quickly taken up the Senate, now under GOP control, in 2003.[60] On April 9, 2003, a stripped-downed version of Bush's original proposal finally passed the Senate 95–5.[61] The House passed its version of the plan, 408–13, on September 17. A final agreement remained delayed, however, through the end of 2003.

Bush's executive orders still remained, and charitable choice survived, albeit through executive order that could be overturned by another administration or restricted by congressional action. Legislatively, however, Bush's initial plan had not succeeded: "I applaud the passage of the bill, but it's a shadow of what was hoped for," Marvin Olasky commented. For DiIulio's replacement at the White House, James Towey, it was "a big step forward" and the latest in Bush's "procession of victories." Failure, in his view, was not the initial strategy, but the work of "a couple of Democratic senators."[62]

The White House's position had also apparently hardened, now that charitable choice seemed legislatively doomed. In late June 2003 the White House issued a position paper, sent to Congress, which sought to ease the ability of religious groups to base hiring decisions on religious principles, including a religion's stand on sexual orientation. The administration called on Congress to clarify what it viewed as conflicting federal laws and to let the courts decide if state and local antidiscrimination laws were applicable to those working in federally funded, faith-based programs. According to one report, "The White House position paper does not change administration doctrine, but it puts Bush in a much more aggressive position on a highly charged issue. . . . [T]he policy, months in development, takes a stand Bush has long held but has not previously stated."[63] The White House chose not to resolve those issues itself (at least for the moment), but it did place Congress and the courts on the political hot seat. The administration's position was no longer that its initiatives would neither add to nor subtract from existing civil rights laws, as John DiIulio had once held. The reach and applicability of those laws was now up for interpretation, perhaps ultimately by the administration itself, should neither Congress nor the courts choose to act.

Healthcare Initiatives: Patients'
Bill of Rights and Prescription Drugs

The early Bush agenda also had two major initiatives in healthcare: a patients' bill of rights and a prescription drug coverage plan for senior citizens. Both had arisen during the campaign in response to alternative Democratic proposals. On the patients' bill of rights, the White House chose not to present its own proposal. Rather, on February 6, 2001, Bush laid out criteria for legislation in a letter sent to congressional leaders. The key element in Bush's "principles for a bipartisan bill" was a more limited right to sue than in current legislation proposed by Senators McCain (R-AZ) and Kennedy (D-MA). Yet the legislation that the Senate, now controlled by the Democrats, began to consider in June paid little heed to Bush's criteria. The bill passed 59–36.

The White House threatened to veto a patients' rights bill that did not meet Bush's conditions. But while a veto remained a possibility, White House aides also signaled that Bush was open to compromise.[64] By July, Bush appeared to have some success. Although the initial House GOP plan lacked sufficient votes, the White House was able to persuade Representative Charles Norwood (R-GA), a leading advocate in Congress, to abandon his cosponsorship of a largely Democratic-backed alternative. Bush personally lobbied Norwood and was able to incorporate some of Norwood's concerns in a compromise bill that passed the House a day later and that the White House supported.[65]

The White House then agreed to deal directly with the Senate rather than proceed to a conference committee. Senators Kennedy, McCain, and John Edwards (D-NC) began negotiations with the White House in November 2001. The White House continued to insist that federal rules for appeals should trump state rules and that health management organizations have the power to require arbitration before cases were filed in courts. The administration also wanted to set limits on damages for certain types of injuries, but Democrats wanted any limits to be determined by the courts. While McCain and Edwards publicly noted that the White House had made a good faith effort to reach a compromise, positions were too far apart and no deal was reached. By August 1, 2002, talks between the White House and Senate had broken down. No major effort was undertaken in the 108th Congress.[66]

Bush's plan for prescription drug benefits for seniors fared no better, at least while the Democrats controlled the Senate. On January 29, 2001, Bush asked Congress to give states grants to help poor elderly Americans to pay for prescription drugs: temporary block grants of $12 billion for each of the next four years. The proposal, interestingly, was unveiled more quietly than his other recent initiatives: no White House event, just six sentences about it in a photo opportunity. Nor did his aides set up a press briefing on the plan. According to Press Secretary Fleischer, "It's just a sign of a very busy day today. We have other busy events tomorrow and the following day. It's always just a question of scheduling."[67]

The Bush proposal encountered immediate opposition from two key GOP legislators, Senator Charles Grassley (R-IA), chair of the Senate Finance Committee, and Representative Bill Thomas (R-CA), chair of the House Ways and Means Committee; both believed a more comprehensive proposal was needed. Yet it would take almost another year and a half for legislation to receive serious consideration on the floor of either the Senate or the House.

In June 2002 the House passed its version of a prescription drug plan that relied on private insurers to provide coverage, close to the White House plan. But a month later the Senate was unable to come to agreement among a number of different plans that had been proposed, voting down four different bills. For the time being, prescription drug coverage was dead. Efforts revived in 2003, and although the House and the Senate voted in favor of different versions of a plan, by November a GOP-dominated conference committee was able to agree on the details of a compromise, estimated to cost $400 billion over ten years, and it passed both the House and the Senate later in the month.[68] The 678-page bill established a complex formula for determining benefits covering 40 million seniors. However, it fell short of the administration's initial goal of forcing Medicare to compete with managed care programs; competition was restricted to future pilot projects in six metropolitan areas and set to begin in 2010. The bill's passage was aided by the support of the 35 million-member American Association of Retired Persons, which congressional Republicans and the White House had assiduously courted.

Social Security

Bush's campaign proposal to allow workers to invest a part of their social security contributions in personal retirement accounts was not actively pushed by the White House in its early days in office. Instead, Bush announced, in his address to Congress on February 27, 2001, that he would create a commission to further study the proposal. The sixteen-member commission was unveiled on May 2, and was cochaired by former senator Daniel Patrick Moynihan (D-NY) and Richard Parsons, then the vice chairman of AOL–Time Warner. The committee met for the first time on June 11, and by July 19 issued a preliminary report that offered a bleak appraisal of the system and recommendations for its overhaul but no concrete proposals. The latter would come in December 2001, in a lengthy report in which the commission outlined several possible courses of action.

Yet the administration chose not to pursue a legislative proposal in 2002 or 2003. On November, 10, 2002, appearing on *Meet the Press,* Chief of Staff Card noted, "It is important that we have a debate about social security reform. It is imperative that it comes. I'm not sure it can happen next year."[69]

Card's prognostication proved accurate. For the time being, social security reform was on the back burner. By the end of 2003, reports indicated that it might still be part of the administration's 2004 agenda or an initiative the White House might pursue in a second Bush term.

Beyond the Bush Agenda

Although the White House enjoyed some success in moving its policy agenda forward, a number of unanticipated issues and problems would at times arise through its first months in office that would require the administration to respond. Off the Bush game plan, these issues sometimes put the White House on the defensive and enmeshed it in political controversies.

One area that quickly cropped up concerned executive orders and other rules and regulations, a number of which were promulgated in the final weeks and months of the Clinton presidency. Many raised technical issues, but with important regulatory consequences. Some also were potentially politically unpopular. For example, the White House was forced to countermand tougher standards for arsenic levels in drinking water, rules dealing with repetitive-stress injuries in the workplace, and limits on carbon dioxide emissions. Bush also reinstated restrictions on abortion counseling in foreign aid programs, refused to support the 1997 Kyoto agreement on global warming, and argued for delays in water pollution cleanup regulations.

Energy

Although energy policy had figured on occasion in Bush's campaign speeches, it was not at the top of the agenda. However, a severe shortage of electrical power and skyrocketing prices in California that had developed by January 2001 forced Bush to undertake a major effort in developing a comprehensive energy policy earlier than it might otherwise have done. On January 29, Bush placed Vice President Cheney in charge of a task force to address not only the crisis in California, but also ways of reducing dependence on foreign oil and expanding domestic output. Key members of the group were economic adviser Lawrence Lindsey, Treasury Secretary Paul O'Neill, and Energy Secretary Spencer Abraham.

The group's work proved somewhat controversial on two counts. First, it raised once again the issue of whether the Bush administration was too close to business interests in its policy deliberations and recommendations. The task force's May report to the president emphasized production rather than conservation and placed the administration on the defensive, particularly with its call for increased domestic oil drilling, coal production, and use of nuclear energy. In the view of Senator Susan Collins of Maine, a moderate Republican, "A lot of the unfortunate negative perceptions are driven by the energy issues." Bush's plan to open oil drilling in the Arctic National Wildlife Refuge (ANWR) was particularly controversial,[70] and the energy plan quickly became linked to some of the more controversial decisions that were being made on rescinding some of the Clinton-era environmental orders and regulations.[71]

The second source of controversy concerned that fact that the energy task force kept its meetings secret, including the names of participants from outside groups and interests that met with its members. This eventually led to a call by some Democratic members of Congress to turn over the list of those who had been involved and other information and documents, which was then countered by a claim of executive privilege by the White House and a refusal to comply. Some information and documents were eventually turned over, but the matter ended up in federal court.[72] In February 2003 the administration won a major victory when a federal judge ruled that the General Accounting Office (GAO), the plaintiff in one of the suits and the investigative arm of Congress, had no standing to bring the case in federal court.[73] However, in a report to Congress issued in late August 2003, the GAO was highly critical of how the task force had undertaken its work, as well as its failure to produce the documents requested by the GAO. According to Comptroller General David Walker, the head of the GAO, the lack of cooperation raised questions about "a reasonable degree of transparency and an appropriate degree of accountability in government."[74]

The White House also had to endure continuing congressional opposition to its plans for increased production. In June and July 2001 the House rejected proposals to expand drilling in the Great Lakes and off the Florida coastline. The House did vote in early August in favor of the Bush plan, including drilling in the ANWR. In July the Senate voted 57–42 to bar new oil drilling in national monuments. But other parts of the bill lingered in the Senate through 2001 and 2002. The need for swift movement on a new energy policy also dissipated. By September 2001 the electricity supply in California had returned to normal, and evidence was surfacing that some energy suppliers had artificially manipulated supplies of electricity to inflate prices and had taken advantage of poorly designed state energy regulations.

In 2003 the House once again passed a bill close to the Bush plan. In late July, in a parliamentary maneuver, the GOP Senate leadership passed a bill that the Democrats had proposed a year before, with the differences with the House bill to be resolved by a conference committee dominated by Republicans. On November 17 the committee finished its work, sending a ten-year, $32 billion, 1,000-plus-page bill to the full Congress. It quickly passed the House 246–180 after just one hour of debate. In the Senate, fifty-eight members favored the bill. However, despite heavy lobbying by the president and vice president, the White House could not gain two additional votes to stop a filibuster. Provisions for exempting liability from lawsuits for manufacturers of a fuel additive, increased subsidies for ethanol production, and the inclusion of a number of "pork barrel" projects in the bill proved especially controversial.

Campaign Finance Reform

Along with energy, perhaps the most politically charged issue that the White House was forced to deal with, not on its political agenda, was campaign finance reform. Here the White House confronted the dogged efforts of Bush's chief primary opponent, Senator John McCain, to make sure his legislation—cosponsored with Senator Russell Feingold (D-WI)—did not once again die in the Senate as it had the previous six years. In 2001, McCain was dealt a stronger hand when Senator Thad Cochran (R-MS) came out in support of the bill, bringing it close to the sixty votes needed to overcome a possible filibuster.[75] Prospects for its companion bill in the House—the Shays-Meehan bill—also looked promising; it had been passed by the House in 1998 and 1999.

On January 24, Bush met with McCain. The meeting was described as friendly (a "good meeting," according to Bush), with Press Secretary Fleischer labeling McCain an "ally."[76] Yet Bush remained opposed to the centerpiece of the proposal: a ban on "soft money" contributions.[77] Despite White House hopes that the issue might be postponed and not deflect attention from the Bush agenda, McCain persisted and five days later began a "town hall" campaign in several key states, with a kickoff in Little Rock, Arkansas.

By mid-March, the McCain-Feingold bill was under consideration by the full Senate. Rather than simply threatening a veto, the White House outlined several broad guidelines that Bush supported—a ban on soft money donations from corporations and unions (but not individuals) as well as a "paycheck protection" provision that would enable union members to block use of their dues for campaign contributions. The White House also had been working closely with Senator Chuck Hagel (R-NE) on a less stringent alternative to McCain-Feingold.[78] Yet despite behind-the-scenes efforts, Bush's alternatives went nowhere.[79] On April 2 the Senate passed an amended version of the McCain-Feingold bill 59–41, with twelve GOP senators joining all but three Democrats in support.[80] The fate of the companion Shays-Meehan bill was less rosy. It and a competing GOP bill were introduced on the House floor, but the issue became caught up in partisan procedural wrangling. On July 12, further debate was shelved when the House rejected Speaker Hastert's ground rules for debate.[81]

Yet the issue did not go away. By late January 2002, supporters of the Shays-Meehan bill, which had been stalled by parliamentary maneuvers in the House, had 218 signatures on a discharge petition, which would force the

House to consider the bill. Only eleven such petitions since 1967 had been successfully employed to force a House vote. Although opponents of the bill offered up a number of amendments to weaken it, the effort failed. On February 14 at 2:43 A.M. the House voted 240–189 in favor of the bill.[82]

On the day of the vote, Bush was cautious in his remarks to the press, saying that he would "look at it very carefully" if it passed the House. "I want to sign a bill that improves the system. We'll see what comes my way." Press Secretary Fleischer also sought to claim some credit for the White House: "If campaign finance reform is enacted into law, I believe you can thank President George W. Bush, because he changed the dynamics of how this phony debate has finally ended in Washington D.C."[83] In late March the Senate passed the bill by a 60–40 vote.[84]

The White House had hoped the bill would either fail to pass or die in parliamentary maneuvers. At the same time, it was caught in the position of not appearing to vigorously oppose a bill that had a good amount of congressional and public support. Although Karl Rove had been privately in touch with the Senate's leading GOP opponent of reform, Senator Mitch McConnell of Kentucky, publicly the White House kept its distance from the debate. "Karl is not going to be talking to the press about campaign finance reform," one aide was reported to have said.[85]

On March 27, President Bush signed the bill at 8:00 A.M. in the Oval Office, without cameras and reporters present, and with none of the traditional fanfare normally associated with a major piece of legislation. Bush's signing statement, however, indicated that he had "serious constitutional concerns" with some aspects of the bill. Senator McCain, at home in Arizona during the congressional recess, was informed of Bush's action by a call from a White House aide. Another White House aide said Bush wanted no public signing ceremony in order to avoid "sticking it in the eye" of the bill's GOP opponents.[86] Opponents of the bill were dealt a final blow on December 10, 2003, when the U.S. Supreme Court ruled in favor of all of the major provisions of the bill, thus rendering moot all of the constitutional objections raised by President Bush and its congressional opponents.[87]

Worsening Economy

Looming over all of Bush's efforts during his first eight months in office (and continuing until 2003) was a worsening economic picture. The downturn had begun before Bush took office, but its full impact would be felt later on. On April 6, 2001, the Labor Department released first-quarter statistics indicating that the job loss in March was the biggest in nine years. Unemployment rose to 4.3 percent (up from 4.2 in February and 3.9 percent in October). By early September it had reached 4.9 percent, a four-year high. The stock market also began to suffer heavy losses, especially as many of the new dot.com firms of the 1990s collapsed. The Standard & Poor's 500 had lost 18 percent of its value since January; Nasdaq had dropped 12 percent (but had lost almost two-thirds of its value from its high in 2000). Scandals in corporate accounting procedures, especially at Enron, created further pessimism. By mid-summer 2001, articles began to appear indicating that the projected $5 trillion budget surplus over the next ten years was disappearing as the economic picture worsened and as federal revenues declined. Although the depth of the economic decline was not as severe as prior recessions in terms of a downturn in economic activity, what was hoped to be a short period of economic decline proved to last much longer once the events of September 11, 2001, took place.

One piece of welcome news for Bush was his rise in the polls in the post–July 4, 2001, period. Two weeks before, Bush had slipped to 52 percent in his approval rating. But in a Gallup poll done the week of July 9, Bush had bounced back to 57 percent. By comparison, Clinton's rating at the same point in 1993 was only 45 percent. The public approved of Bush's handling of the economy, foreign affairs, healthcare reforms, and taxes. But his positions on campaign finance reform, faith-based initiatives, energy, and the environment garnered less than majority support. Bush also scored well on measures of him personally, with 70 percent responding that they approved of Bush as a person, and 78 percent respecting him no matter what their political and policy views; 73 percent also accepted him as the legitimate winner of the 2000 election, although half still thought he won on a technicality or had stolen the election.[88] Yet by early September, the polls had again begun to slide. In a Gallup poll taken right before September 11, Bush's approval rating stood at 51 percent.

*   *   *

By the end of summer 2001 the verdict on the Bush policy agenda still largely remained out. He succeeded in his tax cut plan and the House had moved forward on a number of other White House proposals. The Senate, since June under Democratic control, was a different matter. Shortly before leaving for his August vacation at his ranch in Crawford, Texas, Bush, standing before his assembled cabinet, offered a positive assessment of his administration's achievements. He also told reporters that once he returned to Washington in September he would launch a "personal crusade" emphasizing community spirit and family values. "I'll be proposing creative ways to tackle some of the toughest problems in our society," he told reporters.[89] Other events, however, would intervene.

Notes

1. See Burke, *Presidential Transitions,* pp. 3–36, 75–80.

2. Telephone interview with Bruce Reed, June 4, 1999. Also see Burke, *Presidential Transitions,* pp. 302–305.

3. Richard Berke, "Bush Praised for Smooth Transition," *New York Times,* January 28, 2001.

4. R. W. Apple Jr., "This Episode of 'The Clintons' Makes Bush the Star," *New York Times,* February 18. 2001.

5. Light, *The President's Agenda,* p. 218.

6. In fact, Harrison enjoyed a much wider electoral vote margin—233 to Cleveland's 168—than Bush's 271-to-266 victory over Gore.

7. Kenneth T. Walsh, "A Right-Stuff Kind of Guy," *U.S. News & World Report,* April 9, 2001.

8. As best as I can ascertain, this change in party control of a house of Congress was the first ever to occur once a session was under way. According to the Office of the U.S. Senate Historian, it "has not happened before. Even when party ratio changed enough to change the majority/minority status within a Congress, no reorganization has taken place. For example, in the 83rd Congress, the Republicans controlled the Senate at the beginning. During that congress, nine members died or resigned, repeatedly altering the party ratio. When the second session began in January 1954, the Democrats actually had a one-seat advantage over the Republicans, but the Senate leadership of both parties agreed to maintain the Republican majority throughout the remainder of that Congress." Author correspondence with Office of U.S. Senate Historian, December 29, 2003. According to the Office of the Clerk, U.S. House of Representatives, "Our research has not found any changes of the House after a session has begun. There was a close political division during President Martin Van Buren's first term in 1837–1839, but there does not appear to have been a change of party control." On two occasions, the party that seemed to have majority status *at the start of a session* was unable to secure party control. In the 72nd Congress, 1931–1933, "the Democrats, even though they were in the minority 216 to 218 Republicans, managed after the election to organize the House and elect the Speaker. . . . Another close division was in the 65th Congress, 1917–1919. The Democrats organized the House even though they trailed the Republicans 214 to 215." Author correspondence with the Office of the Clerk, U.S. House of Representatives, January 16, 2004.

9. On December 18, while still president-elect, Bush met with French president Jacques Chirac at the French embassy in Washington.

10. Mike Allen, "Bush Reverses Abortion Aid," *Washington Post,* January 23, 2001.

11. Interestingly, *Time* magazine did not carry a 100-day assessment of the Bush administration, only a cartoon parody of the first 100 days of a Gore presidency. *Time,* May 7, 2001.

12. Kenneth T. Walsh, "A Right-Stuff Kind of Guy," *U.S. News & World Report,* April 2, 2001.

13. Katherine Q. Seelye, "Lunch at the White House Proves No Big Draw," *New York Times,* May 1, 2001. The event, however, was scheduled on a Monday, a day when fewer members of Congress are in Washington.

14. Bush visited twenty-six states, Carter seven, Reagan two, and Bush Sr. and Clinton fifteen each. Mike Allen, "Reluctantly, Bush to Mark His First 100 Days in Office," *Washington Post,* April 24, 2001.

15. Bush did hold two press sessions in the press room of the White House. Bush's public approval rating stood at 62 percent at the 100-day mark, compared with 67 percent for Reagan, 57 percent for Bush Sr., and 55 percent for Clinton.

16. Bill Kovach and Tom Rosensteil, "The Unexamined Presidency," *New York Times,* May 1, 2001.

17. Anne Kornblut, "First 100 Days: A Low Profile for Bush," *Boston Globe,* April 29, 2001.

18. David Gergen, panel discussion, "How Bush Is Governing," American Enterprise Institute, Washington D.C., May 15, 2001.

19. David Broder, "We're Not Hearing Enough of Bush," *Washington Post,* April 11, 2001.

20. Karen Tumulty, "Five New Rules of the Road," *Time,* February 5, 2001.

21. Dan Morgan, "Business Backs Bush Tax Cut," *Washington Post,* March 4, 2001.

22. On March 8 the income tax cut portion of the plan passed the House; and on March 29 two other key parts of the proposal passed, one lowering rates for married couples and the other doubling credits for families with children (both garnered more Democratic support than the cut in the income tax rates on March 6). On April 4 the House passed a repeal of the estate tax, phased in until 2011, by a 274–154 vote. Fifty-eight Democrats joined nearly all GOP members. One of the key elements of contention was over who benefited most from the Bush plan. According to data released by the White House on March 2, the richest 1 percent of tax payers would get 22 percent of the cut, lower than the 43 percent Democrats estimated; 51 percent of the cut would go to those with incomes over $100,000. Bush administration estimates, however, did not include repeal of the estate tax ($185 billion over eleven years). Under the Bush plan, the richest 1 percent would see their share of taxes rise from 31.5 percent to 32.6 percent. In 2000, OMB analysis indicated that the highest 20 percent of taxpayers (with a mean income of $141,000) paid 65.1 percent of income taxes. The next quintile (with a mean income of $81,960) paid 20 percent. The third quintile paid 10.2 percent, the fourth paid 3.9 percent., and the lowest quintile paid 0.7 percent.

23. Bush chose to embrace rather than oppose the rebate program. Single persons or married persons filing separately received up to $300, heads of households received up to $500, and married couples filing jointly received up to $600. The Internal Revenue Service notified those receiving the rebate over the summer, and checks began to be sent out in August, 2001.

24. As the Senate was considering Bush's tax cut, it was also preparing the budget resolution for the 2002 fiscal year. In early April the Democrats' plan was defeated 61–39; the next day, a budget resolution passed by a vote of 65–35, with provisions only for a $1.27 trillion cut. The tax cut itself had yet to pass, but the politics of the situation were clear to the White House. By May, the White House was in agreement on a $1.35 trillion cut over eleven years (including $100 billion in immediate rebates). The White House had also done reasonably well in getting a congressional budget resolution for fiscal year 2002 that was close to its targets. Although the resolution set only overall spending levels that are then reconciled with particular appropriations by congressional committees, it can be an important symbolic victory for the White House, as it was for Ronald Reagan in the spring of 1981. Bush had initially sought an increase of only 4 percent (compared to the 8.5 percent increase in the last Clinton-era budget) in discretionary spending (including the defense budget but excluding Medicare, social security, and other entitlement programs). The final agreement, reached in May, was slightly less than 5 percent. The House passed the resolution on a near party line vote on May 9, and the Senate followed 53–47 on May 10. Five Democratic senators voted in favor of the proposal—Breaux (LA), Miller (GA), Cleland (GA), Baucus (MT), and Nelson (NB)—while two Republicans voted against it—Jeffords (VT) and Chafee (RI).

25. The proposals were part of the reauthorization of the 1965 Elementary and Secondary Education Act.

26. Dana Milbank, "Bush Makes Education First Initiative," *Washington Post,* January 24, 2001. Bush also seemed to signal his willingness to compromise on vouchers in his first Saturday radio address on January 27 when he acknowledged there were "some honest differences of opinion in Congress" about the "better options" parents should be given in failing schools. "Others suggest different approaches, and I'm willing to listen." Frank Bruni, "In First Radio Address, Bush Softens on School Vouchers," *New York Times,* January 28, 2001.

27. Jeffords, *My Declaration of Independence.* In his subsequent longer memoir, Jeffords discusses in greater length his reservations with the Bush education plan and the legislative strategy that the White House employed: "The White House and I started out a little rocky on this legislation, as the administration was wedded throughout February to a strategy of ignoring the deliberations in the [education] committee and concentrating its attention on the House and Senate floor. This seemed unwise in my view, as the committee could, would, and did give the president most of what he sought." Interestingly, in the next paragraph, Jeffords also discusses his reaction to not being invited to the White House ceremony honoring the teacher of the year, who happened to be from Vermont, a first for the state. Jeffords was informed that no member of Congress had been invited to the ceremony, and as he notes, "I left it at that." But then he goes on to state, "But it was hard not to wonder if the decision not to invite me was designed to send a message. . . . As the press began to focus on the decision of the White House, the rationale for why I had not been invited began to sound a little thin." Jeffords, *An Independent Man,* pp. 264–265.

28. The Senate Health and Education Committee, then under GOP control, eliminated vouchers in the bill it reported to the full Senate on March 8. So too with the House Education and Workforce Committee, which voted 27–20 to eliminate vouchers on May 2. Although conservative Republicans in the House took their fight to retain vouchers to the floor of the House, their efforts failed on May 23, when the House voted down an amendment to restore vouchers 273–155. In the full Senate, now under Democratic control, vouchers lost by a lopsided vote of 58–41 on June 12.

29. Mike Allen and Michael Fletcher, "Bush Campaign Aims to Put Education on Fast Track," *Washington Post,* September 7, 2001. In the conference committee, funding, some of the details and timetables on testing, and how to measure "failing" schools proved to be sticking points and an impasse persisted through the summer of 2001.

30. The bill required states to conduct state-administered reading and math tests for grades three through eight, and it penalized schools that failed to meet a minimum proficiency level within twelve years. It targeted federal aid better by providing more of it to failing schools and increased funding for schools with disadvantaged students, as well as allowing school districts greater flexibility in using up to 50 percent of the federal funds they received. It also allowed parents to transfer students from failing schools to other public schools and it also provided them with $500 to $1,000 in federal funds for tutoring and other remedial aid. Federal funds of $1 billion were specifically targeted to improve reading skills by the third grade. Implementation of the bill began to run into problems almost immediately. Some school districts began to balk at implementing the school transfer plan for failing schools. Ohio fiddled with test scores to reduce the number of failing schools to 212. In Los Angeles, the school district pleaded overcrowded schools, while in Baltimore, where 30,000 students were enrolled, only 200 openings were deemed available in nonfailing schools. In the Chicago school district, 125,000 students in 179 schools were deemed eligible for

transfer. Chester E. Finn, "Leaving Many Children Behind," *Weekly Standard,* August 26, 2002. In November 2002, the Department of Education sought to rectify the delay by announcing new regulations that would facilitate parents' ability to transfer their children from failing public schools. The regulations said that a transfer had to be offered even if spaces were not available in other schools. The bill also had other problematic consequences, particularly the absence of a national standard on what constituted a "failing" public school. As a result, states with higher testing standards might yield higher numbers of failing schools and then become subject to federal regulations, sanctions, and requirements such as busing to alternative schools. Richard Rothstein, "How U.S. Punishes States with Higher Standards," *New York Times,* September 18, 2002. For a more positive assessment of the No Child Left Behind Act and a rebuttal of its critics, see Katherine Mangu-Ward, "No Demagogue Left Behind: The Dishonest Assault on Bush's Education Reform," *Weekly Standard*, March 29, 2004.

31. Dana Milbank, "With Fanfare, Bush Signs Education Bill," *Washington Post,* January 9, 2002.

32. Legislative authorization and actual budgeted spending can differ. In a January 20, 2003, article, *Time* magazine's Joel Klein noted, "Bush decided to spend only $22.1 billion of it, which was less than he had been spending before the extravagantly titled Leave No Child Behind Act was passed." Joel Klein, "Is Leadership in the Details?" *Time,* January 20, 2003. Bush's 2004 budget request was another $6 billion short of what legislation had authorized.

33. Mike Allen, "Bush Tries to Maintain Grade on Education," *Washington Post,* March 3, 2002. Respondents were asked whether the following statement was true or false: "Congress passed an education reform bill this year and President Bush has signed it into law."

34. The argument for vouchers was given a major boost on June 27, 2002, when the Supreme Court ruled, 5–4, that the voucher system used in Cleveland Ohio passed constitutional muster, even though the vast majority (over 95 percent) of parents used the vouchers to send their children to parochial schools. In a July 1, 2002, speech in Cleveland, President Bush lauded the decision and said it was "just as historic" as the 1954 Brown decision outlawing segregation in public schools.

35. Jim VandeHei, "Education Law May Hurt Bush," *Washington Post,* October 13, 2003.

36. Charitable choice provisions were also added in 1998 to the block grant program for community services, and, in 2000, to block grants for the treatment of substance abuse and the program for assistance in transition from homelessness.

37. Dana Milbank, "Defending 'Faith-Based' Plan," *Washington Post,* March 7, 2001.

38. Bush's 2001 tax reform bill, however, did not include a new deduction for charitable contributions, a measure that might have raised upward of $15 billion more for charities each year but would lead to a loss, over ten years, of $84 billion in revenue. Estimate comes from Independent Sector, an association of nonprofit organizations. Dana Milbank and Thomas Edsall, "Faith Initiative May be Revised," *Washington Post,* March 12, 2001.

39. Although DiIulio had met with Gore in 1999 to discuss faith-based efforts, he had also been contacted by members of the Bush campaign, and had advised Bush on a July 1999 speech on compassionate conservatism. During the GOP convention in Philadelphia, he met with Bush and two of Bush's domestic advisers, former mayor Stephen Goldsmith of Indianapolis and Governor Tom Ridge (R-PA). Fred Barnes, "The Minister of Ministries," *Weekly Standard,* February 12, 2001. The other leading contender for the position was Goldsmith. Goldsmith, according to reports, turned

down the offer to head the new office and he had earlier been passed over as secretary of housing and urban development. Goldsmith was then tapped to serve as an unpaid adviser and chair of the Corporation for National Service, which was to work with DiIulio's new office and other national service programs such as AmeriCorps. Dana Milbank, "Bush Unveils 'Faith-Based' Initiative," *Washington Post,* January 30, 2001. According to another account, Goldsmith had pressed Cheney to elevate the faith-based position to cabinet status, but Cheney refused: "You don't make a counterproposal to the president." Yet when Bush turned to DiIulio, the latter won an important concession of his own: "faith-based" would precede "community initiatives" in the title of the new White House office. Fred Barnes, "The Minister of Ministries," *Weekly Standard,* February 12, 2001.

40. The two were Don Willett, a lawyer who had worked in Bush's gubernatorial administration, and Don Eberly, a former Reagan administration official and consultant to the Bush campaign on faith-based programs; Eberly later became DiIulio's deputy at OFBCI.

41. Tenpas, "Can an Office Change a Country?" pp. 4–5.

42. Ibid., p. 8.

43. Laurie Goodstein, "Nudging Church-State Line, Bush Invites Religious Groups to Seek Federal Aid," *New York Times,* January 30, 2001.

44. Laurie Goodstein, "Bush's Call to Church Groups to Get Untraditional Replies," *New York Times,* February 14, 2001.

45. Thomas Edsall, "Robertson Joins Liberals in Faulting Bush's 'Faith-Based' Plan," *Washington Post,* February 22, 2001.

46. Dana Milbank and Thomas Edsall, "Faith Initiative May be Revised," *Washington Post,* March 12, 2001.

47. Dana Milbank, "In Bush Cabinet, It's Both Advise and Dissent," *Washington Post,* March 10, 2001.

48. Elizabeth Becker, "Head of Religion-Based Initiative Resigns," *New York Times,* August 18, 2001.

49. As the bill encountered opposition in the House, the White House agreed to add stricter language that would require the same self-auditing requirements as other government contractors, would have accounting requirements separating federal from private contributions, and would permit individuals to opt out of the religious components of the program without losing services. Mike Allen, "Bush Aims to Get Faith Initiative Back on Track," *Washington Post,* June 25, 2001. The bill also reduced the charitable deduction for nonitemizers from $84 billion over ten years to $6.3 billion, a major departure from the Bush proposal. The House did this by reducing the deduction to $25 (for single filers) and $50 (for joint filers), small amounts given the estimated $328 contributed by the average nonitemizer. The House bill contained a provision to allow federal agencies to provide vouchers to clients rather than pass money directly to service providers. It required that any religious activities be funded privately, and that individuals must be able to choose a competing secular program when religious groups are directly funded.

50. The House bill provided that religious groups had a right to control "the definition, development, practice, and expression" of their religious beliefs in faith-based programs. In an article for the *Weekly Standard,* written after he had left the White House, DiIulio maintained that the "beliefs and tenets" provision of the amendment that would have permitted discrimination had been removed by the House Judiciary Committee in June. Moreover, according to DiIulio, it was the White House's consistent position that the proposal should neither add to nor subtract from existing civil rights and other laws. In his view, this would permit hiring practices that allow religion

to be taken into account (consistent with the 1964 civil rights act, a 1972 statute, and rulings of the Supreme Court) and it would have maintained the so-called ministerial exception that allowed exemptions for service providers with under fifteen full-time paid employees. John J. DiIulio Jr., "Bush Keeps the Faith," *Weekly Standard,* February 18, 2002.

51. In March, GOP leaders decided to split the proposal in two: it would move more quickly on a charitable deduction proposal that had bipartisan support, but it would proceed more slowly on "charitable choice." The White House reportedly concurred with the new, albeit slower, approach. Dana Milbank, "Senators Slow Action on Faith-Based Aid," *Washington Post,* March 14, 2001.

52. For example, on May 20, Bush gave the commencement address at Notre Dame University, especially urging a new war on poverty through faith-based initiatives. On June 5, Bush was in Florida, working at a Habitat for Humanity project.

53. On July 25, 2001, Bush met with Senators Joe Lieberman (D-CT) and Rick Santorum (R-PA) and indicated his willingness to support revision of the controversial portions of the House bill dealing with state and local civil rights laws. "Everything is on the table," according to one Republican Senate aide. Frank Bruni, "Senator Says Bush Is Open to Revising Charity-Aid Bill," *New York Times,* July 27, 2001. On August 1, Santorum, floor leader of the bill on the GOP side, announced that he would drop the provision in his Senate version of the House bill that would have provided exemption from state and local antidiscrimination laws: "Let's remove the issue and move on," he told reporters. Dana Milbank, "Senate Faith Initiative Backer to Drop Disputed Provisions," *Washington Post,* August 2, 2001.

54. Health and personal reasons were also cited as underlying his departure. DiIulio had retained his residence in Philadelphia, commuting to Washington on the 4:05 A.M. train each morning. It took until February 2002 to have a replacement for DiIulio on board: James Towey, a former aide to Senator Mark Hatfield (R-OR) who had also worked for Mother Teresa's organization.

55. John DiIulio to Ron Suskind, "Your Next Essay on the Bush Administration," October 24, 2002; Drudge Report, "Bush Aide's Letter to Esquire Reporter Revealed," www.drudgereport.com, December 2, 2002. DiIulio would later note that the hiring issue became the "most contentious" of the issues surrounding the proposal. But despite his entreaties, his colleagues in the White House failed to focus on the "important practical question" of whether most religious groups took religion into account in their hiring practices; in his view the number was "trivial." John DiIulio, panel discussion, "Still Keeping the Faith? President Bush and the Faith-Based Initiative," Annual Meeting of the American Political Science Association, Philadelphia, August 29, 2003.

56. John J. DiIulio Jr., "A View from Within," in Greenstein, *The George W. Bush Presidency,* p. 255.

57. The White House hoped, however, that some charitable choice provisions might be retained to aid children of prisoners and other more limited applications. See Elizabeth Becker, "Bush Is Said to Scale Back His Religion-Based Initiative," *New York Times,* October 14, 2001.

58. The committee's bill reduced Bush's proposal that those who do not itemize taxes be allowed to deduct $800. The thinking was that the standard deduction for non-itemizers was already generous. Instead, the committee proposed that the first $500 of contributions not be deductible, but that contributions from that amount up to $1,000 be eligible for the deduction. It also attempted to overcome some of the barriers that the Office of Faith-Based Initiatives and the five departmental analysis units had identified in their August 2001 report to the president. Its cost was estimated at $10 billion over ten years. In late June and early July 2002, Bush made several public appearances

in Ohio, Florida, and Wisconsin to continue to push his faith-based initiatives program as well as his proposals for education vouchers. Press Secretary Ari Fleischer declined to comment on whether Bush would sign the much-reduced faith-based initiative bill that was still under Senate consideration. Scott Lindlaw, "Bush Touts Religion-Based Program, Welfare Overhaul," *Washington Post*, July 2, 2002.

59. A second executive order expanded the number of department-based centers for faith-based initiatives to include the Department of Agriculture and the Agency for International Development. Bush also ordered the Federal Emergency Management Agency to revise its policies on emergency and disaster-relief aid to include faith-based groups. According to some analysts, the executive orders were close to the compromise legislation on faith-based initiatives that had been worked out by Senators Santorum and Lieberman, but that had not been passed. Lieberman felt that the new orders did not ignore existing state and local civil rights laws and "on the surface it sounds like a sound plan for realizing the principal of equal treatment for faith-based groups." Richard Stevenson, "Bush Will Allow Religious Groups to Receive U.S. Aid," *New York Times*, December 13, 2002. Bush's orders also allowed religious groups to display religious objects in the physical settings where services were provided but not to engage in religious instruction.

60. Senator Santorum continued to press for congressional action that would enact charitable choice and Bush's executive orders into law. But even when the GOP regained control of the Senate in 2003, charitable choice continued to generate strong opposition. In March, Santorum agreed to strip it from his version of the bill, in hope that the Senate would speedily pass the surviving parts of the proposal, largely dealing now with tax deductions for charitable contributions. See Sheryl Gay Stolberg, "Senators Set Deal on Religion-Based Initiative," *New York Times*, March 29, 2003.

61. Bush's original $90 billion plan, spread over ten years, was reduced to $13 billion (16.6 percent of the original proposal), much of it going to its tax deduction provision of $250 (above the first $250) in charitable contributions for nonitemizers. Also included were $150 million per year to help faith-based and community groups apply for federal funding and $1.4 billion over two years in block grants to states for social welfare programs. The White House was not happy, however, with the block grant allocation, which exceeded Bush's budget request.

62. Dana Milbank, "Bush Legislative Approach Failed in Faith Bill Battle," *Washington Post*, April 23, 2003.

63. Mike Allen and Alan Cooperman, "Bush Backs Religious Charities on Hiring," *Washington Post*, June 25, 2003.

64. James Carney, "A Few Small Repairs," *Time*, July 8, 2001; also see Frum, *The Right Man*, p. 73.

65. On August 1, 2001, Norwood met with Josh Bolten, deputy chief of staff and the senior domestic policy adviser, then had a twenty-minute session with Bush. At 5:30 P.M., Bush and Norwood appeared before press and announced a deal. On August 2 the House voted 226–203 in favor of the compromise bill, with no GOP defections. Key to swift passage was an amendment that incorporated the deal with Norwood, which passed by 218–213, with three Democrats and Virgil Goode (I-VA) joining 214 GOP members.

66. Bush touched briefly on patients' bill of rights in his 2003 State of the Union address (one sentence); no bill was filed in the Senate, while Representative Norwood introduced a bill in the House but without any cosponsors. Amy Goldstein, "For Patients' Rights, a Quiet Fadeaway," *Washington Post*, September 12, 2003.

67. Amy Goldstein, "Prescription Drug Plan Sent to Skeptical Congress," *Washington Post*, January 30, 2001.

68. The bill passed the House shortly before dawn on Saturday, November 22, 2003, by the narrow margin of 220–215 and following an unprecedented three-hour roll call. Attempts at a filibuster failed in the Senate, and the bill finally passed by a 54–44 vote on November 25, 2003. Bush signed the bill on December 8. In March 2004, media reports disclosed that the administration had been informed by one of its own analysts, before the bill passed, that its projected costs would be $534 billion rather than $400 billion and that this information had been kept from Congress. Richard S. Foster, the chief actuary of Medicare who had compiled the higher projection, also disclosed that an administration official had threatened to fire him if he informed Congress of his findings. Amy Goldstein, "Official Says He Was Told to Withhold Medicare Data," *Washington Post*, March 13, 2004.

69. Michael Fletcher, "Social Security Changes Put on the Back Burner," *Washington Post,* November 11, 2002.

70. On March 29, Bush did announce at a press conference, in the face of strong opposition in Congress, that he was prepared to look for oil and gas resources elsewhere, but not necessarily the ANWR. See Katherine Q. Seelye, "Facing Obstacles on Arctic Oil, Bush Says He'll Look Elsewhere," *New York Times,* March 30, 2001.

71. How to respond to the negative coverage of both energy policy as well as some of the environmental recommendations that Bush planned to rescind presented a particular problem to Karen Hughes, Bush's chief media and communications adviser. In April, Hughes convened a strategy meeting to try to tailor a strategy for turning the energy and environment issue around: in her view, they were "killing us." James Carney, "A Few Small Repairs," *Time,* July 8, 2001.

72. In one suit, brought by public interest groups, the Energy Department was the defendant and ordered to turn over documents relating to matters it possessed related to the task force's work.

73. The GAO, acting under a request by Representatives Henry Waxman (D-CA) and John Dingell (D-MI), sought information about meetings, attendees, and costs of the task force, as well as matters discussed and who met with Cheney personally. The White House refused the request, citing the GAO's lack of authority to request the material. The White House claimed that the GAO could only investigate under the statutory authority of "existing law," but that Cheney's task force operated under the broader cover of the president's constitutional authority. The GAO was not satisfied with the explanation and on July 18, after two months of unsuccessful effort, issued a letter of demand, the final step before a court order. Ryan Lizza, "Go Away," *New Republic,* July 9, 2001. White House spokesperson Anne Womack told reporters the letter "was under review, and we're going to continue to work with the GAO to resolve this issue appropriately." Some federal records of the task force were subsequently released, but not all that the GAO had requested. The issue went to federal district court in 2002 and on February 7, 2003, the district court ruled that the GAO lacked legal standing to sue. The GAO decided not to appeal the decision. In separate litigation brought by the Sierra Club and Judicial Watch, a federal district court judge denied a motion to dismiss the case; the Justice Department then appealed the ruling on Cheney's behalf, but lost 2–1 at the D.C. federal appeals court in July 2003. On September 11, 2003, the full D.C. appeals court, by a vote of 5–3, also found against the administration and upheld the lower court's decision to let the case go forward and for the administration to produce the documents requested by the plaintiffs. On December 15, 2003, the Supreme Court agreed to hear Cheney's appeal. Cheney was also criticized, one week after the energy proposal was released, for hosting a reception at the vice president's residence that honored donors who had given more than $100,000 to the Republican Party, some of whom were energy industry officials and

lobbyists who had contacts with the task force. The White House was quick to empha-size that it was not a fundraising event, but merely a "thank you" to donors, who were also in town to attend a fundraising event that President Bush was to hold. The inci-dent also led to one of the few reports of internal White House bickering. In this instance, Cheney aide Mary Matalin was singled out for criticism by unnamed White House aides as the one responsible for getting Cheney to agree to the event. Accord-ing to one report, Matalin "has always been suspect among the Bush team. It's well known in the inner circle that the new president feels she didn't serve his father well as a 1992 campaign adviser, and he had to be talked into letting her join W.'s White House staff. . . . Bush sources also claim that Matalin is talking too much to the press, citing anonymous quotes that aren't 'on message'—a capital offense in the Bush camp." "Texas Posse Wants Cheney to Give Matalin the Boot," *Washingtonian,* July 2001. Within the Cheney camp, the culprit was Karl Rove and the Republican National Committee (RNC), plus the explanation that Cheney only agreed to the event as a favor. Mike Allen and Ruth Marcus, "White House Is Divided over Big Donors Ses-sion," *Washington Post,* May 25, 2001.

74. Mike Allen, "GAO Cites Corporate Shaping of Energy Plan," *Washington Post,* August 26, 2003.

75. Senate Majority Leader Trent Lott, after considerable negotiation with Sena-tors McCain and Feingold, also promised that the Senate would consider the bill early on in March and that he would discourage attempts to filibuster or other procedural maneuvers to kill debate and prevent a floor vote.

76. Alison Mitchell, "Bush and McCain Meet on Campaign Finance," *New York Times,* January 25, 2001.

77. In the 2000 election cycle, Democrats and the GOP were almost equal in soft money: $244 million for the GOP, $243 million for Democrats. The difference was in hard money: $447 million for the GOP, $270 million for the Democrats. In 1988 the total amount of soft money was only $45 million.

78. Hagel's bill would have limited rather than banned soft money contributions and would have raised the amounts in hard money that could be contributed to candi-dates and parties. Hagel, according to reports, had met on a number of occasions with Karl Rove and Josh Bolten, deputy White House chief of staff. See Dan Balz and Ruth Marcus, "Bush to Offer Campaign Finance Guidelines," *Washington Post,* March 15, 2001.

79. On March 21 the Senate rejected a "paycheck protection" amendment 69–31. By a 60–40 vote, the Senate also rejected an amendment requiring unions and corpo-rations to disclose their political activities and contributions. On March 27 the Senate defeated important parts of Hagel's alternative bill 60–40, particularly his proposal to only limit soft money. McCain also continued to hold on to his Democratic allies after a successful amendment that raised the contribution limit on hard money donations (where Democrats traditionally lag behind the GOP) from $1,000 to $2,000; the vote was 84–16.

80. Democrats voting against the bill were Hollings (SC), Breaux (LA), and Nel-son (NE). GOP members in favor of the bill were Chafee (RI), Cochran (MI), Collins (ME), Domenici (NM), Fitzgerald (IL), Jeffords (VT), Lugar (IN), McCain (AZ), Snowe (ME), Specter (PA), Stevens (AK), and Thompson (TN). As amended, the McCain-Feingold bill had four major components: (1) a ban on soft money donations by corporations, unions, and individuals; (2) higher ceilings on hard money— $2,000—indexed, with a cap of $37,500; (3) restriction on corporations, unions, and many advocacy groups from running ads that mention a federal candidate sixty days before a federal general election and thirty days before a primary for a federal office;

and (4) a requirement that television stations offer discount rates for campaign commercials.

81. Speaker Hastert had wanted to bring each of the proposed changes (in order to match the Senate's bill and to broaden support) that Shays and Meehan had wanted up for individual floor votes, a procedure that the supporters of the bill believed would doom chances of having an acceptable final bill before the House as well as to avoid a conference committee that would have been likely stacked—on the House side—by members opposed to the bill. The House voted 228–203 to reject Hastert's ground rules, with nineteen GOP members defecting. Hastert then announced that he had no further plan for considering the two bills.

82. Forty-one Republicans broke with the GOP leadership and supported the bill, while only twelve Democrats voted against it. The House bill differed in some details from the bill passed by the Senate. The date that it would come into effect was pushed back until after the November 2002 congressional elections, and the House version dropped a Senate provision that would have required discounts on television advertisements.

83. Juliet Eilperin and Helen Dewar, "House Passes Campaign Finance Bill," *Washington Post,* February 14, 2002.

84. Opponents of the bill were thwarted in their efforts to block it. Majority Leader Daschle forced consideration of the House version of the bill, thereby avoiding a conference committee that might have stopped it. On March 20 the Senate voted 68–32 to stop debate on the bill, well over the sixty votes needed to prevent a filibuster.

85. Howard Fineman, "Everything Will Change, Or Not," *Newsweek,* February 25, 2002. Yet reports indicated that the White House had consented to efforts by the Republican National Committee to defeat it by targeting thirty-three GOP House members who had voted in favor of the bill in previous years when it was clear it would not become law because of Senate opposition. Those members were contacted directly by the RNC and encouraged to support amendments that would weaken the bill, and their names were passed on to Washington lobbyists. Revelations of the effort caught the White House in a bit of controversy since it indicated behind-the-scenes opposition. Dan Bartlett, White House communications director, denied that the White House was working through the party to derail the bill. Bartlett also signaled that Bush would not get directly involved in the legislative battle, nor should opponents of the legislation "count on a veto from the president." Richard Berke and Alison Mitchell, "Finance Limits Are Undercut in White House," *New York Times,* February 12, 2002.

86. Mike Allen, "Bush Signs Campaign Bill, Hits Road to Raise Money," *Washington Post,* March 28, 2002. Karen Hughes had argued for the traditional public signing ceremony, but that was opposed by Rove and Calio. Hughes, *Ten Minutes from Normal,* p. 293.

87. *McConnell v. Federal Elections Commission* (2003). The Court issued a number of rulings on various parts of the bill, with a 5–4 vote on the most controversial dealing with soft money contributions and new rules limiting certain types of political advertising by individuals or groups shortly before federal primary or general elections. The only provisions in the law that the Court struck down, both unanimously, dealt with prohibitions on campaign contributions by minors and a requirement that parties be forced to choose between the types of expenditures ("unlimited independent" versus "limited coordinated") provided to their federal nominees.

88. *USA Today,* July 13, 2001.

89. Edwin Chen and Janet Hook, "President Basking in Victories," *Los Angeles Times,* August 4, 2001.

7

After September 11: Continuity and Change

The events of September 11, 2001, present a difficult challenge for understanding the effects a presidential transition and the early days and months of a new presidency can have upon its subsequent history and its success and failures. No U.S. presidency before George W. Bush's—at least those elected to office—encountered an event or a series of events during its first year that would so thoroughly mark a disjuncture from what had proceeded before it. The closest historical parallels of presidencies whose first years in office were fraught with grave challenges are those of Abraham Lincoln and Franklin Roosevelt. Yet for both, the difficulties they would face were clearly apparent before they took office. For Lincoln, the Civil War indeed erupted after his inauguration, but secession had already occurred and the Confederacy had been established. For Roosevelt, coping with the Great Depression was the centerpiece of his campaign for office and the major preoccupation of his transition. Nor have vice presidents who assume power faced a similar challenge, perhaps with one exception. Their predicament is indeed significant and not forewarned, but it is more personal and immediate: their preparation and ability to assume office, not an external and unexpected event(s) of grave consequences. Only Truman's accession to office presents a case where a vice president both took office and was forced to cope with a series of events that would significantly alter a presidency—the end of a world war and the challenges of demobilization, reconstruction, postwar foreign policy, the onset of the Cold War, and most unpredictably (at least for Truman), the dilemmas posed by the use of nuclear weaponry and the dawning of the nuclear age.

Whether Harry Truman or George W. Bush had the most difficult go of it, I do not propose to settle. But the events of September 11 and its aftermath forced an administration that valued discipline, order, and preparation to deal with an environment that was constantly in flux: the catastrophes of that day, the war against the terrorists, homeland security, war in Afghanistan, and war and postwar reconstruction in Iraq, to name only the most important. It was also a presidency that enjoyed an unusual degree of public support for at least a year after the attacks. Presidents typically gain in their approval ratings following dramatic events, usually in the area of foreign policy. The degree of gain and its length vary (although most are usually short-lived). Bush's "rally around the flag" was unusual. As Michael Nelson has noted, it "was steeper (Bush's thirty-five point jump in approval nearly doubled the previous record), higher (his peak of 90 percent was the highest any president has ever achieved), and longer lasting (Bush remained above his pre–September 11 peak for more than a year) than any in recorded history."[1]

Much clearly changed in this presidency and, perhaps, in this president. The lessons learned earlier that prepared for what can reasonably be regarded as a successful transition to office were not the ones that could serve as a ready and reliable guide for the challenges posed after September 11. What past historical case, challenge, or context could?

Yet while September 11 marked a clear disjuncture and others would follow, what came before also mattered. As Martha Joynt Kumar has observed:

> When terrorists struck on September 11, 2001, President Bush's responses would develop from information and decision-making channels established well before he entered the White House. Organizational work during the transition and the people he brought into his administration shaped the structure he needed to respond. While transitions color the start of an administration and its good will, they are even more significant for how the administration operates.[2]

Bush and His War Cabinet

A Wartime President: Change?

Conventional wisdom suggests that September 11 transformed this president. And in some ways—but only some—that is correct. Foreign policy had not been a major theme of the campaign. Bush himself, prior to assuming office, had traveled little abroad; during the campaign he had been tripped up even knowing the names of some foreign leaders, much less claiming some personal acquaintance with them. Here was a presidency that, over its first eight months in office, had been largely preoccupied with its domestic political agenda. And some of the foreign policy initiatives that had taken place signaled a posture of unilateralism rather than multilateralism, of disengagement rather than more muscular involvement: withdrawal from the anti–ballistic missile treaty with Russia, disavowal of the Kyoto protocol on global warming, concerns about peace talks between North and South Korea, and a more cautious and less direct approach to resolving the Israel-Palestine conflict, most notably. The administration's greatest successes were in forging new agreements with one of America's closest neighbors, Mexico. But after September 11, foreign affairs would come to preoccupy this presidency and likely even define it historically. "This is now the focus of my administration," Bush publicly declared.[3] September 11, according to Colin Powell, "hit the reset button" on U.S. foreign policy.[4] Disengagement, to the degree it existed, was no longer possible, but unilateralism would remain, culminating in what would come to be termed the Bush doctrine of "preemption."

Not only was there a transformation in agenda, but there was significant change in this president as well. During his early months in office, Bush had successfully put the issue of how he had become president behind him and had established his legitimacy. But after September 11, his leadership was more firmly entrenched; who he was as president became more firmly established, if not embraced, in the public's mind. As Bob Woodward has noted, "He had assumed the aura of president, had it imposed on himself."[5] For the American public, that change was most notable in Bush's remarks, on September 14, at the memorial service held in the Washington National Cathedral and, later that day, during his visit to the site of the World Trade Center, followed by an address to a joint session of Congress on September 20. Bush's more tentative rhetorical performance on the day of September 11 was replaced by a surer, more confident leader. His remarks at the National Cathedral, as Bush speech writer David Frum has noted, "reassured Americans that the war would be fought for just purposes," while his impromptu comments at the trade center site "promised it would be fought with decisive methods."[6]

In the aftermath of September 11, Bush's focus of attention clearly shifted to the issues and decisions that the war against the terrorists raised. His working day would begin with the "threat assessment," a written compilation from a variety of intelligence and law enforcement sources. His so-called war cabinet—Cheney, Powell, Rumsfeld, Rice, Card, O'Neill, Central Intelligence Agency (CIA) director Tenet, and on occasion some of their deputies—met frequently with him, including an almost daily meeting in the Situation Room of the White House. Bush's daily briefing by the director of the CIA at 8:00 A.M. stretched longer, and it was now followed by a briefing by the Federal Bureau of Investigation (FBI) and Attorney General Ashcroft at 8:30.[7] Full meetings of the National Security Council (NSC) were convened more frequently: three times a week in the period shortly after September 11, then increasing to four or five a week, and sometimes even twice a day.[8]

A Wartime President: Continuity

Yet what emerged from within the inner core of this presidency was in continuity with its past. Bush himself would prove to be decisive, willing to make decisions, and willing to stick to them, as he had been before. As Frum observes, "Within hours of the attack, he had made two crucial decisions that would determine the aims and conduct of the whole war on terror. . . . The first crucial decision was to recognize that this war *was* a war. . . . The second big decision was to hold responsible for those acts of war not merely the terrorists who committed them, but also the governments that aided, abetted, financed, and shielded terrorism."[9] Both would mark a profound change in U.S. foreign policy.

Implementing those broad decisions largely followed the pattern developed earlier in his presidency: delegate the crafting of plans to his subordinates, but with more active involvement when matters reached the presidential level for decisionmaking. According to journalist Bill Sammon in his book on the post–September 11 Bush presidency, Bush continued his practice of "working on a problem diligently, surrounding himself with thoughtful people, soliciting their advice, and then making decisions without a lot of anguished second guessing. More often than not, this strategy proved successful."[10]

Bush's engagement began immediately. According to one aide, "From the very beginning the president decided he wanted to chair the NSC meetings . . . because I think he didn't want a process where options were coming up to him, where we had to say 'A thinks this, B thinks this, the consensus should be this.' . . . In the earliest phases, he chaired and we had our intellectual discussions about strategy—everybody, with the president there. It was great."[11] According to Bob Woodward, "This was a commander in chief function—it could not be delegated. He also wanted to send the signal that it was he who was calling the shots, that he had the team in harness."[12]

Those meetings were especially crucial in Bush's decision to focus on Al-Qaida rather than to go after a range of terrorist organizations and (at the time) Iraq, as some of Bush's more hawkish advisers, Rumsfeld's deputy Paul Wolfowitz most notably, were pressing for. In particular, on Friday, September 14, and continuing on through the next day, Bush convened a series of meetings at Camp David with his foreign policy principals and their deputies: the general consensus was that Al-Qaida and the Taliban regime in Afghanistan would be the immediate targets. Back at the White House the next day, Bush told NSC adviser Rice that his mind was made up: Iraq would wait.[13] More generally, according to Bill Sammon, "few people were more directly involved in America's response than the commander in chief himself. It was Bush who decided when and how to unleash the punishing, relentless counterattacks. It was Bush who took responsibility for sending young Americans into harm's way, knowing that some would surely die."[14] Similarly, as journalist Frank Bruni reports in his book on the early Bush presidency, "Aides said he was asking more questions in . . . meetings, grilling his advisers with more requests for explanations and often demanding to talk not only to the deputy from an administration agency who was giving him a briefing but to the head of the agency."[15]

A campaign of sustained air strikes against the Taliban began on October 7. Several weeks later, critics were questioning the progress of the war, particularly the strategy of relying heavily on the ground efforts of the Northern Alliance, a loose conglomeration of warlord-led groups opposed to the Taliban. But by mid-November the Afghan capital of Kabul had fallen, and by early December the Taliban regime had been defeated. Later that month an interim government was set up. Opposition to the new regime, however, periodically flared through 2002 and 2003.

By the summer of 2002, Iraq was on the front burner. Once it was clear that war might occur, Bush pressed his advisers as he had done earlier. According to one account, "Aides said he questioned whether the plan was too conventional, what the Iraqis might have learned from the 1991 Persian Gulf War, and he constantly asks what can go wrong with the plans and how ready the generals are if something does go wrong." On September 12, 2002, Bush took his case against Iraq to the United Nations, asking for the destruction of its weapons of mass destruction (WMD). On September 19, Bush asked Congress for the authority to "use all means" to disarm Iraq, which Congress approved by October 11.[16] The action then shifted to the UN Security Council, where Resolution 1441 was passed demanding a new round of weapons inspections. The UN's inspection teams, however, essentially came up empty-handed (some noncompliant missiles were found, but not WMD). The administration charged that the Iraqi government's formal declarations of compliance constituted a material breach of 1441; in a February address to the UN, Secretary of State Powell presented further evidence of Iraqi noncompliance. The UN Security Council, however, did not support a second resolution that the White House proposed, which would have authorized war against Iraq. On March 19, after giving Saddam Hussein forty-eight hours to leave Iraq, air strikes began, followed the next day by the introduction of U.S. and coalition ground forces.

Once the war was under way, Bush continued to press questions about Iraqi troop strengths, coalition troop morale, and the effectiveness of U.S. media communications with the Iraqi people.[17] But two notable areas of possible omission would emerge after the war was over: Had the president pressed his inner circle with sufficient vigor concerning the reliability of some of the evidence on which the case for war was based? Had the political, economic, and military situation in a postwar Iraq been sufficiently anticipated and had Iraq's pacification and reconstruction been adequately planned for?

Other strands of Bush's decisionmaking carried over after September 11. While willing to decide and act in the end, Bush was not hasty in his deliberations. As Frum observes:

[Bush] had another guiding principal. . . . He would not commit himself to any one course of action until he must. If Colin Powell wanted to try a diplomatic solution to a problem—and Donald Rumsfeld promised to have a military solution ready to go within three weeks—Bush would not say, "Right—we're doing it Don's way." He would say: "Colin—you have three weeks."

Furthermore, according to Frum, such a deliberative style fit Bush's own decisionmaking needs: "Sometimes, instead of trying one course of action first and then another later, Bush would allow both to develop, to give himself more time to decide which was superior."[18] Here, too, there was not a new deliberative style; rather, it was a willingness to listen to a variety of voices that Bush had exhibited earlier in his presidency and even during his governorship.

Once decisions had been made, strategy determined, and plans set, Bush did not micromanage the effort, as Lyndon Johnson had done during the Vietnam War. According to Chief of Staff Card, "He gets consulted, but consistent with how does that tactic help us achieve the overall mission. He isn't saying 'I want eight more tanks here,' [or] 'Why are you taking this division up this road.'" In the view of another aide, "He does not and will not micromanage the plan. Instead, what he does is pepper people with questions to ascertain how the plan is going and to get the latest details and the latest information."[19]

Another strand in Bush's conduct as a wartime president was a carryover from the past—a desire to stick with decisions and plans once they had been decided. According to one aide, "The plan is set, the plan is being implemented."[20] Bush's determination in this regard was especially notable as the war in Afghanistan began to take longer than some had anticipated. And it was Bush who pressed his war cabinet either to stick with the plan or come up with a better alternative: "We did agree on this strategy, didn't we?" Bush asked them.[21] According to Woodward's account of the meeting, Bush queried, "I just want to make sure that all of us did agree on this plan, right? . . . Anybody have any ideas they want to put on the table?" According to Woodward, Bush wanted "a precise affirmation from each one [and] each affirmed allegiance to the plan and strategy." As Bush later told Woodward: "If there is going to be a sense of despair, I want to know who it is, and why. I trust the team, and it is a team. And I trust them because I trust their judgment. And if people are having second thoughts about their judgment, I needed to know what they were, and they needed to lay them on the table."[22]

Bush also continued to take a direct role in providing suggestions to his speech writers and then editing their proposed rhetoric. In his televised address to the public on the evening of September 11, for example, it was Bush who inserted the word "harbor" in his call for action not just against the terrorists, but also against those who aided and abetted them. And according to Woodward, he wasn't happy with his speech writers' draft of his address to Congress on September 20: "He wasn't satisfied with a first draft. He wanted to conclude with a personal pledge to the American people, an ending along the lines of: This is my mission, my purpose, this is the nation's purpose. 'This is what my presidency is about.'" Late one evening, Bush called Michael Gerson, his head speech writer, went over the draft again, and proposed two dozen changes; further changes would be made on the day of the speech.[23]

A Wartime Cabinet

Within the broader circle of Bush's advisers, although the war against terrorism was first and foremost on the agenda and the war cabinet consumed more of the president's time and attention, decisionmaking and deliberative patterns before September 11 continued to be present. That Osama bin Laden and Al-Qaida represented a "tremendous" and "immediate" threat to the United States had been emphasized to then-president-elect Bush at a briefing by CIA director Tenet during the transition. In April 2001 the NSC deputies committee adopted a recommendation that the Northern Alliance in Afghanistan be armed on a large scale, a policy that the State Department had opposed under Clinton. By early September the "principals" had approved a plan that would provide the Northern Alliance with up to $200 million in arms a year to fight the Taliban regime. Ironically, on September 10, NSC adviser Rice had just finished a National Security Presidential Directive for Bush's approval that would have put the policy into effect.[24]

Another carryover before and after September was the principals themselves: Powell, Rumsfeld, Cheney, and Rice. Bush had already assembled an impressive foreign policy and defense team who could quickly adapt to the new and uncertain context of a war against terror. All had served in the White House before, two had been secretaries of defense in previous administrations (Rumsfeld and Cheney), one had been NSC adviser and then chairman of the Joint Chiefs of Staff (Powell), and two had been principals at the time of the first Gulf War (Powell and Cheney). In fact, according to one estimate, of the about dozen top foreign policy advisers to George W. Bush, more than half had played a key role, in some capacity, during the 1991 Gulf War: Rumsfeld's deputy, Paul Wolfowitz; Powell's deputy, Richard Armitage; Cheney's chief of staff, I. Lewis Libby; Powell's assistant secretary for policy planning, Richard Haass; Rice's deputy, Stephen Hadley; as well as Powell, Cheney, and Rice.

Yet unlike his father's foreign policy team, which had been more like-minded in their approach to foreign affairs, significant differences both strategically and in overall philosophy existed, most notably between Powell's multilateralism, on the one hand, and Rumsfeld's[25] and (to a lesser extent) Cheney's more hawkish approach, on the other. Those differences had been manifest early in the Bush presidency (the *New York Times* reported about them as early as late March 2001)[26] and they continued after September 11.

Despite the policy differences that would sometimes separate them, that Cheney and Powell had worked together before brought a degree of familiarity if not respect. So too did the even closer relationship between Rumsfeld and Cheney, one extending back to the Nixon presidency, when Rumsfeld had hired Cheney as his assistant in charge of congressional liaison when he was director of the Office of Economic Opportunity.[27] In Cheney's view, "Contrary to other administrations, you don't have to watch your backside when you go down to the Situation Room. What gets argued stays down there." According to Powell, "We argue but we almost always find the answer. We have political views. I am considered moderate. But everyone knows where everyone else is coming from." All three were past the age to harbor presidential ambitions of their own ("We're old," Rumsfeld told reporters in January 2002; "We're not positioning ourselves for the next job," Powell noted at the time).[28] Moreover, according to Powell, "creative tension" among Bush's principals served Bush's interests and "is quite manageable and appropriate. . . . The president would not be well served by cabinet officers and others in the administration who did not have strong views."[29]

Other Bush aides questioned whether the supposed differences among the principals were as deep as portrayed in the media. In the view of NSC adviser Rice, "I don't believe the caricature was right before [September 11]. And the caricature afterward is not right." In her view, "It's not a formal debating society," where participants lay out predictable positions. Rather, "These sessions are problem solving, so an issue will come on the table and some who were advocating one way at the beginning might be advocating the opposite at the end."[30]

Powell's and Rice's comments indicate the presence of healthy and constructive debate within the Bush inner circle. But some elements of the decisionmaking process remain troubling. For example, the positions taken by some of the principals, especially Powell and Rumsfeld, were often in line with the differing perspectives of their respective departments. Most notable was the urgency to enter into the Iraq war and, after the war was over, how and who should undertake Iraq's reconstruction. Bureaucratically grounded divisions also emerged between the CIA and the White House over the reliability of the evidence for going to war and, later, over the issue of whether White House aides, through leaks to the press, had blown the cover of a CIA operative. Bureaucratic politics is not usually a recipe for deliberative quality or successful policy decisions.

Another issue is whether the decisionmaking of this administration always took place within the collective context of the war cabinet, one in which—whether based on bureaucratic politics or not—the president was likely to be exposed to a range of views within a lively context of give-and-take and tough questioning. As Fred I. Greenstein has noted, some evidence seems to indicate that "Bush may sometimes be shielded from instructive debate." In August and early September 2002, for example, Colin Powell's *private* meetings with Bush and NSC adviser Rice seem to have been instrumental in the president's decision to take his case to the UN. "The shortcoming of policymaking by end run," Greenstein observes, "is that it places a premium on an adviser's bureaucratic skill and not just the merits of his or her recommendations."[31]

It is generally the responsibility of the NSC adviser to right any imbalances in the decisionmaking process; this is one of the functions of a "neutral broker" and a "managerial custodian."[32] Did Rice step into the breach? After September 11, Rice's role as NSC adviser seemed to evolve a bit, but not apparently in the direction of a better neutral broker or a strong and effective custodian of the decisionmaking *process*.[33] She remained the most intimate adviser to Bush, often spending weekends with him at Camp David and frequently meeting with him or otherwise being in contact during the workday. She reportedly became a bit more proactive in her advisory role rather than just serving as a policy coordinator. According to one administration official, "She started as a filter for competing views. Now she actively shapes the decisions."[34] When asked—in an October 2002 profile in *New Yorker* magazine—whether she tendered private advice to Bush, she acknowledged that she did, but without offering any clues as to the content of that advice or whether it differed from that of the other principals: "I have a very strong view about this, which is that the president does not need to read my views in the newspaper. Our discussions about my views are private."[35]

Her visibility as a spokesperson for the administration continued (although once war was under way, Rumsfeld became the daily face and voice of the administration). According to one White House aide, "The initial response is always to put Condi out first. She always has the exact tone and response the president wants. She's someone everyone feels entirely safe with."[36] It was Rice, for example, who briefed the press and the public before Bush's address to Congress on September 20, 2001.

Yet some of Rice's performance did not escape criticism, particularly her role in managing the flow of information, especially in making sure that all sides to an issue or a dispute were fairly and fully presented and their assumptions probed—activities at the core of the neutral broker or custodian role. Rice was a "yes man," according to one former government official. "She thinks her job is just to figure out what the president is trying to say and say it more articulately."[37] More generally, according to one account, some State and Defense Department officials complained that the policy process had become "dysfunctional": "Decisions go unmade at the deadlocked 'deputies' meetings or get kicked back or ignored by the president's 'principals,' his top advisers. The principals themselves tend to revisit unresolved issues or reopen decisions already made by the president."[38] At interagency meetings at lower levels in the process, according to one report, "the Defense Department sometimes doesn't even bother to show up," and at higher levels, the disagreements among the principals "have been allowed to spin out of control."[39] According to *Newsweek's* Evan Thomas, however, Rice "does not bear all the blame. She is dealing with some huge egos who have known each other for years, respect and by and large trust each other, but aren't afraid to fight."[40] The prospects of Rice's ability to ride herd over the NSC's deliberations were enhanced, after the Iraq war, with the appointment of Robert Blackwill, once Rice's boss in the Bush Sr. NSC staff, to the new NSC post of coordinator of strategic planning, a position designed to achieve better cohesion and long-range planning.[41]

One incident is particularly revealing about some of these inner tensions. In October 2003, Rice was placed in charge of a new "Iraq Stabilization Group," which was designed to ensure a stronger White House role in decisionmaking about that nation's postwar reconstruction. That the new group was needed is telling in its own right, particularly about perceptions of the effectiveness of the Defense Department's efforts in Iraq. But its public announcement as a "major restructuring" (by "a senior administration official" quoted in the *New York Times*—likely Rice) also led to some testiness on the part of Defense Secretary Rumsfeld. According to reports, Rumsfeld had only recently learned of the new group via a memo sent from Rice. Pressed by reporters, he seemed to indicate that not much was new here; such coordination was "what the responsibility of the NSC is and always has been, which is what's been going on."[42] Pressed further, Rumsfeld told them to ask Rice why the changes were necessary.

Not only were Rumsfeld's responses to press queries a bit testy, but the incident also raised the issue of the extent to which Rumsfeld had been involved in the decision to create the new group. Rumsfeld's own comments seemed to indicate that he had learned of it only in Rice's one-page memo. White House Press Secretary Scott McClellan later told reporters that Rumsfeld had been "very involved" in the change, a statement he seemed to retract a few days later when he told the press, "Maybe I should not have characterized it that way."[43] Other White House aides indicated that the creation of the new group had been discussed by members of the NSC, including Rumsfeld, as recently as the week before.[44] Whatever the level of Rumsfeld's knowledge of and participation in the creation of the new group, Rice's and the NSC's mandate had clearly been expanded. Whether she and the NSC staff would be able to assert control over the process and achieve better coordination and compliance remained the open questions.

War with Iraq: A Failure of Process?

While contentious debate may have been the usual order to the day among Bush's foreign policy principals, the decision process that led to the Iraq war raised the opposite concern: that a decision to go war had been made—"slipped into"—with deliberations turning to issues of "how" and "when," not "why" or "whether." Richard Haass, director of policy planning in the State Department, recalled a meeting with Rice in the first week of July 2002, when he raised the issue of whether Iraq should be the focus of concern in the war on terrorism: "She said essentially, that the decision's been made, don't waste your breath." Meetings were held in the spring of 2002, according to Haass, and "my staff would come back to me and report that there's something in the air here. So there was a sense that it was gathering momentum, but it was hard to put down." When Colin Powell had his August 2002 meetings with Bush, where he successfully pressed the case to secure a UN resolution, "the agenda was not whether Iraq, but how."[45] According to another account, when administration officials were asked "to recall how and when the president decided to invade Iraq, they had a hard time picking out one turning point." In the view of one State Department official, "We never had a decisive moment. It was like water dripping."[46]

But other accounts stressed the linkage to discoveries during the Afghanistan war that Al-Qaida had attempted to obtain weapons of mass destruction and that Iraq would be a likely supplier. According to one senior former official: "The eureka moment was that realization by the president that were a WMD to fall into [terrorist] hands, their willingness to use it would be unquestioned. So we must act pre-emptively to ensure that those who have that capability aren't allowed to proliferate it." Bush, moreover, became increasingly concerned about Saddam's brutality if not his basic sanity: "This fascination with Saddam's cruelty, says a source close to the White House, was neither ghoulish nor an expression of Bush's propensity to identify evil in the world. The point, says this adviser, is that Bush thinks Saddam is insane," according to one account. "If there is one thing standing between those who want WMDs and those who have them," according to this official, "it is this madman. Depending on the sanity of Saddam is not an option."[47]

That Saddam Hussein possessed weapons of mass destruction, however, remained an open question in the weeks and months after the war ended, as no weapons were found (based on a CIA assessment, the White House claimed, however, that two Iraqi vehicles that had been seized were in fact mobile weapons-producing labs, a claim that was in turn disputed by others). Other claims—particularly some of the evidence produced by Colin Powell in his presentation before the UN Security Council, assertions about the links between Iraq and Al-Qaida, and statements made by the president in his 2003 State of the Union address (notably the assertion, based on forged documents, that Iraq had purchased uranium "from Africa" for its nuclear weapons program)—were also called into question.[48] The issue of whether the administration had properly heeded CIA warnings about some of the evidence was also thrown into the mix.[49] In June 2003, Powell and Rice labeled the charges as "revisionist history" (a phrase that Bush would also later use),[50] with Rice noting that "successive CIA directors" in "successive administrations" had drawn the same conclusions as had Bush's foreign policy team.[51] However, the issue raised the question whether the administration had based its decision to go to war on faulty evidence or had overexaggerated or otherwise misinterpreted the evidence it did have. By early July 2003 the White House publicly acknowledged that Bush should not have included the claim about uranium purchases in his State of the Union address.[52] In the view of Senator Pat Roberts (R-KA), chairman of the Senate Intelligence Committee, the error indicated that "the process was broken" and was a sign of "sloppy coordination between State and CIA and the NSC and the White House."[53]

How the administration handled the controversy also raised concerns, especially given its track record of dealing with disagreements internally and rolling out a disciplined message. Initially, CIA director Tenet took the blame for allowing the reference to African uranium purchases, based on questionable foreign intelligence, to appear in the State of the Union address. But further investigation (helped along by leaks) revealed that Tenet had personally intervened with deputy NSC adviser Stephen Hadley to prevent a similar reference in Bush's October 7, 2002, speech, a major address in Cincinnati on the rationale for war against Iraq. Moreover, Hadley had received two memos from the CIA in October warning against claims about uranium purchases. On July 22, 2003, Hadley accepted blame for not remembering the CIA's counsel during the drafting of the State of the Union address. One positive development did come out of the controversy: a CIA officer was now assigned to participate in the speech-writing process.[54]

The issue also raised questions about NSC adviser Rice's role. One of the CIA's October 2002 warnings listed her as a recipient, although she later claimed that she did not know of the CIA's concerns then. CIA concerns were also raised in the National Intelligence Estimate issued in October 2002, perhaps the most important prewar assessment of Iraqi weapons programs. The CIA's reservations were in an annex to the ninety-page report. In July 2003 a senior administration official, asked if Rice had read the report, said that she may not have fully read it: "We have experts who work for the national security adviser who would know this information." As for the annex, she "did not read footnotes in a ninety-page document. . . . The national security adviser has people who do that." Nor had Hadley discussed with her the removal of the reference to uranium purchases in the October speech: "There was no need," he told reporters. As for the CIA memo listing her as a recipient, "I can't tell you she read it. I can't tell you she received it," Hadley noted.[55]

On July 24, former CIA director John Deutch, in testimony before the House Permanent Select Committee on Intelligence, said that the failure to find weapons of mass destruction in Iraq would signify "an intelligence failure . . . of massive proportions." It would mean that the "leaders of the American public based support for the most serious foreign policy judgments—the decision to go to war—on an incorrect intelligence judgment."[56] In late September 2003 the House Intelligence Committee issued an interim report, based on four months of study, in which it took the administration to task for building its case against Iraq on evidence that was "circumstantial," "fragmentary," overly reliant on "past assessments" dating before 1998, with only some new "piece-meal" evidence, which "were not challenged as a routine matter."[57] Administration officials, however, immediately disputed the claims; according to NSC adviser Rice, "There was an enrichment of the intelligence from 1998 over the period leading up to the war."[58]

As these controversies brewed in June and July 2003 and as the postwar situation in Iraq continued to take American lives, public support for the administration began to suffer. In mid-July 2003 a Washington Post/ABC News poll indicated that Bush's approval rating had dropped nine points to 59 percent over a two-week period. A poll by the Pew Research Center indicated that only 23 percent of the public felt that the U.S. involvement in Iraq was going "very well," down from 61 percent in April.[59] On October 29 the number of Americans killed in the postwar period (115) exceeded the death toll from the onset of the war through its official end on May 1 (113).

In short, the general strengths (and potential weaknesses) of the policy processes and the president's own patterns of decisionmaking that were present before September 11 also continued after that date. Bush was a central and active participant on those issues that merited presidential attention. He made the early call that the events of September 11 demanded a war against terror as a response. His views, instincts, and intuitions were central in the expansion of that effort to include a war against Iraq. And the so-called Bush doctrine of preemption was indeed *his* doctrine in the end. But his surety in making those decisions often rested on the responsibilities of others to whom much was delegated. The impact of the latter would be especially manifest before and after the Iraq war: Was the U.S. prepared to undertake the nation-building required? And had the rationale for war—particularly the claim that Iraq possessed weapons of mass destruction and was seeking to once again develop a nuclear capability—been based on reliable evidence?

Beyond the War Cabinet

A White House in Control

Although Powell, Rumsfeld, Tenet, and Ashcroft took up a considerable amount of the president's time and attention, other post–September 11 events continued to be handled by the White House–dominated policymaking process that held sway before that date. The most notable was the anthrax crisis that emerged a few weeks later. When the first case of anthrax occurred in Florida, Health and Human Services (HHS) Secretary Thompson, appearing in the White House press room, downplayed it by saying that the victim might have contracted it from a polluted stream in South Carolina. Thompson's role as crisis manager and spokesman was quickly eclipsed by Governor Ridge, now heading the White House Office of Homeland Security, as other cases developed, especially contamination in congressional offices and U.S. postal facilities. According to one account, Bush told Ridge: "Tom, get these people together. We need to get to the bottom of this."[60] Nor was Thompson and the HHS the major player in the debate over a prescription drug benefit for Medicare recipients. According to one report, "The administration managed the issue mostly from the White House, where health care adviser Mark McClellan was seen as the point person. Most members of Congress and their aides called McClellan—not Thompson— when they had a Medicare question."[61]

Even Attorney General Ashcroft was at times on the White House's leash, albeit one longer than those of some of his colleagues. In the domestic war against terror, he was a key player, perhaps becoming the most visible and powerful attorney general since Robert Kennedy. Shortly after September 11, Bush told him, "This can't happen again." And over the subsequent months Ashcroft was the driving force behind the drafting of the USA Patriot Act and the reorientation of the Justice Department's mission (including the addition of 2,400 more staff members), as well as serving as the public face announcing the apprehension of suspected terrorists and personally briefing Bush daily.[62] Yet Ashcroft, too, operated within parameters set by the White House. For example, according to one report, as the Patriot bill was working its way through Congress, "he had planned to be the administration's deal-cutter on Capitol Hill, but the White House informed him that the White House counsel's office would make those calls."[63]

Other cabinet members not involved in the war against terror continued to pursue the initiatives set out in the Bush campaign and early months of the Bush presidency, generally under White House direction. In a column on Housing and Urban Development Secretary Mel Martinez, David Broder labeled him "the mystery man of the Bush Cabinet," and observed, "His goals are commendable but modest—and appear to come straight from the Bush campaign or the White House Domestic Policy Council."[64] The White House, not Interior Secretary Gale Norton, took the lead in pressing for oil exploration in the Arctic National Wildlife Refuge. Environmental Protection Agency (EPA) administrator Whitman told a reporter that Colin Powell had dubbed her the administration's "wind dummy": "It's a military term for when you are over the landing zone and don't know what the winds are," Whitman said. "You push the dummy out the door and see what happens."[65] On May 21, 2003, Whitman announced she was leaving the administration in order to spend more time with her family.[66] In June, shortly before she was set to leave, the White House edited a major report on climate change that the EPA had prepared under Whitman's direction. Sections of the report that analyzed the risks from global warming were deleted and, according to one report, "whittled to a few noncommittal paragraphs." Several EPA officials reportedly protested the deletions.[67] In September 2003, Whitman and the EPA again faced criticism, now from the EPA's own inspector general, that the agency had downplayed air quality hazards in New York City following September 11 and had permitted some concerns by EPA scientists to be toned down by the White House's Council on Environmental Quality.[68]

Nor, despite the increased visibility of some cabinet members, was this a period in which they felt free of White House control and able to take advantage of the president's and the White House's greater attention to the war against terror. Delegation but with discipline remained the order of the day. According to one White House aide: "This is not a presidency in which there's a lot of freelancing within the cabinet. It's a very tight team, very regimented, very tight message discipline, and I think the cabinet officers realize a large part of their job is to be shields."[69]

In Andrew Card's view, cabinet members are not just implementers, "they also consult. They are advisers." But their access to Bush was controlled by Card or one of his deputies. Moreover, Card admitted, "The White House tends to believe that we can do whatever it is that we can do without going outside this building, and that is so wrong."[70] According to one January 2003 report: "As was the case in Bill Clinton's White House, the West Wing drives policy. And Bush, like his immediate predecessor, seems to think of his cabinet secretaries as glorified staff. He does not view his cabinet departments as think tanks, brewing the newest ideas. Bush applauds an innovation most readily if his White House aides have vetted it first."[71] That analysis could readily fit Bush's relationship with and use of the cabinet either before or after September 11. In fact, in Card's view, "I'm not sure that there would be a dividing line."[72]

Organizational Continuity and Change in the White House

The absence of a bright dividing line before and after September 11 was especially so for the White House staff: some organizational changes were made and some responsibilities shifted but earlier organizational patterns and workways persisted. The pace in the White House heightened, but given its discipline and organization, it managed to cope. According to one top aide, the Bush team had faced unsettled times before: "We had a kind of baptism by fire because of the [Florida] recount. We've never really had smooth sailing. The president's here to do good, big things. We've got a pretty seasoned, now-veteran team with a lot of the original people still here who have been tested."[73]

Bush's preoccupation with foreign policy put more of a burden on the White House staff to continue working on his domestic political agenda.

According to Karl Rove, Bush told his staff that he still wanted a "robust" domestic agenda, but "I am not going to be able to spend as much time on it," and the staff would need to fill in the breach.[74] Policy processes and decisionmaking structures developed before September 11 enabled the staff to cope with the new demands and heightened dangers. And Bush himself was mindful of the political difficulties his father had faced in 1991 and 1992 when he failed to turn from his success during the first Gulf War to domestic and economic issues.

A number of existing White House units were adapted to deal with the war on terror. One was the creation of a "Domestic Consequences Group." It was chaired by deputy chief of staff Josh Bolten to deal with the impact of September 11 on the domestic front; it usually convened daily and included several cabinet members as well as White House aides.

The second cluster of changes occurred in the White House's communications operations—Karen Hughes's domain until her departure from the White House in July 2002. Shortly after September 11 the White House created temporary Coalition Information Centers (CIC) in an attempt to get the administration's message out into the international arena. Headed by Hughes, the centers were also designed as a rapid response team to terrorist propaganda. In November 2001, for example, the team was able to arrange for a spokesman to appear on Al-Jazeera—the independent Arab television station—to respond to a taped message from Osama bin Laden that denounced the United States.[75] On January 21, 2003, the Coalition Information Centers were replaced by a more permanent White House unit, the Office of Global Communications (OGC). It was headed by Tucker Eskew, who had been head of the White House's media affairs office and then ran the CIC office in London during the Afghanistan war. The OGC's purpose, according to the White House website, was "to coordinate strategic communications with global audiences, integrating the president's themes into new and ongoing programs."[76]

The third organizational change was the creation of the USA Freedom Corps by executive order on January 29, 2002. It was designed to serve as a coordinating unit for the Office of Faith-Based and Community Initiatives (OFBCI), AmeriCorps, the Peace Corps, Senior Corps, and other citizen volunteer efforts. It was the organizational embodiment of the president's call, in his 2002 State of the Union address, on all Americans to make a lifetime commitment of two years to volunteer service. John Bridgeland, a key member of the Domestic Policy Council (DPC), was appointed to head the new office.[77]

White House Office of Homeland Security

The most significant organizational change within the White House occurred on September 20, 2001, when, in his speech before Congress, Bush announced that Governor Ridge would be appointed as director of a new White

House Office of Homeland Security. Ridge, sworn in on October 8, quickly assembled a staff of over 100, with an operating budget of $25 million. A new Homeland Security Council was also created to replicate the NSC and the other White House policy councils.[78] Yet from the start, some members of Congress, academic experts, and media commentators questioned whether Ridge had sufficient bureaucratic clout to do the job.[79] Within just days of Bush's announcement of the new office, proposals were being discussed on Capitol Hill that would create a "super" agency or department, not a White House office.[80]

Although well liked within the administration, over time Ridge reportedly encountered increasing resistance to his efforts. As the head of a White House office, Ridge particularly lacked direct authority over agencies and departments involved in homeland security. And despite his mandate from the president, Ridge was occasionally not in the loop. When air patrols were suspended over New York, Ridge was not consulted beforehand. "We don't tell the Office of Homeland Security about recommendations, only decisions," according to one Pentagon official.[81] Ridge especially encountered resistance to his effort to better organize border security through the reorganization of the Immigration and Naturalization Service (INS) and the U.S. Customs Service. Even within the White House, some of Ridge's efforts met with resistance. Ridge's office reportedly sought to use the basement "Situation Room" for high-level meetings, but the NSC staff balked at the idea.[82]

Nor were his relations with Congress always smooth. Congressional attempts to have him testify before committees were rebuffed by the White House. Executive privilege, specifically Ridge's status as a presidential adviser not confirmed by the Senate, was invoked on a number of occasions. By April 2002 an agreement was reached that Ridge would meet "informally" with House committees.

A Troika Continues, Later Minus One

Bush continued to rely on his three principal staff members—Card, Rove, and Hughes—through the summer of 2002, when Hughes left the staff. Their responsibilities basically remained the same, although with some adjustments to reflect the administration's shift in focus to the war on terror. After September 11, for example, Card became part of the war cabinet and he attended Bush's 8:00 A.M. CIA and FBI briefings along with Cheney and Rice. In April 2002, as we shall see, Card became the key player in determining that a full-blown Department of Homeland Security needed to be created, and then was a central participant in its design.

The domestic policy apparatus also remained basically the same as it had before September 11. There were some personnel changes, with Jay Lefkowitz replacing John Bridgeland at the DPC when the latter was tapped to head the USA Freedom Corps.[83] Other personnel changes on the domestic staff took more time: it took from mid-September 2001 until February 1, 2002, for the White House to find a replacement for DiIulio at OFBCI.[84] The National Economic Council (NEC) also was reportedly functioning better once Lindsey left in December 2003, when Stephen Friedman, the former chairman of Goldman Sachs, replaced him. According to Office of Management and Budget (OMB) director Daniels, "I think Steve's brought the element he was first associated with—that is, strong business credibility and real-world street credibility. But also, he's proved a good broker, a good coordinator of policy. . . . Meetings are likely to have a clear agenda now, and more likely to reach an outcome, and that's been useful." Other parts of the new Bush economic team—Treasury Secretary John Snow and Council of Economic Advisers Chair N. Gregory Mankiw (who was nominated to replace R. Glenn Hubbard in February 2003)—were also reportedly operating more smoothly than their predecessors.[85]

But policy initiatives, whether from the NEC, the DPC, or other sources, continued to funnel through Josh Bolten, Card's deputy, until his departure to head the OMB in the summer of 2003. According to one senior White House aide, during the transition, Card and his associates sought "just one path in to the president on any particular policy issue, [because] past White Houses have been afflicted with multiple paths, which causes not just rivalries but actually confusion, which is worse."[86] According to Card, "When there are disputes [in the policy councils]—and there frequently are—if they can't be resolved by acquiescence, the president frequently has to make the call."[87]

The emphasis on discipline and loyalty that had been so strong in the early months of the new administration continued after September 11. Unauthorized leaks were rare and not only Card but Hughes and others continued in their roles as watchdogs. After one leak occurred, one staff member recalled Hughes commenting: "Whoever did this did not do the president a service." Some critics complained that the tight lid kept on internal deliberations did not serve the public's interest and was perhaps symptomatic of the lack of internal dissent. But in Hughes's view, the president's senior staff members "all feel very comfortable disagreeing, and yet once a decision has been made, not airing those disagreements because it is the president's decision." For Rove, the lack of unauthorized leaks "allows people to explore things. You don't have to worry about coming up with an idea and having it leaked in an unpleasant way. People have the freedom to think outside the box." In fact, in Rove's view, Bush's emphasis on collegiality and discipline had been ingrained from the start of the presidency by the president himself: "He said 'return each others phone calls. Respect each others opinions.' . . . He wants colleagues to try to come up with a consensus. What it does is to create intense loyalty to him, but also to your colleagues."[88]

Rove's Role Continues

Although some reports in the aftermath of September 11 indicated that Rove's influence might diminish as the White House focused on foreign policy, Rove remained an influential player, if not more so.[89] An April 2002 article in the *National Journal* indicated that Rove was complementing his role as a strategic adviser with "mastery of the substance of governing: effective policy."[90] As one sign of Rove's expanding mandate, his Office of Strategic Initiatives broadened its planning to include analysis of how past presidents responded in times of crisis. And Rove himself reportedly studied reports of Franklin Roosevelt's office of war information, as well as participating in the efforts of Bolten's Domestic Consequences Group.[91]

Rove's influence on the Bush domestic agenda also continued. He publicly called on airlines to be less greedy in applying for bailout funds. In the summer of 2002 he organized a summit of business executives in Waco, Texas, and urged them to support corporate reform measures then before Congress.[92] In June 2002, appearing before a meeting of the National Federation of Independent Business, Rove told the group that he would "wage war" to ensure that the estate tax was permanently repealed.[93] That same month, Rove instructed his Office of Strategic Initiatives to request from all cabinet departments lists of legislation set to expire before Bush's first term ended, a job usually done by the White House's congressional affairs unit.[94] In July, Rove convened a meeting—described as "confrontational"—with members of Congress from farm states to press them not to ease travel restrictions to Cuba.[95] Later in the year, he was a powerful voice in the Bush inner circle, urging the president to sign a bill that created $180 billion in farm subsidies.[96] During the spring 2003 battle over Bush's second round of major tax cuts, Rove also delved into congressional lobbying. He secured the crucial support of Senator George Voinovich (R-OH) for a compromise plan by promising that Bush would create a commission on tax reform. As it neared passage, one important vote broke fifty-fifty, with Vice President Cheney casting the tie-breaking vote.[97] By the end of 2003, Rove was reported to be centrally involved in crafting major proposals for the Bush 2004 agenda, including major changes in immigration laws and a new program that would make it easier for immigrants to work legally.[98]

But Rove's responsibilities, particularly his involvement in foreign policy matters after September 11, did not escape criticism. Although Rove was not a participant in Bush's war cabinet meetings ("There was a conscious decision that he would not sit in on war-related stuff," according to one Defense Department official),[99] he continued to play an important role as a conduit of advice to Bush. In a January 2002 speech at a Republican Party (GOP) meeting in Austin, Rove urged Republican leaders to take political advantage of President Bush's efforts in the war against terrorism. Rove's language not only led to immediate criticism by Democratic party leaders, but, according to at least one report, also raised concerns from Secretary of State Powell. Rove reportedly weighed in on the Israel-Palestine conflict. Rove's political contacts with state and local officials also sometimes led him, rather than Governor Ridge, to serve as their contact point with the White House on issues dealing with homeland security.[100]

Rove's strategic advice was embodied in a number of policy actions taken by the White House. One proved especially problematic. He successfully urged the president to modify his free trade policy by supporting tariff protection for U.S. steel producers, thereby hopefully bolstering the administration's political position in key electoral states such as Ohio, Pennsylvania, and West Virginia as well as helping the steel industry. Eighteen months later, however, the policy was under fire both from within and outside the administration: it may have cost more jobs than it was thought to save, and it may have contributed to price hikes in steel that negatively affected other parts of the economy, automobile production most notably. In November 2003 the World Trade Organization ruled that the tariffs violated international trade rules, leaving foreign countries with the right to impose an array of retaliatory tariffs on U.S. goods. The European Union quickly announced it would levy $2.2 billion in tariffs targeted at commodities from electorally key states, such as oranges from Florida; similar threats were made by Japan.[101] According to one source close to the White House, even "Rove has agreed [the tariffs] should come down."[102] On December 4, 2003, Bush announced that the tariffs would be lifted ahead of their 2005 scheduled expiration. Putting a positive spin on the decision, Bush said, "These safeguard measures have now achieved their purpose, and as a result of changed economic circumstance, it is time to lift them."[103]

While Rove's forays beyond domestic policies were questioned by some, his defenders noted that he had "limited his role to questions of how foreign policy decisions are communicated and how the White House deals with domestic organizations" that have interests in foreign affairs. Furthermore, according to one White House official, "The president has a foreign team that he relies upon, but he also has an open-door policy in which any of his senior advisers can offer a perspective, and that happens routinely."[104] According to Rove himself, his power within the Bush inner circle had not expanded either after September 11 or after the departure of Karen Hughes: "I think my role has remained pretty much what it has been from the start."[105] Organizational decisions made during the transition continued to be consequential and enduring.

Hughes

Given that Hughes's efforts were largely directed at the administration's economic and domestic agenda, her media presence diminished somewhat following September 11 (although on that day she was the first senior official on television—before Bush returned to the White House—to announce, "Your federal government continues to function effectively"). But Hughes remained involved in the White House's communications strategy for dealing with terrorism, the war in Afghanistan, and the Israel-Palestine conflict in the spring of 2002. Most important, communication of the administration's message remained central to this White House both in its organizational structure and in its day-to-day operations.[106]

In April 2002, Hughes announced that she would leave the White House during the summer to return home to Austin in order to spend more time with her family. Although she did state that she would continue to travel to Washington to periodically advise the president and would be in frequent telephone conversation, her departure—the first among Bush's top aides—signaled a change in the Bush inner circle. As testimony to Hughes's tight control, the announcement of her departure came as a complete surprise; even her immediate staff did not know of the move until she told them at her morning staff meeting on the day of the announcement.[107]

Hughes's departure from the White House may also have increased Rove's clout. She had been an important counterweight to him. Moreover, her replacement, Dan Bartlett, was a Rove protégé before joining Hughes's staff.[108] Even Card recognized the potential void. In an interview with a reporter from *Esquire* magazine, Card said: "I'll need designees, people trusted by the president that I can elevate for various needs to balance against Karl. . . . They are going to have to really step up, but it won't be easy. Karl is a formidable adversary."[109] But in the view of another top White House aide: "No one balances Karl. Forget it. That was Andy's cry for help."[110] Card later clarified his remarks, saying that the departure of Hughes "does create a void," but that the staff would continue to function well.[111]

Her departure elevated the importance of White House speech writers, with whom the president continued the habit of working directly on important addresses. Michael Gerson, his chief speech writer, reportedly was often invited into the Situation Room to "soak in the discussion" before drafting major addresses; "White House officials said Gerson's clout has increased even more" once Hughes left. Gerson also was promoted to "assistant to the president." According to one staff member, "Mike has become the arbiter of what Bush would want" in meetings among Bush's senior aides on presidential speeches.[112]

But Hughes was not out of the picture. She continued to frequently advise the White House on its communications strategy from her new position as, reportedly, a $15,000-a-month consultant to the Republican National Committee, including speaking with Bush several times a week and more frequent contact with other high-level White House officials.[113] And she continued to have a hand in the drafting of Bush's speeches and accompanied him on the occasion of his Azores meeting with British prime minister Tony Blair the weekend before the outbreak of the Iraq war. As Mary Matalin, Cheney's senior adviser, noted at the time of her departure, Bush would continue to seek her input: "He will say in every case, 'What does Karen think?' And someone will have to talk to Karen."[114]

Other Personnel Changes

Late 2002 and the first half of 2003 saw the departure of several other White House officials. Mary Matalin announced her resignation as senior adviser to Cheney on December 13, 2002, followed by that of Nicholas Calio—the White House's congressional liaison—on December 17; Calio was replaced by one of his deputies, David Hobbs. In January 2003, White House personnel director Clay Johnson was nominated by the president to serve as deputy director of the OMB, although his confirmation was delayed by the Senate. He was replaced by his deputy, Dina Habib Powell. On May 6, OMB director Mitchell Daniels announced he would be resigning and returning to Indiana, most likely to run for governor. His replacement was Josh Bolten, Card's deputy and a key figure in the economic and domestic policy process. Bolten's slot was then filled by staff secretary Harriet Miers, who did not have his policy background and whose appointment likely signaled that the NEC and the DPC (or perhaps Rove), rather than the chief of staff's office, would figure more centrally in policy decisions.[115] On May 19, Press Secretary Ari Fleischer announced that he would leave the White House in July.[116] On May 23 the White House announced that the director of its political affairs unit and a key figure in Rove's operation, Ken Mehlman, would be leaving to serve as Bush's reelection campaign manager. He was replaced by his deputy, Matt Schlapp. Another White House aide, Nicolle Devenish, also left to join the campaign as its communications director; Devenish had been White House director of media affairs.

    All of the changeovers—following the shakeup in the economic team—were seen as voluntary. They sought to take advantage of a window of opportunity before the election cycle began, as well as moving key White House figures—mostly from Rove's operation—into the 2004 campaign organization. They are also of interest in another way: the continuity of organizational practices for this administration. The new appointments replicated Bush's penchant during his gubernatorial years of promoting insiders rather than searching outside for new faces. As one account noted at the time, "Aides said Bush's preference for promoting from within gives him a hardworking, committed team beholden only to him without their own agendas." At the same time, however, that practice had its potential downside. As the *Washington Post*'s Mike Allen observed: it might produce an "echo chamber," a lack of new ideas, and "a culture so driven by 'loyalty for loyalty's sake' [that] could produce a White House that was deaf to brewing political or governing crises."[117]

Post–September 11 Policy Initiatives: The Response to Terror

The events of September 11 led to a set of new initiatives on the part of the administration to deal with the war on terror. Here a disjuncture with the past is clearly present. Yet the way the White House dealt with Congress was often strikingly similar to the stance it took in the early months of the Bush presidency, the patina of bipartisanship in the immediate aftermath of September 11 notwithstanding.

Aviation Security and the USA Patriot Act

One immediate priority was an aviation security bill that would better regulate and federalize airport employees who screen baggage and passengers. Bush had initially favored a bill that would give the federal government power to supervise airport security but permit private contracting of screening services. The White House's legislative strategy initially followed the one it had successfully used in the past: rely on the House to come up with a bill that reflected the president's position, then strike a bargain with the Senate. But unlike the tax cut plan, the Senate was now under Democratic control, plus it moved more quickly than the House. The White House floated a number of compromise proposals; none proved acceptable. On October 11, 2001, by a vote of 100–0, the Senate passed a bill that provided for full federalization of employees. On November 1, the House version, which gave the federal government the option of hiring or not hiring private screeners, passed 286–139.[118] Given pressure to act quickly, the administration could not rely on a strategy of prevailing in a drawn-out process of compromise. The White House left it up to its supporters to cut the best deal they could, and Bush signaled his desire to resolve the issue quickly by stating he would sign either version. Not surprisingly, the Senate version prevailed, although with some provisions that might allow private contracting in the future.[119] Despite the outcome, the legislative strategy and tactics were not new. According to one account, "Bush's handling of the aviation bill shows he is responsive to the most conservative wing of his party, but remains adept at minimizing the possible political cost. . . . Stay above the fray and claim credit for whatever emerges—his modus operandi, incidentally, when he was Texas governor."[120]

The second major initiative that was quickly undertaken was the USA Patriot Act. The proposal sought to give the Justice Department and law enforcement new powers to combat the domestic activities of terrorists, including broadened wiretapping powers, indefinite detention of noncitizens suspected of terrorist activities or links to terrorists, enhanced abilities to trace Internet activity and library borrowing, and other provisions. Despite the significant civil liberties issues at stake, in the immediate aftermath of September 11 the administration's call for action and its quick response in proposing legislation put Congress, especially the Senate, on the defensive. In the Senate, an agreement was struck with the leadership of the Senate Judiciary Committee to bring a bill before the full Senate. In the House, hearings were held and significant modifications were made—not just liberals but GOP conservatives, including some in the House leadership, were concerned with the act's expansion of federal power. Speaker Hastert, however, crafted an alternative bill, closer to the White House's position, which passed. On October 24, 2001, the final version of the bill passed the Senate 98–1 and the House 357–66. The White House was also able to secure two other September 11–related measures: a $15 billion package to aid the airline industry, which had been hard hit by the drop-off in air travel, and a $40 billion appropriation to aid New York City. In all these measures, the president's agenda had once again largely prevailed, compromise was undertaken when needed, and in the end, the White House was willing to take credit for whatever resulted.

Department of Homeland Security

In a nationally televised address on June 6, 2002, Bush unveiled a massive proposal to reorganize homeland security efforts into a new department. It was the most significant reorganization of the executive branch since the creation of the Defense Department during the Truman administration. It would combine parts of twenty-two agencies and departments and have about 170,000 employees, with an estimated budget of $37.5 billion.[121] The call for a new department had been made by some Democrats ever since Bush had created the White House Office of Homeland Security under Governor Ridge's direction. The change in the administration's position represented a major step. But how the White House changed its thinking and the speed with which it crafted such a major reorganization are also significant: it was a manifestation of the Bush team at work, especially the handicraft of Chief of Staff Card.

The proposal, which took Washington by surprise, had been developed in secret over the preceding six weeks. It had its origins in a proposal that Governor Ridge had put together to reorganize the INS and the Customs Service. But the proposal encountered resistance. In March 2002, Bush called together several of the cabinet members involved, but, according to Card, discovered "obvious examples of bureaucratic inertia that would prevent this from happening."[122]

Although Bush had reservations about creating a new cabinet-level department, Card instructed his deputies Bolten and Hagin to collect information on some of the bureaucratic resistance to Ridge's efforts. "I stuck a microscope in some of the organizations," Card later told reporters, and he became convinced that a more fundamental reorganization was needed and needed to be undertaken in secret.[123] One of those organizations was apparently Ridge's own office. According to Card, he "took a couple of silo looks inside of what Ridge was doing. I drilled down to see the work product," apparently without initially informing Ridge. Card then told Ridge of his concerns and that he was going to bring the issue before the president, an approach to which Ridge agreed.[124] Bush's instructions were simple: "Come to me with what you think is right."[125] Bush was not wedded to his initial position that a White House office could do the job.

A small group, under Card's direction, undertook the effort in late April 2002. Initially, a number of options were under consideration: "Everything is on the table," one White House staffer was quoted as saying in early May.[126] But the group quickly embraced a more fundamental reorganization. By late May, the group—which had met in secret per the president's instructions—had completed its work.[127] Bush approved the plan on May 31.[128]

On the morning of June 6, the day of the speech, other top-level White House aides were told about the proposal for the new department at the morning senior staff meeting, as were key members of Congress later in the day.[129] As occurred with the departments, members of Congress who had been involved in homeland security (such as Senator Lieberman, who had presented a reorganization bill of his own) had been contacted by members of Card's planning team. But the White House concealed its purposes and did not reveal that its own reorganization plan was in the works. According to one White House official, "If we maintained secrecy, it would catch the Hill off guard and [we would] be able to frame the issue for what it was."[130] The White House was also mindful about the controversy that had ensued among some departments and congressional committees when Ridge's more modest proposal to consolidate the Customs Service and INS was made public in March.

Some critics questioned the timing of Bush's announcement, which occurred amid mounting reports that the FBI and CIA had received some information, prior to September 11, concerning the terrorists' activities in the United States and a possible attack but had failed to fully pursue the leads.[131] Although Bush and his aides had begun work on the proposal well before these controversies erupted, they did act swiftly—either to recapture the political initiative or head off leaks (or both)—to unveil the proposal.[132] According to one report, June 6 (the anniversary of D-Day) or June 12 had been proposed as possible dates, but the White House's congressional lobbyist, Nick Calio, according to one report, "insisted that speed was of the essence to capture momentum and give Congress time to act."[133]

On June 18, Ridge presented the administration's bill to congressional leaders, and it was the White House's hope that legislation would be enacted by the first anniversary of September 11. The House proceeded swiftly, passing a measure that was very close to Bush's proposal by a 295–132 margin by late July.[134] In the Democrat-controlled Senate, however, the bill stalled—largely over Bush's attempt to give the new department greater flexibility in hiring, firing, disciplining, and moving workers than existed under civil service rules for other agencies and departments.

The impasse lasted until after the 2002 midterm congressional elections, and Democratic opposition to Bush's plan may have figured in the loss of their majority in the Senate. Once the lame duck session was under way, Bush prevailed, especially on the issue of more flexible civil service rules. On November 13 the House approved the bill 299–121, followed by passage in the Senate 90–9.[135] It was not clear that Ridge would be selected to head the new department.[136] However, on November 25, 2002, at the signing ceremony for the bill, Bush announced that Ridge would indeed become the new department's first secretary.[137]

The White House had achieved a major victory. Critics were (at least temporarily) stilled, especially those who had faulted the administration for not creating a department in the first place. There was also some logic to the administration's initial path: create a White House unit quickly and by executive order rather than move to a lengthy and likely contentious legislative process for creating a department. As it was, at least some type of homeland security apparatus was put quickly in place. Moreover, if the departmental option had been pursued initially, the White House would likely have found itself in a more strategically defensive position, especially given the Democrats' control of the Senate, and it likely would have required more compromise lest the administration appear to be dragging its feet over legislative details. Recall that it took the Democrats' midterm loss of Senate control to break the logjam.

It is too far a step to impute the moves that were taken to some grand strategy at the outset: White House unit first, then spring the department option at a more auspicious time. Yet how acceptance of the department option came about is revealing. Problems were noticed. Card did his organizational digging. Bush was open to a range of remedies and not wed to his initial position. A skilled team quickly put together a plan, catching its potential adversaries off guard. Homeland security raised new challenges, but it was the administration that was in place before September 11 that had the skill and ability to respond to them.

Domestic Initiatives Continue: Guns and Butter?

Although September 11 posed new policy and priority challenges, the Bush White House did not abandon its domestic political agenda. As noted in Chapter 6, by December 2001 a compromise had finally been reached with Senate Democrats on Bush's education plan—it contained most of the reforms Bush wanted, but without the controversial voucher program. The faith-based initiatives effort, however, foundered, although Bush was able to achieve much of what he wanted through executive orders.[138] On November 5, 2003, Bush signed into law a bill banning partial birth abortions.[139] Later in the month, a prescription drug benefit for seniors finally passed Congress. Other proposals, however, remained in the pipeline: limits on class action suits, a patients' bill of rights, and energy legislation, which passed the House but was blocked by a filibuster in the Senate. By the end of 2003, reports surfaced indicating that the White House was exploring a number of initiatives for the administration's 2004 agenda, including new space missions to Mars and the moon, children's universal healthcare and a campaign against childhood diseases, a program that would make it easier for immigrants to work legally, as well as moving forward with Bush's proposal to partially privatize social security.[140]

Regaining Control of the Senate

Wartime presidents have followed different tracks in dealing with midterm congressional elections. Some, such as Franklin Roosevelt in 1942, have shied away from heavy partisan involvement. Others, such as Woodrow Wilson in 1918 and Richard Nixon in 1970, have sought to bolster their party's standing in Congress. Regardless of strategy, no twentieth-century wartime president succeeded in increasing the number of his party's seats in the House. Indeed their losses were often significant: nineteen seats under Wilson in 1918, fifty under Roosevelt in 1942, twenty-nine under Truman in 1950, forty-seven under Johnson in 1966, twelve under Nixon in 1970, and eight under Bush Sr. in 1990. (Of course it must also be borne in mind that the president's party generally loses House seats in midterms; since 1862, sitting presidents have gained more seats than the opposition party only in 1934 and 1998.)[141] In the Senate, Wilson lost six seats, Roosevelt lost nine, Truman lost six, Johnson lost three, and Bush Sr. lost one. Only Nixon achieved positive results with a net gain of two seats in 1970.[142] Over the six previous wartime presidencies, the average loss in the House was 27.5 seats and in the Senate 3.8 seats.

Bush broke the pattern with a gain of six House seats and two Senate seats, the latter regaining GOP control of the Senate by a 51–48–1 margin (the first time that occurred in a midterm election since senators began to be elected by popular vote in 1914). Bush's high level of political activity in the 2002 races was a decided and tough gamble. Although the dynamics of congressional races are generally set by forces outside a president's direct influence (and they continued to be in 2002),[143] the White House did what it could for GOP candidates despite possible negative consequences for Bush's popularity (likely to decline as the president appeared more partisan).[144] Karl Rove was instrumental in persuading a number of candidates to run (and dissuading others). Bush was an aggressive fundraiser for the GOP and its candidates: some seventy events raised $140–$150 million (by contrast, Clinton raised $50 million in 1994).[145] President Bush personally took on the most active role of any of his wartime predecessors, making some ninety campaign appearances. In the last five days of the campaign, he visited fifteen states and seventeen cities, and logged over 10,000 miles in travel.[146] The strategy ran the risk of backfiring: GOP losses would likely have been taken as a repudiation of the Bush presidency, especially given his rhetorical references to the war on terror, homeland security, and the record of his presidency. Instead, news stories noted Bush's personal victory and increased political clout: "Bush's ten-gallon hat was holding twelve gallons," the *National Journal* observed. "It's now apparent that Bush is an uncommonly popular president who can transfer his goodwill to other Republican candidates."[147]

The 2003 Tax Cut

Whether that clout and goodwill could be transferred to the members of the 108th Congress was another matter. Throughout 2003, despite GOP control, the Senate passed legislation that was often significantly different from House versions, which were closer to those of the White House. Given differences from the House in its internal rules and procedures, a slim majority in the Senate is no guarantee of effective legislative control. Compromise often proved hard to reach, especially over new energy policies. After the Iraq war, perceptions of Bush's political vulnerability also increased; nor was the White House's cause helped in the Senate as four prominent members (Senators Lieberman of Connecticut, Graham of Florida, Kerry of Massachusetts, and Edwards of North Carolina) were actively pursuing their campaigns for the Democratic nomination.

Yet in addition to prescription drug coverage for seniors, the White House did achieve passage of major legislation, although its final product was somewhat different from what the president first proposed: the enactment of another tax reduction package, the third since Bush took office. In early January 2003, Bush proposed a ten-year, $670 billion plan. Touted as an economic stimulus plan, its chief element was the elimination of taxes on stock dividends (estimated to be about $364 billion), immediate phase-in of the tax cuts scheduled to take effect in 2004 and 2006 ($64 billion), reduction in the marriage penalty ($58 billion), and an increase in the child credit ($91 billion), as well as other changes in the tax code. The proposal encountered opposition not only among congressional Democrats, but also among moderate Republican senators and even some conservatives such as Representative Bill Thomas (R-CA), chairman of the House Ways and Means Committee, through which any tax proposal would have to pass.

Given the pending costs of the war in Iraq as well as mounting federal deficit estimates, the Bush plan appeared doomed. Yet by May, both the Senate and the House had passed tax reduction bills, albeit different in details from each other's and from the president's.[148] With Bush pressing for a tax bill on his desk by Memorial Day, an agreement was finally reached on May 21: a $350 billion plan that would reduce taxes on dividends *and* capital gains to a flat 15 percent for most taxpayers, phase in scheduled tax cuts in Bush's 2001 bill earlier, increase the tax credit for children (including immediate $400 per child rebate checks), as well as make some changes in business deductions and depreciation schedules.[149] Bush's Memorial Day deadline had been met, and the president signed the bill on May 28, 2003.

On the surface, the compromise measure appeared to be a significant departure from what Bush had proposed and a victory for GOP moderates in the Senate. Yet the $350 billion cap set by the Senate was achieved by "sunseting" the tax reductions and other provisions in the bill in three to six years, not eleven as Bush had initially proposed. In fact, prorated over eleven years, the compromise plan would actually be higher in cost—$800 billion compared to Bush's proposed $726 billion.[150] And while the longer time frame had been sacrificed, a bill had been produced and future Congresses were placed in the potentially unpopular position of raising taxes and reducing credits back to their previous levels. The peril for Bush was whether the reductions could provide economic stimulus, especially as the lost revenues further deepened the budget deficit. Some 2 million jobs had been lost since Bush took office, compared to the 23 million jobs that had been added during the Clinton presidency. By the end of May 2003, the unemployment rate had risen to 6 percent and fears of economic deflation were being voiced for the first time since the Great Depression (better economic news would emerge later in the year).[151]

Although Press Secretary Ari Fleischer told reporters on May 22 that Bush "is getting less than he would have liked" but was "pleased" with the eventual agreement, the final bill was a significant victory for the White House. In the midst of a lagging economy and mounting deficits, Bush had managed to continue his quest for tax reduction.[152] As had been the case both as governor of Texas and in the battle over the 2001 tax bill, he was firm yet willing to compromise. For example, he was willing to accept the addition of $20 billion in aid to states and local governments that was needed to gain the support of Senators George Voinovich (R-OH) and Ben Nelson (D-NE), and in the final days he indicated his willingness to see some reduction in both dividend and capital gains taxes rather than the full elimination of dividend taxes as he had originally proposed. As he done in 2001, he pressed his case publicly, especially in states where some Senate support might be gained, Ohio and Nebraska most notably. Cheney was brought in during the final days to work out an agreement among GOP leaders. And the president himself was willing at key points to enter into the fray. According to Senator Robert Bennett (R-UT): "By force of his personality, he stepped into the squabble between the House and Senate and brought everyone into the room and said 'You're going to get this done by Memorial Day.'"[153] Bush's earlier efforts to secure a GOP victory in the midterm election also helped his political fortunes: the tax battle of 2003 was a fight among Republicans; the Democrats had been marginalized when they lost control of the Senate.

*   *   *

The events of September 11 and what transpired thereafter clearly marked a set of challenges and turning points in this presidency. Yet past still became prologue. The cast of players remained largely the same through the end of 2002. And while the press of decisions shifted toward foreign affairs and the war on terror, the administration's internal deliberative and decisionmaking processes remained basically the same. So too with President Bush: as a decisionmaker, his pattern of deliberation was markedly consistent, albeit with the war on terror at front and center.

The post–September 11 period also exhibited both the strengths and weaknesses of those decisionmaking processes, often more markedly than was apparent early in this presidency. On the plus side, Colin Powell often acted as a brake on those within the administration's inner circle who favored quick, unilateral action. The administration's response to Governor Ridge's difficulties in gaining departmental and agency cooperation with his White House–based Office of Homeland Security generated a thorough reorganization of the effort into a stronger Department of Homeland Security. The administration also scored a major coup on December 19, 2003, when President Bush and Prime Minister Blair announced that ongoing, secret negotiations had led to an agreement with Libya's Muammar Qaddafi to give up all his biological, chemical, and nuclear weapons. On the other hand, the evidentiary weaknesses that were later revealed in the administration's case for war in Iraq and the issue of whether it was sufficiently prepared to undertake postwar reconstruction of that nation indicated problems in a decision process in which much was delegated to others, as well as, perhaps, limits in the president's ability to ask the right questions and probe the information that was given to him.

The melding of politics and policy through the central role of Karl Rove both aided the administration and generated criticisms. Some of those calculations may prove problematic in the long run; the decision to place tariffs on steel imports even proved problematic in the short run, and they were abandoned. Bush's communications skills did appear to grow after September 11 and some organizational adaptations were made in order to deal with the public relations needs for a war on terror. Yet this was a White House that from the start recognized the centrality of an effective public message and embedded that recognition in Karen Hughes's responsibilities (and they continued under her successor). It was also a White House—and here the contrast with the Bush Sr. presidency is very noticeable—in which the speech-writing staff was front and center and in direct interaction with the president.

But challenges remained for the Bush presidency in retaining the public support at which much of these communications and political efforts were directed. By late September 2003 the president's approval rating, which had begun to slide over the summer, was at the lowest point in his presidency— 49 percent in an NBC News/Wall Street Journal poll, 50 percent for USA Today/CNN/Gallup—an approximately 20 percent decline since the end of the Iraq war. In the NBC News/Wall Street Journal poll, 42 percent favored Bush's reelection, while 40 percent favored an unnamed Democrat.[154] But Bush's approval ratings and electoral prospects would improve over the next several months, especially after the capture of Saddam Hussein on December 13, 2003. In New York Times/CBS News polls taken immediately before and after Hussein's capture, Bush's approval rating rose from 52 percent to 58 percent, while his prospects for reelection against an unnamed Democrat moved from 42 percent to 44 percent (versus 40 percent for his unnamed opponent).[155] By early March 2004, Bush's approval rating had slipped back to 50 percent,[156] and in the presidential race, Bush was backed by 46 percent of respondents in an Associated Press poll, compared to 43 percent for John Kerry and 5 percent for Ralph Nader.[157]

Process aside, the final judgment on whether the *right* decisions were made, however, still remained uncertain by the end of 2003. The effort to secure a Republican-controlled Senate in the midterm elections had paid off, although the 108th Congress often found the Senate and House at odds on a number of policy initiatives. And there were political implications for the president's future. Unified government, as Michael Nelson has noted, "conferred considerable advantages on President Bush [and] also increased his political risks. With full control of the government comes full responsibility for the government's performance. As one White House official said, 'Republicans have the keys to the car.'"[158]

The White House chose to follow through on its domestic policy initiatives, and some came to fruition (although often in somewhat different form than what had been initially proposed). But the costs of some proposals— especially the 2003 tax cut and prescription drug benefits for seniors—raised the issue of whether both "guns and butter" could be easily had. The costs of the war and reconstruction of Iraq mounted: Bush's initial request for $75 billion in April was followed by a September 2003 request of $87 billion, a figure thought too low by some critics and too high by others.[159] Nor was the administration successful in getting other nations to significantly share in the reconstruction's costs. The guns and butter aspect of the Bush wartime presidency was more akin to Lyndon Johnson during the Vietnam War than to the more austerity-minded and sacrifice-demanding wartime actions of Franklin Roosevelt or Harry Truman.

The public, moreover, was registering its concerns, particularly as sporadic fighting and targeted attacks against U.S. forces and installations continued in Iraq, and as it became increasingly unclear when U.S. intervention would end or under what circumstances. In late August 2003, 63 percent felt that the situation in Iraq was worth going to war over, 35 percent did not; one month later the public was evenly divided: 50 percent in favor, 48 percent against.[160] But as with Bush's general approval ratings, public support for the administration's efforts in Iraq would improve after Hussein's capture. According to a New York Times/CBS News poll taken after the capture, 59 percent approved of Bush's handling of the situation in Iraq (35 percent disapproved), up fourteen points since right before the capture; 64 percent felt the U.S. effort in Iraq was going "well" (35 percent "badly"), up seventeen points; and Bush's general handling of foreign policy moved from 45 percent approval to 52 percent approval (while disapproval dropped from 47 percent to 38 percent).[161] By early March 2004, approval of Bush's handling of the situation in Iraq had dropped to 46 percent, while disapproval had risen to 53 percent.[162]

Finally, Bush's efforts, whether foreign or domestic, continued to be dogged by the economy in 2002 and the first half of 2003. By the fall of 2003, however, economic indicators were looking better (especially a whopping 8.2 percent annualized growth in gross domestic product in the third quarter of 2003, the largest percentage increase since 1984; a 9.4 percent annualized growth in productivity, the largest since 1983; and a "core" annualized inflation rate for 2003 of 1.1 percent, the lowest since 1965). Stocks rose across the board through the end of 2003.[163] By the end of the year, new unemployment claims were at their lowest levels since Bush took office.

Yet all news was not perfect. There was still a net loss of jobs since the start of this administration (a decline that President Hoover was the last to experience). Federal deficits were mounting: a deficit of $375 billion for fiscal year 2003 (double the $158 billion for fiscal year 2002), and projections of a $480 to $550 billion deficit for fiscal year 2004. The estimate made at the start of this presidency of a $5.6 trillion surplus by 2011 now was projected to be $2.3 trillion in cumulative deficit.[164]

The legacy of September 11 had presented new challenges to the Bush presidency. Over two years later, some of the challenges remained, with some new ones added: continuing the battle against terrorists; determining the right balance between domestic initiatives and war-related spending; dealing with the political, fiscal, and military repercussions of wars in Afghanistan and Iraq; selling the wisdom of its tax cuts and economic policies amid mounting budget deficits and an economic recovery in which most indicators were up except for the creation of significant numbers of new jobs; and maintaining public support as an election year approached. Organization, structure, process, and players had largely been set before September 11; the consequences of the Bush administration's deliberations and decisionmaking thereafter would determine the success or failure of this presidency.

Notes

1. Michael Nelson, "George W. Bush and Congress: The Electoral Connection," in Gregg and Rozell, *Considering the Bush Presidency,* p. 149.

2. Kumar, "Recruiting and Organizing the White House Staff," p. 35.

3. Doyle McManus and James Gerstenzang, "Bush Takes CEO Role in Waging War," *Los Angeles Times,* September 23, 2001. In his book on the early Bush presidency, journalist Frank Bruni observes, "His push for education reform, his desire to give more government social service money to religious groups—these receded from his schedule and attention. Now he was sometimes coming into the West Wing shortly before 7:00 A.M. instead of shortly after and entering into phone conversations with world leaders and tight clutches with congressional leaders more frequently than ever before." Bruni, *Ambling into History,* p. 262.

4. Bill Keller, "The World According to Colin Powell," *New York Times Magazine,* November 25, 2001.

5. Woodward, *Bush at War,* p. 55.

6. Frum, *The Right Man,* p. 141.

7. Bush's personal briefing (usually) by the CIA director was not an artifact of September 11, but had been established at the start of his presidency on the advice of his father. Also usually attending the meeting were Cheney, Rice, Ridge, and Card. Elisabeth Bumiller, "CIA Chief Prospers from Bond with Bush," *New York Times,* December 17, 2002. After September 11, the FBI director's briefing was added and Homeland Security Director Ridge became a regular attendee; according to one account, "The addition of the FBI director and the homeland security director has created what Rice has described as a 'fusion of intelligence.'" Walter Pincus, "Under Bush, the Briefing Gets Briefer," *Washington Post,* May 24, 2002.

8. Maura Reynolds and Doyle McManus, "For Bush, Burdens of Office Multiply," *Los Angeles Times,* January 26, 2003. Technology also assisted: absent principals could participate through the White House's "secure video teleconferencing system."

9. Frum, *The Right Man,* pp. 141–142.

10. Sammon, *Fighting Back,* p. 8.

11. Doyle McManus and James Gerstenzang, "Bush Takes CEO Role in Waging War," *Los Angeles Times,* September 23, 2001.

12. Woodward, *Bush at War,* p. 38.

13. Bill Keller, "The World According to Colin Powell," *New York Times Magazine,* November 25, 2001.

14. Sammon, *Fighting Back,* p. 7.

15. Bruni, *Ambling into History,* p. 248.

16. The vote in the House was 296–133, with 6 Republicans, 126 Democrats, and 1 independent voting against. In the Senate, the vote was 77–23, with 21 Democrats, 1 Republican, and 1 independent voting against it.

17. Dan Balz and Mike Allen, "CEO Bush Takes Over Management of Message," *Washington Post,* March 28, 2003.

18. Frum, *The Right Man,* p. 168.

19. Dan Balz and Mike Allen, "CEO Bush Takes Over Management of Message," *Washington Post,* March 28, 2003.

20. Ibid.

21. Evan Thomas, "Chemistry in the War Cabinet," *Newsweek,* January 28, 2002. For a longer account of the meeting, see Woodward, *Bush at War,* pp. 258–263.

22. Woodward, *Bush at War,* pp. 259, 261.

23. Ibid., pp. 30, 102. On the speech, also see Hughes, *Ten Minutes from Normal,* pp. 256–260.

24. Ibid., pp. 34–36. The administration's efforts to develop new plans for dealing with Al-Qaida before September 11 came under fire after the March 2004 publication of a book, *Against All Enemies,* authored by Richard Clarke, the adminnistration's former top counterterrorism expert. Clarke, who had resigned in March 2003, charged (among other things) that the Bush administration had failed to take Al-Qaida seriously before September 11, was slow in the steps it did take, and after the attacks tried to pressure him into finding links between the terrorists and Iraq, a preoccupation in Clarke's view that eventually led to a costly and unnecessary war with Iraq. Clarke reiterated his charges in an appearance on CBS's *60 Minutes* program the day before the release of his book. That same week, the independent commission investigating September 11 also held its first public hearings, which included testimony by Clarke as well as a number of other Bush and Clinton administration officials. Clarke's televised testimony and the charges made in his book generated immediate and strenuous rebuttals by the White House and the Republican congressional leadership.

25. The impact of what transpired before September 11 is especially interesting in Rumsfeld's case in another way. His pre–September 11 battles with a military that he perceived as overly bureaucratic, cautious, and cumbersome in its planning, played out once again once the war against terrorism was under way, but with Rumsfeld winning. Rumsfeld's relationship with General Tommy Franks, chief of the U.S. Central Command during both the Afghanistan and Iraq wars, was especially crucial. During the Afghanistan war, according to one senior Pentagon official, Rumsfeld "pushed Franks to be creative and to seek what's needed." Eric Schmitt, "Bush's War Troika Seeking Blend of Military and Civilian Decision Making," *New York Times,* October 24, 2001. The pattern repeated itself with Iraq, when Rumsfeld repeatedly pressed Franks to develop a leaner, tighter plan for waging war against Iraq. And, "under the persistent questioning of his boss [Rumsfeld] . . . Franks transformed himself into an avatar of a whole new way of war." Evan Thomas and Martha Brant, "The Education of Tommy Franks," *Newsweek,* May 19, 2003; also see Mark Thompson and Michael Duffy, "Pentagon Warlord," *Time,* January 27, 2003; and Peter J. Boyer, "The New War Machine," *New Yorker,* June 30, 2003.

26. See Jane Perlez, "Bush Team's Counsel Is Divided on Foreign Policy," *New York Times,* March 27, 2001.

27. Indeed, those associations also extended to some of their deputies. Cheney's chief of staff and foreign policy adviser, I. Lewis Libby, had been a student of Rumsfeld's deputy Paul Wolfowitz at Yale; both also had worked at the State Department during the Reagan presidency and in the Defense Department in the Bush Sr. administration.

28. Evan Thomas, "Chemistry in the War Cabinet," *Newsweek,* January 28, 2002.

29. "Think of the President Without Him," *National Journal,* January 25, 2003, p. 245.

30. David E. Sanger and Patrick E. Tyler, "Wartime Forges a United Front for Bush Aides," *New York Times,* December 22, 2001. In line with Rice's observations, Rumsfeld's and Powell's deputies dismissed the notion of a deep chasm and internal feuding. According to Paul Wolfowitz, Rumsfeld's deputy, it was "sophomoric." For

Richard Armitage, Powell's deputy, it was "utter nonsense," and, in his view, far from the deeper divisions that he recalled between Defense Secretary Caspar Weinberger and Secretary of State George Shultz during the Reagan years: "Now there was a constant battle. We used to sit there and cringe. I've never seen Powell or Rumsfeld be dismissive or rude to each other." Steven Weisman, "What Rift? Top Aides Deny State Dept.-Pentagon Chasm," *New York Times,* June 1, 2003.

31. Greenstein, *The Presidential Difference,* p. 208.

32. On the role of NSC adviser as managerial custodian, see George, *Presidential Decisionmaking in Foreign Policy,* pp. 195–195; and Burke, *The Institutional Presidency,* pp. 98–102.

33. Rice's NSC staff also expanded on October 9, 2001, with the inclusion of a new deputy position on counterterrorism (who would report to both Rice and Homeland Security Director Ridge). The new occupant of the position was former General Wayne A. Downing, who had headed the U.S. Special Operations Command. A second appointment was also announced that day: Richard A. Clarke, who was tapped as "special adviser" to the president on cyberspace security. Clarke had been national terrorism coordinator in the Clinton White House, where he was reportedly frustrated in his efforts. Elisabeth Bumiller, "Bush Picks Two for Senior Posts in the War Against Terror," *New York Times,* October 10, 2001. After he left the administration in March 2003, Clarke became a prominent and controversial critic of the Bush administration's antiterror efforts and the war against Iraq

34. David E. Sanger and Patrick E. Tyler, "Wartime Forges a United Front for Bush Aides," *New York Times,* December 23, 2001.

35. Nicholas Lemann, "Without a Doubt," *New Yorker,* October 14, 2001.

36. Richard Berke, "White House Aides Trying to Balance Attention on Terrorism, the Economy, and Politics," *New York Times,* December 26, 2001.

37. Evan Thomas, "The Twelve Year Itch," *Newsweek,* March 31, 2003.

38. Evan Thomas, "The Quiet Power of Condi Rice," *Newsweek,* December 16, 2002.

39. Evan Thomas, "The Twelve Year Itch," *Newsweek,* March 31, 2003. Similar criticisms appeared in a *Washington Post* piece on Rice published in October 2003 based on four dozen interviews. One senior State Department official, "voicing an opinion that few in the government disputed," stated that "if you want a one-word description of the NSC since January 21, 2001: dysfunctional." According to one former senior NSC staff member, in Rice "you've never really had a national security adviser who's ready to discipline the process, to drive decisions to conclusions and, once decisions are made, to enforce them. [In particular] she will never discipline Don Rumsfeld. . . . Never any sanctions. Never any discipline. He never paid a price." Glenn Lessler and Peter Slevin, "Rice Fails to Repair Rifts, Officials Say," *Washington Post,* October 12, 2003.

40. Evan Thomas, "The Quiet Power of Condi Rice," *Newsweek,* December 16, 2002.

41. Blackwill had been a member of Rice's "Vulcans" during the transition, then had served a stint as U.S. ambassador to India. Robin Wright, "Foreign Policy Guru Tapped to Aid Rice, a Former Employee," *Washington Post,* December 23, 2003.

42. Peter Spiegel, "Rumsfeld 'Not Told' of Postwar Shake Up," *Financial Times,* October 7, 2003.

43. David Sanger, "White House to Overhaul Iraq and Afghan Missions," *New York Times,* October 6, 2003; Peter Slevin and Mike Allen, "Rice to Lead Effort to Speed Iraqi Aid, *Washington Post,* October 7, 2003; Mike Allen, "Iraq Shake-Up Skipped Rumsfeld," *Washington Post,* October 8, 2003.

44. David Sanger and Thom Shanker, "Rumsfeld Quick to Dismiss Talk of Reduced Role in Iraq Policy," *New York Times,* October 9, 2003.

45. Nicholas Lemann, "How It Came to War," *New Yorker,* March 31, 2003.

46. Evan Thomas, "The Twelve Year Itch," *Newsweek,* March 31, 2003.

47. Michael Elliott and James Carney, "First Stop, Iraq," *Time,* March 31, 2003.

48. One prominent Powell critic was a member of his own intelligence staff, Greg Theilman. Appearing on CBS's *60 Minutes II* program, broadcast on October 15, 2003, Theilman said, "The main problem was that senior administration officials have what I call faith-based intelligence. They knew what they wanted the intelligence to show. They were really blind and deaf to any kind of countervailing information the intelligence community would produce." The issue of whether there were stronger links between Al-Qaida and the Iraqi government resurfaced with the publication, in the *Weekly Standard,* of parts of a confidential October 27, 2003, memo from Douglas J. Feith, undersecretary of defense for policy, to Senators Pat Roberts (R-KA) and Jay Rockefeller (D-WV) of the Senate Intelligence Committee. The sixteen-page memo listed fifty raw intelligence reports of such links. Stephen Hayes, "Case Closed," *Weekly Standard,* November 23, 2003; Walter Pincus, "Memo Exacerbates Defense-CIA Strains," *Washington Post,* November 20, 2003; Douglas Jehl, "More Proof of Iraq-Qaeda Link, or Not?" *New York Times,* November 20, 2003; Editorial, "About That Memo," *Weekly Standard,* December 8, 2003.

49. On problems with the CIA's analysis, especially the National Intelligence Estimate of October 2002, see Spencer Ackerman and John B. Judis, "The Operator," *New Republic,* September 22, 2003.

50. Mike Allen, "President Assails Iraq War Skeptics," *Washington Post,* June 18, 2003.

51. David E. Sanger, "Bush Aides Deny Effort to Slant Data on Iraq Arms," *New York Times,* June 9, 2003.

52. Walter Pincus, "White House Backs Off Claim on Iraqi Buy," *Washington Post,* July 8, 2001.

53. Walter Pincus, "Tenet Says He Didn't Know About Claim," *Washington Post,* July 17, 2003.

54. The President's Foreign Intelligence Advisory Board, following a study requested by President Bush, was also reportedly critical of the internal processes dealing with intelligence within the Bush White House, particularly in the case of the claims about uranium purchases. The board, chaired by former NSC adviser Brent Scowcroft, reportedly briefed Bush in early December 2003 and, according to one report, raised concerns that "there was no organized system at the White House to vet intelligence, and the informal system that was followed did not work in the case [of Bush's State of the Union address]." Walter Pincus, "White House Faulted on Uranium Claim," *Washington Post,* December 24, 2003.

55. Dana Milbank and Mike Allen, "Iraq Flap Shakes Rice's Image," *Washington Post,* July 27, 2003; David Sanger and Judith Miller, "National Security Aide Say's He's to Blame for Speech Error," *New York Times,* July 23, 2003. Perhaps in response, the White House announced on August 15 that Robert D. Blackwill, former U.S. ambassador to India, had been appointed deputy assistant to the president with responsibilities to coordinate strategic planning at the NSC.

56. Walter Pincus, "Deutch Sees Consequences in Failed Search for Arms," *Washington Post,* July 25, 2003.

57. Dana Priest, "House Probers Conclude Iraq War Data Was Weak," *Washington Post,* September 28, 2003; Carl Hulse and David E. Sanger, "New Criticism on Prewar Use of Intelligence," *New York Times,* September 29, 2003.

58. Glenn Kessler and Dana Priest, "Iraq Data Not Old, Bush Aides Insist," *Washington Post,* September 29, 2003.

59. Dana Milbank, "Intelligence Dispute Fester as Iraq Victory Recedes," *Washington Post,* July 17, 2003.

60. Michael Duffy and Nancy Gibbs, "Defender in Chief," *Time,* November 5, 2001.

61. "Taking a Shine to a Second Choice," *National Journal,* January 25, 2003, p. 274. Yet Thompson was not wholly out of the picture, particularly when McClellan was appointed as head of the Food and Drug Administration and under Thompson's jurisdiction. In a fall 2002 White House meeting convened to strategize on the administration's proposal for the next Congress, Bush reportedly pointed to Thompson and said: "You're the team. You're the team leader."

62. Wayne Washington, "A Change in Mission for Ashcroft," *Boston Globe,* December 8, 2002.

63. "From the Ashes of 9/11: Big Bad John," *National Journal,* January 25, 2003, p. 255.

64. David Broder, "HUD Secretary Quiet, Interesting," *Burlington Free Press,* April 3, 2002.

65. Katherine Q. Seelye, "After Rocky Start, Whitman Attains Measure of Influence," *New York Times,* March 11, 2002.

66. Her replacement was Michael O. Leavitt, the Republican governor of Utah. Leavitt was confirmed by the Senate on October 28, 2003 (by a vote of 88–8), following a fifty-six-day attempt by a group of Democrats to block his nomination.

67. Andrew C. Revkin and Katherine Q. Seelye, "Report By E.P.A. Leaves Out Data on Climate Change," *New York Times,* June 19, 2003.

68. According to Whitman, the evidence was open to interpretation and there was a concern not to unduly alarm the public; Whitman also noted in an interview, "We were not told to lie." Eleanor Clift and Julie Scelfo, "'We Were Not Told to Lie' About 9/11 and Health," *Newsweek,* September 8, 2003.

69. Todd S. Purdum, "Mr. Heat Shield Keeps Boss Happy," *New York Times,* December 6, 2001.

70. "Governing the Cabinet," *National Journal,* January 25, 2003, p. 237.

71. Ibid.

72. "The Cabinet's Keeper," *National Journal,* January 25, 2003, p. 238.

73. Maura Reynolds and Doyle McManus, "For Bush, Burdens of Office Multiply," *Los Angeles Times,* January 26, 2003.

74. Elisabeth Bumiller and David Sanger, "Threat of Terrorism Is Shaping the Focus of the Bush Presidency," *New York Times,* September 11, 2002.

75. Martha Brant, "Bush's New War Room," *Newsweek,* November 12, 2001.

76. See www.whitehouse.gov/ogc. According to the website, it "advises on strategic direction and themes that United States government agencies use to reach foreign audience [and] to disseminate truthful, accurate, and effective messages about the American people and their government." The CIC, in the White House's view, had proven successful in delivering messages about the liberation of women in Afghanistan in 2002, and more recently the new OGC had been disseminating information about the president's views on Islam and U.S. efforts at regime change in Iraq. As well, the OGC distributed daily a one-page e-mail digest of important news items and administration activities ("The Global Messenger"), distributed Bush's speeches and remarks, was working to set up a U.S.-sponsored television network in the Middle East, and during the Iraq war had a team in place at the U.S. Central Command in Doha, Qatar. Alexis Simendinger, "Shepherding the Story," *National Journal,* March

22, 2003, pp. 922–923. According to one report, "The unit's plan for the Iraq war, mimicking the real war plan, was to orchestrate the information 'battlefield' and to control the outcome—the message of the war." Peter J. Boyer, "The New War Machine," *New Yorker,* June 30, 2003. In the immediate aftermath of September 11, Hughes and Rove cochaired a daily "message meeting," which was "designed to communicate the White House's dual message of fighting terrorism and promoting recovery from the attacks." Mike Allen and Alan Sipress, "Attacks Refocus White House on How to Fight Terrorism," *Washington Post,* September 26, 2001. The message meeting followed a short meeting with the president in the Oval Office designed to craft the White House's daily message; also in attendance were Cheney, Card, and Rice. Mike Allen, "An Unvarnished President on Display," *Washington Post,* September 19, 2001. A daily communications meeting had also been used when the crew of a U.S. Navy surveillance plane was held captive by the Chinese government in spring 2001.

77. In addition to the office, a USA Freedom Corps council was established; its membership included the heads of relevant cabinet departments (e.g., secretaries of state, commerce, education, veterans affairs, and health and human services, as well as the attorney general), White House units (Office of Faith-Based and Community Initiatives), and other federal agencies (the Federal Emergency Management Agency, the Peace Corps, and the Agency for International Development). Bush designated himself as chair of the council, with Cheney and then Bridgeland to preside in his absence.

78. Early on, it met regularly on Tuesday and Thursday, but by 2003 was meeting on an "as needed" basis. Maura Reynolds and Doyle McManus, "For Bush Burdens of Office Multiply," *Los Angeles Times,* January 26, 2003.

79. See, for example, Douglas Waller, "A Toothless Tiger," *Time,* October 15, 2001; and Alison Mitchell, "Disputes Erupt on Ridge's Needs for His Job," *New York Times,* November 4, 2001. For a more general assessment of the Office of Homeland Security, see Relyea, "Homeland Security"; Wise, "Organizing for Homeland Security"; and Donley and Pollard, "Homeland Security." On the later creation of the Department of Homeland Security, see Relyea, "Organizing for Homeland Security."

80. Eric Pianin and Bradley Graham, "New Homeland Defense Plans Emerge, Fearing Ridge Lacks Clout, Lawmakers Float Proposals for Super Agency," *Washington Post,* September 25, 2001.

81. Elizabeth Becker, "Big Visions for Security Post Shrink Amid Political Drama," *New York Times,* May 3, 2002.

82. Douglas Waller, "The Sit-Room Waiting List," *Time,* November 26, 2001. Ridge did manage to secure a small office in prime West Wing real estate: between Card's office and the Oval Office. Ridge also attended Card's morning senior staff meeting and received a personal CIA briefing.

83. More ideological than Bridgeland, Lefkowitz's appointment offered reassurance to Bush's conservative base. Lefkowitz had also played a major role in Bush's deliberations on stem cell research. Although Lefkowitz nominally reported to Margaret LaMontagne Spellings, he reportedly coordinated domestic policymaking and he met with the president usually twice a week, according to his aides. Before joining the administration as general counsel for the OMB, Lefkowitz had been a litigator at Kirkland & Ellis, Whitewater prosecutor Kenneth Starr's law firm. His tenacity as a lawyer earned him the nickname "Viper," although Bush dubbed him "Lefty." Dana Milbank, "A Hard-Nosed Litigator Becomes Bush's Policy Point Man," *Washington Post,* April 30, 2002. On October 7, 2003, Lefkowitz announced that he would be leaving the White House to return to his legal practice.

84. The new appointee, James Towey, had served as Florida secretary of health under Governor Lawton Chiles, a Democrat, but he was also reportedly a close asso-

ciate of Governor Jeb Bush. Towey had also served as legal counsel to Mother Teresa's organization and had lived for a year in an AIDS hospice the organization ran in Washington, D.C. Unlike DiIulio, who was an "assistant to the president," Towey was appointed at the deputy assistant level. Elisabeth Bumiller, "New Leader Picked for Religion-Based Initiative," *New York Times,* February 1, 2002.

85. Alexis Simendinger, "The Broker's Burden," *National Journal,* April 26, 2003, pp. 1306–1308. In February 2004, Mankiw did find himself at the center of political controversy when he remarked that the "outsourcing" of jobs to foreign countries—an issue that had arisen in the presidential campaign—was simply another form of free trade and an economic "plus." He also drew fire for items in the Council of Economic Advisers' Annual Report for 2004: overly optimistic projections of a 2.6 million growth in net jobs and a query whether the hamburgers made at fast-food restaurants should be classified as a "service" or combining inputs to "manufacture" a product. According to one report, "officials who were steeped in Bush's first campaign have moved out of the West Wing or out of government and their replacements—especially in the economic arena—have weaker political antennae." In place of the outspoken O'Neill and Lindsey, "Bush swung the team in the opposite direction, filling it with replacements who would stick to the White House message and keep it out of the news. But those officials have not generated fresh policies." Jonathan Weisman and Mike Allen, "Missteps on Economy Worry Bush Supporters," *Washington Post,* March 13, 2004. Also see Edmund Andrews, "Economics Adviser Learns the Principles of Politics," *New York Times,* February 26, 2004.

86. "Governing the Cabinet," *National Journal,* January 25, 2003, p. 236.

87. "The Cabinet's Keeper," *National Journal,* January 25, 2003, p. 238.

88. Richard L. Berke, "This Time Dissent Stops at the White House Door," *New York Times,* December 16, 2001.

89. See, for example, Dan Balz, "Bush's Political Guru Finds Himself on Periphery," *Washington Post,* October 31, 2001.

90. Carl Cannon and Alexis Simendinger, "The Evolution of Karl Rove," *National Journal,* April 27, 2002, p. 1211.

91. Dan Balz, "Bush's Political Guru Finds Himself on Periphery," *Washington Post,* October 31, 2001.

92. James Carney and John Dickerson, "W. and the 'Boy Genius,'" *Time,* November 18, 2002.

93. Mike Allen, "Rove Urges 'War' for Permanent Repeal of Estate Tax," *Washington Post,* June 14, 2002.

94. Dana Milbank, "Karl Rove, Adding to His To-Do List," *Washington Post,* June 25, 2002.

95. Christopher Marquis, "It's Republican vs. Republican on Cuba," *New York Times,* July 28, 2002.

96. Matt Bai, "Rove's Way," *New York Times Magazine,* October 20, 2002.

97. The final vote was 51—49, with three Democrats in favor and three Republicans opposed. Jonathan Weisman, "Senate Approves Tax Cut Proposal," *Washington Post,* May 16, 2003.

98. Mike Allen, "Immigration Reform on Bush Agenda," *Washington Post,* December 24, 2003; Adam Nagourney and Richard W. Stevenson, "Bush Advisers, with Eye on Dean, Formulate '04 Plans," *New York Times,* December 26, 2003.

99. Richard Berke and David Sanger, "Some in Administration Grumble As Aide's Role Seems to Expand," *New York Times,* May 13, 2002.

100. Ibid.

101. Mike Allen and Jonathan Weisman, "Steel Tariffs Appear to Have Backfired on Bush," *Washington Post,* September 19, 2003.

102. Paul Blustein and Jonathan Weisman, "U.S. Loses Appeal on Steel Tariffs," *Washington Post,* November 11, 2003.

103. Jonathan Weisman, "Bush Rescinds Tariffs on Steel," *Washington Post,* December 5, 2003.

104. Richard Berke and David Sanger, "Some in Administration Grumble As Aide's Role Seems to Expand," *New York Times,* May 13, 2002.

105. Elisabeth Bumiller, "Minus One, Bush Inner Circle Is Open for Sharp Angling," *New York Times,* July 15, 2002.

106. For an extensive analysis of the Bush communications operation, especially its continuities before and after September 11, see Kumar, "Communications Operations in the White House." According to Kumar, the pattern of extensive strategy and communications meetings continued after September 11, including Hughes's daily meeting with the communications staff, monthly or biweekly meetings of Rove's "strategery group," and biweekly meetings of a communications strategy group chaired by Hughes (and later by her successor, Dan Bartlett). The one major change after September 11 was the institution of daily meetings on communications and strategy with the president, with Hughes, Rove, Card, Rice, and Cheney in attendance. On President Bush's pattern of personal communication with the press and additional material on the organization of the White House communications operation see Kumar, "The White House and the Press."

107. For a fuller account of Hughes's departure, see Hughes, *Ten Minutes from Normal,* pp. 306–311.

108. While not as close to Bush personally as Hughes, Bartlett reportedly had a close relationship with him stemming from his time as a young aide in the governor's office. According to one colleague, "We kidded him and called him 'the vice' as in vice governor. It was pretty clear to everyone that Dan had a special relationship with the governor." As for his ties to Rove, Bartlett joined Rove's consulting firm while in college, and it was Rove who involved him in Bush's run for the governorship in 1994. Dana Milbank, "Message Man Is Like a Younger Bush," *Washington Post,* April 28, 2002.

109. Ron Suskind, "Mrs. Hughes Takes Her Leave," *Esquire,* July 2002. According to Card, "The key balance around here has been between Karen and Karl Rove. That's what I have been doing from the start of this administration. Standing on the middle of the seesaw, with Karen on one side, Karl on the other, trying to keep it in balance. One of them just jumped off."

110. Ron Suskind, "Why Are These Men Laughing?" *Esquire,* January 2003.

111. "Bush Aide Clarifies Remark on Void," *New York Times,* June 10, 2002.

112. Mike Allen, "For Bush's Speechwriter, Job Grows Beyond Words," *Washington Post,* October 11, 2002.

113. Elisabeth Bumiller, "Still Advising from Near and Far," *New York Times,* October 21, 2002.

114. Elisabeth Bumiller, "Minus One, Bush Inner Circle Is Open for Sharp Angling," *New York Times,* July 15, 2002.

115. Miers's position as staff secretary was filled by associate White House counsel Brett Kavanaugh.

116. On June 20 the White House announced that Fleischer's deputy, Scott McClellan, would replace him.

117. Mike Allen, "Bush Fills Key Slots with Young Loyalists," *Washington Post,* May 29, 2003.

118. The final vote indicated an overwhelming majority for the administration's position, but the actual split was much narrower. A vote to substitute a Democratic-sponsored proposal was narrowly defeated on an almost straight party line vote of 218–214, with the White House putting considerable pressure on wavering GOP House members to defeat it. See Juliet Eilperin, "House Passes Security Bill," *Washington Post,* November 2, 2001.

119. Experimentation with private contracting was permitted after the first year, and airports were given the option of requesting private contracting after three years. Bush signed the final bill into law on November 19, 2001.

120. Mike Allen, "Airport Bill Could Be Repeated," *Washington Post,* November 19, 2001.

121. The Bush proposal envisioned four subdivisions of the new department plus movement of the Secret Service from the Treasury Department. (1) Border and Transportation Security (including the Coast Guard, the Immigration and Naturalization Service, the Customs Service, the Transportation Security Administration, the Federal Protective Service, and the Animal and Plant Health Inspection Service); (2) Emergency Preparedness and Response (including the Federal Emergency Management Agency, the Office of Domestic Preparedness, chemical, nuclear and biological response teams, the National Domestic Preparedness Office, and the Domestic Emergency Support Team); (3) Chemical, Biological, Radiological, and Nuclear Countermeasures (including the Lawrence Livermore National Laboratory, civilian biodefense research programs, the National Biological Warfare Defense Analysis Center, and the Plum Island Animal Disease Facility); (4) Information Analysis and Infrastructure Protection (including the National Communications System, the National Infrastructure Protection Center, the Critical Infrastructure Assurance Office, the National Infrastructure Simulation and Analysis Center, and the Federal Computer Incident Response Center). The budget for the new department was less than the $50 billion for the Department of Education, and about 10 percent of the budget for the Defense Department. The CIA and FBI remained separate entities, with only the mandate to coordinate their intelligence gathering efforts with the new entity. The new department, in the president's words, would be a "customer" of the intelligence activity of the FBI and CIA.

122. David Von Drehle and Mike Allen, "Bush Plan's Underground Architects," *Washington Post,* June 9, 2002.

123. Ibid.

124. Howard Fineman and Tamara Lipper, "Bush's Homeland Shuffle," *Newsweek,* June 17, 2002.

125. Romesh Ratnesar, James Carney, and John Dickerson, "Can He Fix It?" *Time,* June 17, 2002.

126. Tamara Lipper and Michael Isikoff, "Can Card Save the Incredible Shrinking Czar?" *Newsweek,* May 13, 2002.

127. The effort was essentially the work of four of Bush's closest White House aides: Ridge, Card, OMB director Daniels, and White House counsel Alberto Gonzales. Card and Ridge also met daily with the president to keep him informed of their progress. Card's deputies, Josh Bolten and Joseph Hagin, were also involved in providing information and analysis. Meeting daily, the group was ready with a tentative plan for the president on May 3. A handful of other aides in Ridge's, Daniels's, and Gonzales's offices worked on pieces of the plan as it was further refined. During the first week of May, NSC adviser Rice, her deputy, Stephen Hadley, and congressional lobbyist Nick Calio were brought in for advice, as was I. Lewis Libby, Vice President

Cheney's chief of staff. However, Bush's closest advisers—Karen Hughes and Karl Rove—as well as Press Secretary Fleischer and chief speech writer Michael Gerson, were not informed of what had been under way until a week before it was publicly unveiled. According to one account, deputy chief of staff Hagin was the "enforcer" of secrecy and discipline, limiting the process "to those who truly needed to be involved," and reminding participants that "this is the president's news to make." Dana Milbank, "Plan Was Formed in Utmost Secrecy," *Washington Post,* June 7, 2002.

128. On May 21 the group presented its work to Cheney. The next day, while flying to Europe, Card went over the group's recommendations—a document, three-quarters of an inch thick, complete with diagrams and the pros and cons of each recommended change—with Bush. Final presidential approval came on May 31, just one week before his address to the nation. At that point, White House media and communications aides were told of the plan in order to devise a "roll-out" plan. On June 5, Bush met with most of the cabinet, informing them of the plan. Although cabinet officials were not briefed until that point, members of the group had contacted a variety of agencies and departments with the ostensible purpose of just seeking information. According to Card, "We consulted with them, but without their really knowing about what we had in mind." David Sanger, "In Big Shuffle, Bush Considered Putting FBI in His New Department," *New York Times,* June 9, 2002.

129. Dan Milbank, "Plan Was Formed in Utmost Secrecy," *Washington Post,* June 7, 2002; David Von Drehle and Mike Allen, "Bush Plan's Underground Architects," *Washington Post,* June 9, 2002.

130. Elisabeth Bumiller and Alison Mitchell, "Bush Aides See Political Pluses in Security Plan," *New York Times,* June 15, 2002. Following his speech, Bush held a series of meetings to brief members of Congress. Ridge also met with them, including a meeting of 200 House members on June 12. The White House also permitted Ridge to testify before Congress, which it had vigorously opposed before, claiming executive privilege. The White House cited the precedent of James Schlesinger's testimony before Congress on the creation of a new energy department in 1977; Schlesinger was a White House aide at the time and headed up the task force that crafted the Carter administration's plan for the new department. Ridge also told reporters that there would be limits on his comments before Congress: "The testimony on the Hill will not be as an adviser [to the president] and there will not be any discussions relevant to the advice and counsel" he had offered the president. Jim VandeHei, "Lawmakers: Bush's Plan Will Pass, with Changes," *Washington Post,* June 8, 2002.

131. In fact, Bush's speech occurred in the midst of Senate Judiciary Committee hearings and on the very evening of testimony that day by FBI director Robert Mueller and FBI agent Coleen Rowley. Rowley, an FBI lawyer in its Minneapolis office, had sought, before September 11, to pursue computer evidence concerning one of the terrorist suspects, but was prevented from doing so by higher-ups in the FBI (Rowley and her office especially wanted to obtain a search warrant to examine the laptop computer of Zacarias Moussaoui, the suspected "twentieth hijacker"). After September 11, his computer was searched and contained data about cockpit layouts for passenger planes as well as telephone numbers of Al-Qaida operatives in Germany.

132. On April 10, 2002, OMB director Mitchell Daniels had signaled White House willingness to consider elevating Ridge's office to departmental status during his testimony before the Senate Governmental Affairs Committee: "The president has said from the outset that the structure for organizing and overseeing homeland security may evolve over time as we all learn more and as circumstances change." Daniels also said Bush might consider creating a White House working group to analyze the issue. Elizabeth Becker, "Bush Is Said to Consider a New Security Department," *New*

York Times, April 12, 2002. Card's efforts later in the month to organize a group to study the issue were also reported in *Newsweek.* Tamara Lipper and Michael Isikoff, "Can Card Save the Incredible Shrinking Czar?" *Newsweek,* May 13, 2002.

133. David Von Drehle and Mike Allen, "Bush Plan's Underground Architects," *Washington Post,* June 9, 2002.

134. The House permitted its standing committees that have oversight over existing agencies to weigh in, but they were required to convey their recommendations, by July 12, to a select committee, headed by House Majority Leader Richard Armey (R-TX) and composed of House leaders, with a five Republican and four Democrat balance in membership.

135. Controversial provisions inserted in the House bill almost derailed passage: provisions for protecting vaccine manufacturers against legal liability, a provision to allow companies that incorporate offshore to contract with the new department, and a provision for creating a homeland security research center at Texas A&M University. Senate GOP leaders promised moderates, however, that the provisions would be rescinded in the first spending bill for the department when the new session opened in January. The Democratic alternative was defeated 52–47.

136. Several names surfaced in the days following Bush's June 6 address: FEMA director and longtime Bush friend Joe Allbaugh; Norman Augustine, former CEO of Lockheed-Martin; Richard Armitage, deputy secretary of state; former New York City mayor Rudy Giuliani; and General Barry McCaffrey, Clinton's former drug czar. Elizabeth Becker, "Ridge May Be Reluctant to Take New Cabinet Job," *New York Times,* June 12, 2002. On June 18, even Card's name surfaced. The story was posted on the *Washington Post*'s website. But it was subsequently pulled by the *Post,* and another version was substituted a few hours later. The latter noted that Bush had rejected the proposal from several aides that Card be named. Mike Allen, "Bush Rejects Card as Homeland Security Chief," www.washingtonpost.com, June 18, 2002; Mike Allen, "Bush Rejects Card for Top Security Post," *Washington Post,* June 19, 2002. The next day, the White House indicated that although Card's name had been promoted by several White House aides, it was not formally presented to the president. Mike Allen and Bill Miller, "Lawmakers Fear Costly Price Tag to Create Homeland Dept.," *Washington Post,* June 20, 2002.

137. Ridge, however, was not made a formal member of NSC (which would have required legislative changes). But he could attend at the president's invitation. A separate Homeland Security Council was also created.

138. Different versions of the part of the original proposal dealing with tax deductions for charitable contributions also passed the Senate and the House by the fall of 2003, but differences remained to be ironed out.

139. The bill had passed the House on October 2, 2003, by 281–142 and then the Senate on October 21 by 64–34.

140. Mike Allen and Kathy Sawyer, "Return to Moon May Be on Agenda," *Washington Post,* December 5, 2003.

141. The Republicans also gained seats in 1902 under Theodore Roosevelt, although that year the Democrats gained even more since the size of the House had recently been expanded.

142. Data are from James A. Barnes, "Wartime Presidents, Midterm Losses," *National Journal,* October 13, 2001, pp. 3198–3199.

143. In the House races, the GOP benefited from the redistricting that occurred after the 2000 census. At the same time, Bush mattered too: he had won seven of the eight states that had gained seats. In the Senate races, the GOP was more vulnerable with twenty seats at stake versus fourteen for the Democrats. Moreover, there were

four open GOP seats, and none for the Democrats. But here too 2000 may have had an impact: seven of the fourteen Democrats were in states Bush won, while only three of the twenty GOP seats were in states Gore carried. Nelson, "George W. Bush and Congress," p. 151.

144. As Michael Nelson notes, it cost Bush about a 5 percent decline in his approval rating. Yet as Nelson also notes, this was typical of Bush's view that political capital needed to be spent and that the return on his investment—a Republican Congress—was worth the cost. The GOP also benefited from the political agenda of September and October: the possibility of war with Iraq and the president's request for a congressional resolution. Nelson, "George W. Bush and Congress," pp. 152–153.

145. Andrew E. Busch, "On the Edge: The Electoral Career of George W. Bush," in Gregg and Rozell, *Considering the Bush Presidency,* p. 198.

146. Pika and Maltese, "George W. Bush," p. 11.

147. Carl M. Cannon and David Baumann, "Performance Pressure," *National Journal,* November 9, 2002, pp. 3269–3270.

148. By late March, estimates of the Bush plan's costs had risen to $726 billion over an eleven-year period. Packaged as part of the yearly budget resolution, the House passed a plan 216–211 that would provide a tax cut of some $550 billion. But in the Senate, moderate Republicans forced the figure even lower—$350 billion, which passed 51–50 on a tie-breaking vote by Vice President Cheney. Prospects for an agreement looked dicey: House GOP leaders were angered by the deals made by their counterparts in the Senate. However, the White House indicated its willingness to accept the reductions passed by the House, and it signaled a willingness to compromise even further. As well, once the Iraq war ended, President Bush took to the political hustings to make a case for his plan, often targeting states (once again) that he had won in 2000 but that were represented by moderate Republicans and potential swing-vote Democrats. By mid-May, both the Senate and the House had narrowly passed tax legislation, but with their respective differences in proposed tax reductions remaining to be worked out by a conference committee (which the GOP would now dominate, since it controlled both houses of Congress).

149. The bill provided for $320 billion in tax reductions, $20 billion in aid to states, and $10 billion for low-income families with children. On May 23 (the Friday before the beginning of the Memorial Day weekend holiday), the bill passed the House 231–200 (at 2:00 A.M.) and then (just after 10:00 A.M.) the Senate passed it by a 51–50 vote, with Vice President Cheney again breaking the tie. In the Senate, two Democrats voted in favor—Senators Miller (D-GA) and Nelson (D-NE)—and three Republicans were opposed—Senators McCain (R-AZ), Snowe (R-ME), and Chafee (R-RI). In the House, seven Democrats voted in favor of the bill, one Republican voted against it— Representative Jim Leach (R-IA).

150. The compromise plan was estimated by the Congressional Budget Office to reduce taxes by $61 billion in fiscal year 2003 and by $149 billion in fiscal year 2004; Bush's initial proposal would have reductions of $35 billion in fiscal year 2003 and $117 billion in fiscal year 2004. David E. Rosenbaum, "A Tax Cut Without End," *New York Times,* May 23, 2003.

151. Richard Stevenson, "In Bush Math, Economy Equals Votes," *New York Times,* May 25, 2003. The White House had estimated that Bush's initial proposal would create some 1 million jobs by election day 2004, still leaving Bush with a net deficit of 1 million jobs since starting his presidency.

152. Bush had been less successful in pushing his efforts at tax reform. His initial proposal of eliminating dividend taxes had been linked to corporate tax reform:

only those companies that paid corporate taxes would have their dividends tax-free. This provision was dropped from final legislation.

153. David E. Rosenbaum, "A Tax Cut Without End," *New York Times,* May 23, 2003.

154. In a late September 2003 Gallup poll, the leading Democratic candidates were close to Bush (in some cases ahead): Clark 49 percent, Bush 46 percent; Dean 46 percent, Bush 49 percent; Gephardt 46 percent, Bush 48 percent; Kerry 48 percent, Bush 47 percent; Lieberman 47 percent, Bush 48 percent. In a NBC News/Wall Street Journal poll taken after Hussein's capture, Bush had moved to healthy lead over front-runner Dean, 52 percent to 31 percent; while a Newsweek poll taken December 18–19 showed Bush handily ahead of all his major Democratic opponents: Dean 40 percent, Bush 53 percent; Clark 41 percent, Bush 53 percent; Gephardt 38 percent, Bush 54 percent; Lieberman 40 percent, Bush 52 percent. John Harwood and Jacob Schlesinger, "Democrats' Risky Gambit: Tax Talk," *Wall Street Journal,* September 25, 2003; USAToday/CNN/Gallup Poll Results, www.usatoday.com; www.pollingreport.com.

155. Approval of Bush's handling of the economy also rose from 37 percent in September to 44 percent right before Hussein's capture, and 49 percent immediately after. On the question of the country's direction, 56 percent of those polled before the capture felt that the country was on the "wrong track," while 39 percent felt it was headed in the "right direction"; after the capture, 43 percent felt it was on the wrong track, while 49 percent felt it was headed in the right direction. Adam Nagourney and Janet Elder, "Bush's Approval Ratings Climb in Days After Hussein's Capture," *New York Times,* December 17, 2003.

156. Washington Post/ABC News Poll Results, March 7, 2004, www.washingtonpost.com.

157. Will Lester, "Poll Shows Vulnerabilities of Kerry, Bush," March 24, 2004, www.washingtonpost.com. A CNN/USA Today/Gallup poll released on March 29, 2004, had 51 percent of likely voters backing Bush to 47 percent for Kerry in a two-person race, and Bush's overall approval rating stood at 53 percent. "Poll: Bush's Position Against Kerry Strengthens," www.cnn.com, March 29, 2004.

158. Nelson, "George W. Bush and Congress," p. 157.

159. The Bush request passed both the Senate and the House. However, the Senate initially approved a $20 billion loan rather than a grant for the portion that was to go to reconstruction projects in Iraq. The conference committee on the bill, however, replaced the loan with Bush's initial request for a grant. On October 31, 2003, the House approved the appropriation 298–121. On November 3 the Senate passed it on a voice vote with only six members present; only Senator Robert Byrd (D-WV) voted no. Some specific appropriations in the bill differed from the administration's initial requests, such as lower amounts for building prisons, emergency oil supplies, solid waste management, and road and housing construction, to name but a few.

160. USAToday/CNN/Gallup Poll Results, www.usatoday.com.

161. Adam Nagourney and Janet Elder, "Bush's Approval Ratings Climb in Days After Hussein's Capture," *New York Times,* December 17, 2003.

162. Washington Post/ABC News Poll Results, March 7, 2004, www.washingtonpost.com.

163. The Dow Industrials closed at 10,453 (a yearly gain of 25.3 percent), the Standard & Poor's 500 index gained 26.4 percent, and the Nasdaq composite index gained 50 percent; none of the measures, however, had reached their earlier peaks.

164. These figures are from the Congressional Budget Office's best-case scenario issued in September 2003. David Firestone, "Dizzying Dive to Red Ink Poses Stark

Choices for Washington," *New York Times,* September 14, 2003. However, as a percentage of gross domestic product, the fiscal year 2003 deficit stood at 3.4 percent, far lower than its high mark of 6 percent in 1983. Federal spending also increased by the highest percentage since 1990: in fiscal year 2002 it grew by 7.9 percent and in fiscal year 2003 by 7.3 percent.

8

Lessons from the Bush Experience

As I noted in Chapter 1, transitions are highly consequential for the successes and failures of new presidencies. They begin before election day so that the president-elect and his team can "hit the ground running" once their electoral victory is secure and not have to wake up the morning after the first Tuesday in November and ask, "What do we do now?" They are times when the American public is "reintroduced" to a soon-to-be president, not the candidate who has been running for office. They are times when appointments are made, a White House staff is crafted, and more tightly defined policy agendas begin to form from a myriad of campaign issues and promises. Most important, they are decisionmaking about decisionmaking processes: they begin to set out the organization and management of the information and advice that modern presidents rely upon to make policy decisions, as well as establishing the ways presidents can effectively communicate those decisions and sell them politically.

A successful transition does not guarantee a successful presidency—strengths can devolve into weaknesses, opportunities can be squandered. Likewise, a botched transition need not doom a presidency—mistakes can be rectified, omissions corrected. Furthermore, a range of other causal forces also powerfully affect success or failure—the partisan balance of power in Congress, the tenor of other parts of the political environment, the impact of events, political, economic, and international, to name but a few.

Yet even conceding this, the way a president assumes power can have influence on these forces: How are relations with Congress handled early on? How are other parts of the political environment—media, interest groups, the public—dealt with? What considerations are given to planning for the unexpected? More generally, as I found in my study of the four transitions from Carter through Clinton, transitions matter because "the decisionmaking underlying policy choices has great effect; and the way in which transitions craft, or do not craft, those processes has consequences, sometimes severe."[1]

209

While the broad sweep of activities undertaken during presidential transitions is roughly similar, there is tremendous variation in how recent presidents and their associates went about these tasks, which were deemed more significant than others, which were given short shrift, what was successfully accomplished, and what was not.

Lessons from the Transition

Individually and collectively, presidential transitions offer important lessons about what can contribute to—or detract from—successful performance once in office. What lessons can we learn from the transition to power of George W. Bush?

The Importance of Starting Early

The first lesson, and earliest chronologically, derives from the preelection work undertaken by Clay Johnson. Johnson started in the spring of 1999 and was able, through the summer of 2000, to make contact with a number of former Reagan and Bush Sr. officials. He acquired a broad base of knowledge about how transitions take place, especially the lessons to be learned from the successes and failures of those two previous transitions. By June 2000 he was able to develop a list of transition tasks and priorities (discussed in more detail in Chapter 2). Johnson also planned for the mechanics of a possible Bush transition: its organization, budget, functions, and activities, as well as such technological innovations as a transition website and an online job application process. Johnson's longtime connection to George W. Bush was also an advantage. He knew his principal and what needed to be tailored to Bush's decisionmaking, management, and leadership style. He was also in a position to press Bush to make timely decisions on his recommendations, especially the need to select a chief of staff early. All was in order by election day.

Johnson was in a somewhat unique position to carry out some of these efforts, given that he was working on behalf of the son of a former president and vice president and had easy entree to the collective knowledge of many in the Reagan and Bush Sr. administrations. But, that noted, his activities and their consequences provide a good model for how a preelection effort might be successfully undertaken.

Avoiding Tensions Before Election Day

The Bush preelection effort offers other lessons. Tension between the campaign staff and those involved in transition planning before election day can sour the success of subsequent transition efforts. This was the case for both the Carter and Clinton transitions. Rivalries emerge—campaign staff may look with suspicion on newcomers who now appear to be planning a presidency that campaign staff have been laboring for months, if not years, to win. Attention may also get deflected from the primary task at hand—winning the presidency, not planning for postelection jobs and political spoils.

For Bush, those problems did not emerge. Johnson's early work, coupled with Cheney's later involvement, brought an element of trust and familiarity. Johnson was an Austin insider, Cheney a member of the larger Bush political family. Campaign staff had no reason to worry about their preelection activities. As with the Reagan transition in 1980 and the Bush Sr. transition in 1988, attention to who occupied key roles in the preelection transition effort was critical to its success. Moreover, while operating separately from the campaign, Johnson sought to keep in touch with its key figures—Rove, Hughes, Allbaugh, and Evans—all of whom, like Johnson, were longtime associates of Bush.

Another layer of coordination was also present—oversight by key figures, if not the presidential candidate himself. George W. Bush met with Johnson periodically, often directing his efforts. This level of involvement mirrored his father's practice in 1988 (Bush Sr. was later joined by John Sununu and James Baker) in meeting with Chase Untermeyer, his equivalent to Johnson. Sometimes a high-level surrogate may suffice, as was the case with Ed Meese's oversight of the Reagan preelection effort. Meese was chief of staff for the campaign, as well as a longtime aide to Reagan during his governorship. By contrast, Carter and Clinton invested little time or effort in what their preelection planners were doing, nor did they delegate that task to a trusted associate.

An important element of discretion also was present in the Bush transition. Johnson's activities garnered little media attention. Nor did he seek it. Again, the parallels to 1980 and 1988 are important: little of their preelection activities were publicly revealed. By contrast, in 1976 and 1992, news stories did appear and they fueled the rivalries that would emerge after election day and that had negative impact on their postelection transitions.

A Paradox: A Robust Preelection Effort Can Work

As we saw, Johnson's mandate was broad—not just planning for a postelection transition operation, but garnering information and advice about how a Bush presidency would be organized and structured, organizing a personnel operation, and even beginning to develop lists of potential nominees. In my book *Presidential Transitions,* I note that the more successful transitions—1980 and 1988—had more narrowly defined mandates: planning and organizing a postelection personnel operation. The more problematic transitions—1976 and 1992—were more ambitious efforts, not unlike Johnson's.

The Bush transition of 2000 thus represents a bit of a paradox: more robust mandates can work. Yet the particularities of the Bush effort may make it unique:

- A presidential candidate who could draw on a pool of talent comprising not just his longtime associates but also associates of his father's presidency.
- A trusted aide who could easily tap into that talent pool, especially in learning about the strengths and weaknesses of prior transitions and their subsequent presidencies from those who had a direct hand in them.
- The selection of a vice-presidential candidate, and his assignment to transition planning, who had prior White House, cabinet, and transition experience.
- The presence of a very disciplined team who could focus on their respective tasks and avoid infighting, rivalry, and jealousy.
- A presidential candidate who would heed the advice of his preelection transition, especially in agreeing to tap someone as chief of staff before election day.

The Importance of Recognizing and Making Early Decisions

Johnson's advice that then-candidate Bush settle the issue of who would be chief of staff before election day was especially crucial to this transition's success. As Johnson later reflected:

> One of the primary things we did in the transition—and has borne fruit during the first 100 days—we got the president to do what most people running for the presidency do not want to do [and that is] to decide who their chief of staff is to be and ask him to be the chief of staff before the election. It was critically important that Andy Card had been asked and accepted and was on the ground prior to the election and beginning to have conversations with Governor Bush.

Card's earlier selection, in turn, proved crucial in getting a Bush White House staff in place, even as the controversies in Florida rolled on. In Johnson's view, "I read about the Clinton transition, and Mack McLarty [Clinton's chief of staff] was not on board until mid-December. Well, by mid-December, Andy already had the senior staff done."[2]

Early decisions were also made about the transition's organization and operation. The most important before election day was the selection of Cheney to head the transition, with Johnson to serve as its executive director. Johnson and Cheney had also settled on the transition's budget, organization, and tasks, as noted in more detail in Chapter 2. Chief among these was a recognition of the importance of organizing and filling the White House staff as soon as feasible, development of a policy agenda, setting up a preliminary presidential schedule, building bridges to Congress and key constituency groups, and more generally understanding the importance of the transition period as an indicator for what kind of president the president-elect would be and for setting the foundations of presidential governance. It is fair to say that no other presidential transition in recent history was as prepared to hit the ground running after election day, much less by January 20.

Using the Florida Interlude Wisely

The events from election day through mid-December presented Bush and his associates with the most unique and difficult challenge of any presidential transition. They had to navigate the difficult waters of not appearing to usurp the office yet, at the same time, not squander valuable time by putting aside transition tasks. Card, as we saw, used the period to put together the White House staff; decisions on cabinet positions also commenced. Although not provided with federal funds, following Bush's certification as the winner in late November, Cheney quickly set up a transition headquarters in suburban Virginia, a step the Gore camp did not take.

It was also a time when steps were taken to cement the notion that Bush indeed would become president. Always being ahead in the popular vote count in Florida helped, even though the margins sometimes were dangerously narrow. But, as Don Kettl has noted, more concerted efforts were under way:

> Throughout it all, Team Bush had a clear and straight-forward strategy. By acting as winners, they strengthened their case that they were winners. They pointed to Gore's initial phone call to concede the election and quietly suggested Gore was working behind the scenes to undermine Florida law. But throughout it all, Bush stayed above the fray. Focusing on key issues and assembling his cabinet. It was simple: Playing the part would make it happen. . . . If anything is clear about Bush's transition, it's that he had the right strategy to help him negotiate one of the most contentious election battles in American history.[3]

A thought experiment: What if Bush, perhaps following Gore's example, had waited until the contest over Florida's electoral votes was resolved? In most transitions, it takes eight to ten weeks to fill the cabinet. Had Bush begun after mid-December, he would have hurriedly tried to fill positions—perhaps leading to a number of controversy-prone nominees. Or, had he been more deliberate and slow, he would have found himself on inauguration day with some cabinet slots occupied by Clinton holdovers, hardly an auspicious beginning and potentially detrimental to his political agenda.

Understanding the Key Positions

Once the transition was under way, earlier efforts paid off with the quick unfolding of the top levels of the Bush White House and a successive roll-out of cabinet nominees. But the members of the Bush transition also understood the need to fill key positions first. The most obvious, in addition to Card's, was Condoleezza Rice's at the National Security Council (NSC) staff. Less obvious were Gonzales's appointment as White House counsel and Johnson's as personnel director—both very central to the entire appointments process. Indeed, their White House jobs were functional equivalents of their jobs in the transition itself. And that pattern of slotting the transition's legal counsel and personnel chiefs into White House jobs had occurred in the Bush Sr. transition.

But the 2000 Bush transition bested the 1988 Bush transition in devising an organizational arrangement that would better suit both this president and his performance in office. By bringing Karl Rove and Karen Hughes on board (as well as by having a chief of staff in Card who could tolerate other power centers in the White House) and giving them organizational control of important White House units, the work of the 2000 transition built in better "marketing and selling" and political strategizing and calculation than had been present in the Bush Sr. White House.

Creating "Institutional Memory"

The absence of what has been termed "institutional memory"—knowledgeable personnel or pertinent information that gets carried over from one administration to another—is one of the most vexing problems for presidential transitions. Come inauguration day, White House offices are quite literally empty: files from the old administration have been carted off—according to federal law—to await disposition at the former president's soon-to-be presidential library or to other federal archives. A number of matters need to be constructed or reconstructed, ranging from how most White House units are organized and function to what legislation is up for reauthorization and which executive orders and other actions need to be rescinded or kept in place. Success will turn on being able to create a kind of surrogate institutional memory, whether through the development of pertinent information and a base of knowledge or through the participation in the transition and new administration of persons who themselves have had past White House or other relevant experience.

Vice presidents face a somewhat easier challenge. They bring their own knowledge of how the preceding administration was organized and operated. This has been particularly enhanced, starting with the Carter presidency, by the expanded role of the vice presidency in the administration's inner workings and by the physical location of the vice president's office in the West Wing. Vice presidents also have the advantage of placing their own loyalists in jobs in the prior administration in which they serve, either on their own large vice-presidential staff or in other positions. The Bush Sr. transition provides good evidence of the advantages that accrue. Not only did eight years of the Reagan administration provide George H. W. Bush with an understanding of how he wanted *his* White House to operate, but he was able to assemble a pool of talent who had worked in it, who were associated with him, and who could bring a body of experience to bear in his own transition and presidency.[4]

Andrew Card provides just one example. Card had supported Bush in his 1980 quest for the presidency and later served in two White House units under Reagan—the intergovernmental and the political affairs offices. When he was tapped as John Sununu's deputy chief of staff in the 1988 transition, Card was able to bring a wealth of knowledge about White House operations that Governor Sununu, as a Washington outsider, lacked. As he later recollected:

> I knew where to go in the White House, and I went to the executive clerk's
> office in the White House and got copies of all of the flow charts of presi-
> dents going back to Eisenhower. Then I drew a list of all of the responsibil-
> ities I knew of in the White House from my days there and from talking to
> policy people and the career staff. And then we just went through, deciding
> whether or not those responsibilities appropriately rested in the White House
> and what structure would best serve the president.[5]

By contrast, governors who ascend to the presidency face a more difficult challenge. Not only may they lack the direct experience of vice presidents, but the personnel they may be inclined to rely upon may not have relevant experience either. Jimmy Carter's difficulty during the 1976 transition and, later, in his early presidency is especially telling in this regard; his "Georgia mafia," who were placed in key White House positions, faced a steep learning curve, as did Carter himself.

In the 2000 transition, George W. Bush was in a unique position. Unlike most of his fellow governors who ascended to the White House, he had participated in a transition and remained in close touch as that administration unfolded. Not quite a vice-presidential vantage point, but one that was itself unique given that it was father's presidency. He was also well served by the large body of Bush family loyalists who could provide that "surrogate" institutional memory. Many had provided advice to Clay Johnson in the preelection phase, a number would serve during the transition (Cheney and Card most notably), and in his presidency. In addition, Johnson was an eager recipient of the information and analysis provided by Martha Joynt Kumar and the White House 2001 Project.

Incorporating Personal Knowledge

But providing institutional memory was not the only aim of the Bush transition effort. There was also recognition of the need to craft a working presidency and decision processes and structures that would serve *this* president's needs. Moreover, there was a tacit recognition of Bush's desire to bring on board several key aides who had served him well in Texas—Rove, Hughes, Gonzales, Spellings, and others. Despite media reports during the transition of appointments that were seeming to turn this into "his father's presidency" (other accounts saw links back to the Reagan and even Ford administrations), Bush did not neglect those who had worked for him in the past. Not only did some reflect organizational needs (better communication—Hughes—and better political analysis and strategy—Rove), but they brought elements of trust, loyalty, and close personal knowledge and attachment that presidents also need but that may be lacking if only "Beltway insiders" are picked for key positions. The latter may be strong on some forms of institutional memory but weak on what makes the new president tick effectively; they also may be less allegiant to the new president's policy and political agenda.

Bush, moreover, was in a position to have both pools of talent—the experienced Washington insiders and the loyal, long-serving outsiders—mesh well. Again, the Bush political family was of service: they brought Washington-based experience, but also loyalty and trust. The contrast to the early Reagan presidency is especially marked here. Reagan and his associates also sought to blend both, but created a presidency that was often marked by rival camps and internal competition. This did not occur (at least in major degree) in the George W. Bush presidency. And it was also a presidency in which internal strife would be dampened by the strong, continuing efforts to instill and then reinforce internal discipline and a sense of teamwork, which none of his recent predecessors (including his father) so strongly recognized as needed or so assiduously pursued.

The degree of loyalty and the value placed on teamwork in this administration, however, was not without potential risks to the quality of its internal deliberations and decision outcomes: an absence or stifling of dissenting views, a failure to fully explore policy options and their assumptions and implications, too high a degree of ideological commitment, and an unbending adherence to a set political agenda. The criticisms raised by former members of the administration, such as Paul O'Neill, Richard Clarke, and John DiIulio, of its deliberative processes and inner workings may be idiosyncratic or an artifact of some other set of issues. But they are, at the very least, sobering and to a surprising degree consistent with each other.

Planning a Policy Agenda

While organizing the new administration was a central task of the Bush transition, efforts to prioritize its campaign themes into a leaner political agenda were also undertaken. Bush himself recognized the need for this effort; a lean agenda, focusing on just four or five issues, had been the centerpiece of his campaign for the Texas governorship, and then his early administration. The presidential campaign demanded a response to a wider range of issues, but a successful presidency required a narrow legislative focus. Not only was his own experience useful in this regard, but he was also cognizant of the failure to do so during his father's transition as well as Clinton's early difficulties ("I saw what happened to my dad, who got elected and came in and then said, 'What do we do?' . . . I saw what happened to Clinton.").[6]

Organization and agenda merged with Karl Rove's efforts during the transition and later as senior adviser to the president. Rove developed a long-range action plan for rolling out the president's policy proposals. The first weeks and months of the new Bush presidency—a period crucial to its success—were the products of careful analysis and planning, not matters of happenstance or the daily press of Washington politics.

Campaigning and Governing

As Charles O. Jones argues, especially reflecting on the Clinton transition to office, "campaigning for policy" may be replacing the traditional function of transitions as simply preparing to take office. Jones is right—the transition period has now become marked by greater efforts to project a public image, build public support, and establish alliances with key constituency groups and members of Congress. In effect, the campaign does not end on election day. So too with the Bush transition. From mid-December until inauguration day, Bush undertook a number of public relations efforts to build support for his policy agenda, meeting with a number of groups and individuals in key areas of his political agenda. Bush also sought to build support with members of Congress, both Democrats and Republicans, many of whom served on committees that had jurisdiction over his policy initiatives. Bush's situation was unusually precarious—the events that took place in Florida and the way the dispute was resolved might have completely poisoned any chances of even minimal bipartisan cooperation. The Bush "campaign" succeeded at least to the degree that this did not occur.

But the Bush transition was also successful in another way. While adept at building support for a Bush presidency, the other part of the equation, building toward governance, was not neglected. Here the difference from his predecessor is noticeable. The Clinton transition was long on public relations but short on organizational design and discipline. Media relations soured as the Clinton White House had difficulty adjusting to a more critical White House press pool, a different cast of characters than had been there during the campaign. Nor was the communications operation well organized: different messages sent out by Press Secretary Dee Dee Myers and communications chief George Stephanopoulos, as well as an unusually porous White House where unauthorized leaks were often common. By contrast, the Bush transition was attentive to how these communications and "campaign efforts" needed to be incorporated into the structure of the Bush White House: the wide-ranging mandates of Rove and Hughes and the selection of an experienced congressional lobbying unit, as well as the strategic planning efforts that had been undertaken. Campaigning continued, but how it needed to be linked to ongoing governance once Bush was in office was also recognized as important.

Lessons Once in Office

Recognizing the Management Task

A concern for governance carries over once the president is in office. In *Presidential Transitions,* I note that part of effective governance will turn on the ability to manage the resources—both human and institutional—that impinge on a president's decisionmaking and carrying out the day-to-day duties of the office. Often, these management tasks are delegated to others, especially the chief of staff. Unlike some of his predecessors, Bush clearly recognized this managerial component in his selection of Card as chief of staff: he explicitly and clearly wanted a strong chief of staff but one who would also be a neutral broker and not a strong policy advocate in his own right. Card fit that description well. Card's recognition of his role especially led, in the week or so before inauguration day, to getting the top staff to begin "practicing to be in the White House" as well as his "pin-drop" address to a larger group of soon-to-be staff members.

Others in the Bush inner circle also took on some managerial concerns, especially in stressing the need for discipline and teamwork and adherence to the Bush policy agenda. Their efforts not only pervaded the organizational culture of the White House staff, but also encompassed the working relationships of Bush's top aides, especially Card, Hughes, and Rove. Their division of labor could have been a recipe for the kinds of conflict, competition, infighting, and media leaks that have occurred in some administrations. But it wasn't.

Management as a Presidential Task

What is also of interest is George W. Bush's own active managerial role. Perhaps his MBA and business background came to the fore here, but it is clear that this was a president who in a number of ways recognized the need to set the tone and organizational culture of his presidency—expectations for staff members that ranged from proper attire and punctuality to short memos, cordiality, and prompt return of phone calls. His level of involvement here stands in marked departure from that of his recent predecessors. As I note in *Presi-*

dential Transitions, "Particularly striking in each of these four [transitions] is the rather limited attention to management as an object of ongoing presidential attention and a recognition of its effects on performance in office."[7]

The Dilemmas of Delegation

But there was also a potential downside to the division of labor and decision-making processes of the Bush presidency: the pitfalls of delegation. As noted above and in Chapter 5, delegation matched his own predilections, workways, and comfort level. Nor is Bush unique in this regard; most modern presidents delegate to some degree, even presidents like Kennedy or Lyndon Johnson who favored more fluid collegial styles of operation. Plus, Bush could often be quite engaged in meetings and deliberations, probing those around him with queries and observations about their positions and recommendations.

In some circumstances, delegation worked well: when aides had done their work, when the president himself was directly engaged and interested, and when matters under discussion were part of the ongoing agenda. But in other instances, it proved more problematic. Sometimes difficulties arose when issues emerged quickly and were unfamiliar—Bush's off-the-cuff remarks about defending Taiwan at the time of the Chinese plane seizure incident. Sometimes difficulties arose when the president became too dependent on the advice and information of those around him and the vetting process wasn't working properly—the apparent lack of a more robust domestic policy debate and, more ominously, some of the missteps that occurred in processing the intelligence substantiating the case for going to war with Iraq and in understanding the realities and demands of postwar reconstruction in Iraq.

Dealing with Delegation

The chief pitfall of delegation is reliance on those to whom much is delegated. The lesson here is the need to craft organizational structures, decisionmaking processes, and definitions of individual roles and responsibilities so that they not only play to the president's predilections and strengths, but also take into account and compensate for any potential weaknesses, both of the principal actor—the president—and his agents—the White House staff and cabinet.

The experience of some of Bush's predecessors provides a useful framework for understanding what this administration did right and where it might have been lacking. First, like Bush, Reagan relied heavily on delegation. Yet the Reagan White House sometimes lacked discipline and over time often found itself riven by internal conflicts. Here the managerial concerns of the Bush presidency were of positive benefit and may have staved off the public airing of internal controversies and the use of leaks as ways of settling scores or gaining policy advantage; their relative absence particularly among the

White House staff is especially notable compared to Bush's predecessors. At the same time, the administration did prove more porous when powerful principals and their bureaucracies were at loggerheads: the Central Intelligence Agency and the National Security Council staff over who knew what and told whom what about Iraqi weapons of mass destruction, Defense versus State on preparations for Iraq's postwar reconstruction.

Second, the Clinton experience with the National Economic Council during the early period when it was headed by Robert Rubin is instructive. The benefit here was organizational structure—a council system that worked to bring the White House and representatives of the cabinet departments together; it wasn't perfect, but it was an improvement. So too with some—but not all—of the cabinet councils established during Reagan's first term. The council system, when structured well, can let agreements and disagreements surface and bring different levels of policymakers to the table (some have been "tiered," with deputy-level meetings, then principal-level meetings, and finally those at which the president presides). At the very least, it can offer a powerful counterweight to the more insular perspectives of a White House–dominated policy process, but at the same time giving the White House a measure of control over that process.[8] Although less is currently known about the inner workings of the Bush Domestic Policy Council and National Economic Council, they appear to be less structured than the other cases where council systems have worked well.

Third, the Eisenhower presidency is particularly interesting on the question of effective delegation. That Eisenhower relied on a more formally organized staff system and decisionmaking process is quite clear. Yet as Fred I. Greenstein has noted in his work on Ike's "hidden-hand" leadership style, there were a number of features that made it work.[9] One was Eisenhower's reliance on *informal* sources of information and advice as a check on official channels. We see some of this in the relationship between Bush father and Bush son, and perhaps some may also exist between President George W. Bush and members of the Bush political family who did not serve in his administration. At the same time, it is notable that Brent Scowcroft, NSC adviser under both President Ford and President Bush Sr., chose to make public his concerns about President George W. Bush's decisions to go to war against Iraq in 2003.[10]

Another critical element within the Eisenhower staff system involved attention to how roles were defined: the NSC adviser's role as a neutral broker of the process was taken seriously—someone whose principal concern was the quality of information and advice and the effective and fair working of the deliberative process. Moreover, that role operated within a policy process that was well organized: policy tasks forces, an NSC Planning Board composed of the principals' deputies, frequent (often weekly) meetings of the full NSC at which Eisenhower presided, followed by meetings of the Operations Coordinating Board, which was concerned with the coordination of policy implementation. At meetings of the full NSC, moreover, policy issues were extensively staffed beforehand, options were outlined, and disagreements of the Planning Board were frequently presented in parallel columns on the same page. It is interesting to speculate about how the evidence against Saddam Hussein and the issues of postwar reconstruction in Iraq would have been dealt with in an Eisenhower-era national security process.[11]

Seizing the Agenda

As noted earlier, the Bush transition recognized the importance of agenda politics: defining a coherent political agenda and seizing the initiative so that agenda defines the terrain of political battle. As John C. Fortier and Norman J. Ornstein note, "Those predicting consistent bipartisanship or a cautious and incremental approach to policy were wrong. Bush has been a bold president in the legislative arena."[12]

Success quickly came for the most important part of that agenda, the tax plan, and Congress began to focus on other Bush proposals—education reform and faith-based initiatives, most notably. The pace of the legislative process, however, was typically slow, especially once the Senate was in Democratic hands. Yet, particularly in light of how Bush became president, he and his associates did a remarkable job of defining the terrain of political battle. As Hedrick Smith notes in his book *Power Game,* "In the grand scheme of American government, the paramount task and power of the president is . . . to fix the nation's agenda. Of all the big games of American politics, the agenda game must be won first."[13] It was a game which Bush understood and at which he sought to prevail.

A Legislative Strategy: Flexibility with Firmness

Bush's dealings with Congress varied over the course of his first years in office. However, they can be characterized by several features. First, while attempting to stick to the president's agenda, the White House was often flexible in accepting compromise—but only where a reasonably acceptable compromise could be had. Here, Bush's experience, as governor, with the Texas legislature was an instructive precursor: set out a limited number of goals, assess the political situation, be willing to accept what you can realistically get, and then claim victory.

Second, there was awareness of the wide array of tools for exercising power and influence, not just bargaining and compromise or "going public" to build support, but also interpersonal skill. For this president, this particularly meant George W. Bush's personal charm and its use in establishing bonds and relationships with members of Congress, especially those across the aisle. It proved helpful in getting to know members of Congress during the transition, it was useful in establishing the loyalty of members of the president's own party, it was employed in gaining the support of key members of Congress on particular issues (notably Senator Kennedy on education), and it successfully resurfaced for a time with the Democratic leadership in the aftermath of September 11, 2001. But its utility was limited: it didn't work on Senator Jeffords, by January 2002 a sense of bipartisanship was crumbling, and by 2003 even some House Republicans were willing to strike out on their own.

Third, there was recognition of the political and institutional differences between the House and the Senate. Although the game plan sometimes differed depending on the legislative issue, the White House could generally rely on the internal discipline of Republicans within the House to get a version of legislation that it wanted. The real battle was in the Senate, whether under Republican or Democratic control. Still, House victories helped. As Charles O. Jones notes, it was "win where you can and when you can. (For Bush that meant winning in the House, given Republican Party discipline there and the likely boost from having bills pass in one house for passage in the other.)."[14]

Fourth, where the game plan differed, the White House often showed sensitivity to political context. Its approach to the Senate, in particular, could be partisan or more bipartisan, depending on the issue, timing, and political stakes. It pursued a more partisan approach on its tax cut plans, but selective bipartisanship on education. How it approached Congress also varied. On a patients' bill of rights—a high valence issue—it stuck to vaguer guidelines. On campaign finance reform—another valence issue—it also issued guidelines at the start, then pushed for an acceptable alternative, but was prepared to accept far less. And whatever resulted, it was prepared to claim credit for it—or at least to signal a kind of acquiescent association. Yet there were also boundaries to what the administration would accept: for example, a patients' bill of rights structured so that limits were set on damage awards. The 2001 tax cut process also offers another lesson: cut a deal only when the time is right. Bush waited until the Democrats had drifted away from their initial across-the-board cut proposal of $750 billion to the $1.2 billion that was much closer to the administration's proposal before getting down to serious negotiation. For some issues, such as social security, the time was never right during the first three years to bring that issue onto the legislative agenda.

Political Fortune and Political Environment

Changes in the broader political environment over time also affected how this administration responded to the legislative process. Over its first four months it mounted a fairly aggressive drive for its policy agenda; the weak hand Bush was dealt was not the stronger hand he first played. The situation changed after the loss of Senate control, and outcomes seemed more uncertain. By late August, while the tax cut had passed, other proposals were still caught in the legislative process between a House bent on passing them and a now Democratic-controlled Senate that had begun to balk. The question that cannot be answered is whether the administration's strategy and tactics would have been ultimately successful in achieving most of what had been proposed had not September 11 intervened. A major public relations initiative was planned for September and October, but it obviously did not come to pass.

With September 11, the environment changed again. At least for a time bipartisanship was the order of the day. The White House quickly took the initiative with its transportation safety bill, the USA Patriot Act, and other measures directed against the war on terror. Again, the lessons of agenda politics were understood and played well. A wartime presidency led to congressional acquiescence to wartime measures. By the end of the year, some success also came on education reform (minus Bush's voucher proposal).

By early January 2002, partisanship had begun to return. A number of the initiatives that passed were not central parts of the Bush agenda, had their roots in Senate proposals, or were dictated by new events: bills dealing with corporate fraud, farm subsidies, and campaign finance. Here the White House did what it could to effect a favorable outcome, but acquiesced to the seeming inevitable, again claiming credit where possible. Bush was able, however, to secure trade promotion authority, which had eluded his predecessor.

By the fall of 2002, as attention moved to war in Iraq, the administration used the period to press for a congressional authorization for possible military action and to make the case for Republican control of the Senate in the midterm elections. Both were achieved. In the postelection, lame duck session, the administration's heightened political position was felt when Congress accepted almost all of what the White House wanted in its proposal for a Department of Homeland Security, as well as an administration bill that shifted some of the costs of terrorist attacks from insurance companies to the federal government.

Through 2003, the administration also continued to press Congress on prescription drug coverage for senior citizens, tort reform, a new energy policy, as well as securing the second major installment of tax cuts. The latter was achieved (albeit with significant modifications from the White House's initial set of proposals), as was passage of prescription drug coverage.

Yet as the administration's third year in office drew to a close, Bush's legislative success began to be hampered by the pending 2004 presidential election (hardly an incentive for accommodation by Senate Democrats) and perhaps fatigue on the part of some in Congress with Bush's efforts to date. As Fortier and Ornstein note, "His close partisan victories had alienated potential Democratic allies. There were serious doubts as to whether he could hold together his Republican allies in Congress as he had done early in his presidency."[15] The prescription drug plan was achieved, but the White House and the Republican leadership could not muster the sixty votes needed to save the energy plan from filibuster.

When Fortune Fails, Use Other Presidential Powers

This was also a presidency that recognized that legislation is not the only path to policy success. As scholars such as Phillip Cooper and Kenneth Mayer have noted, there has been a marked increase in presidential use of executive orders and other means of exerting executive control.[16] Although in sheer quantity the number of executive orders issued over the first two years of the Bush presidency was actually less than the number issued in Bill Clinton's first two years (72 versus 109),[17] some proved highly significant. Most notable were the executive orders issued in relation to his faith-based initiatives proposal, especially those that put in place much of what he failed to get from Congress.

However, over his first three years in office, Bush did not use his veto power. He did on occasion threaten to veto legislation (some fifty times according to a count by the Office of Management and Budget).[18] By contrast, Reagan had vetoed twenty-two bills, Bush Sr. twenty-five, and Clinton eleven over their first three years. Part of the explanation for the difference may have resided in Bush's ability to get legislation to his liking or his willingness to sign bills (such as campaign finance reform) that were more problematic, but he also could rely on the Republican–controlled and disciplined House to forestall the emergence of legislation that he strongly opposed.[19]

But the Bush White House was notable for its frequent assertions of a third sort of presidential power—the claim of executive privilege. Claims were made to block the release of presidential papers at the Reagan presidential library, information about the task force on energy policy directed by Vice President Cheney, prosecutorial records on past cases at the Justice Department, national security documents requested by congressional inquiries into September 11 and war decisionmaking concerning Iraq, and to block congressional testimony by some White House officials. The administration's efforts raised some controversies in its relations with Congress and were not without price. Yet as Mark J. Rozell notes, they "were consistent with an overall administration strategy of attempting to tip the balance of federal government powers increasingly in favor of the executive branch."[20] And as he had in his more direct dealings with Congress, Bush was sometimes willing to compromise: Governor Ridge, while serving as head of the White House Office of Homeland Security, was permitted to give "informal" briefings with members of Congress, and an agreement was struck with the independent commission investigating the attacks of September 11 to allow limited access to the daily intelligence briefings prepared for Presidents Clinton and Bush as well as to allow public testimony by NSC adviser Rice.

Dealing with the Unexpected

The Bush team was less skillful in dealing with the unexpected. During the transition, it responded quickly to the problems in Linda Chavez's nomination as labor secretary; there would be no lingering difficulties as had beset his father's nomination of John Tower for defense secretary or Clinton's travails in finding an attorney general. But other unforeseen early developments proved more perilous. Clinton's last-minute executive orders and regulatory rulings placed Bush in a difficult position politically. The energy crisis in California called for a response. And the White House had to deal with the defection of Senator Jeffords from the Republican Party and the loss of control of the Senate. None were handled crisply. Looming over all was an economic decline and a sluggish recovery that dramatically changed the projections of budget surpluses and would eventually yield significant budget deficits. These parts of the nation's political agenda did not readily yield to Bush's control.

Yet George W. Bush and his administration did rise to the immediate challenges posed by September 11. His public performance seemed a bit wobbly on the day of the attack, but he recovered quickly. In his address at the memorial ceremony at the National Cathedral, his impromptu remarks at the World Trade Center site, and his speech before Congress, the president established his stature as a national leader who was capable of rising to this most difficult of challenges. In the aftermath of September 11, he was also well served by his principals and by a deliberative process that quickly assembled the information needed to assess the situation and craft a response. Whether he was as well served in his decisions on Iraq still remains an open matter.

Finally, whatever their strengths or weaknesses, the decisions that were made and courses of action settled upon were the products of deliberative and decisionmaking processes, of organizational routines, of management practices, and of the predilections and behavior of individual actors that had largely been put in place at the start of this presidency. Change occurs, and it occurred in this presidency. But continuity also remains, as it surely did here. And that is why presidential transitions are enduring and consequential.

* * *

Let me end with an observation from Charles O. Jones in his work *Passages to the Presidency:* "Presidents-elect who win convincingly with a clear message and collateral support in Congress have an advantage in effecting the conventional transition."[21] What is interesting about this president and this transition is how a president-elect whose electoral win was hardly convincing and who had collateral support in Congress by the narrowest of margins imaginable, nonetheless created an advantage in effecting the most unconventional of transitions. The shadows and outlines are there—many positive, some less so—but history will still determine whether it also abetted a successful presidency.

Notes

1. Burke, *Presidential Transitions,* p. 377.
2. Clay Johnson, panel discussion, "Bush Transition to the Presidency: Planning and Implementation," American Enterprise Institute, Washington, D.C., December 11, 2001.
3. Kettl, *Team Bush,* pp. 55–56.
4. Vice presidents also enjoy easier relations with the outgoing administration, which may even extend to contacts that occur before election day, as occurred in 1988. For further discussion, see Burke, *Presidential Transitions,* pp. 193–195.
5. Telephone interview with Andrew Card, September 17, 1998.
6. Karl Rove, "A Discussion with Karl Rove," American Enterprise Institute, Washington, D.C., December 11, 2001.
7. Burke, *Presidential Transitions,* p. 389.
8. On the Clinton National Economic Council and the Reagan-era cabinet councils, see Burke, *Presidential Transitions,* pp. 144–151, 330–334.
9. Greenstein, *The Hidden-Hand Presidency.*
10. On Scowcroft's reservations, see Mann, *Rise of the Vulcans,* pp. 336–339.
11. For an analysis of how the Eisenhower system did operate within an important foreign policy crisis of his early presidency—intervention in Indochina in 1954—see Burke and Greenstein, *How Presidents Test Reality.*
12. John C. Fortier and Norman J. Ornstein, "President Bush: Legislative Strategist," in Greenstein, *The George W. Bush Presidency,* p. 139.
13. Smith, *The Power Game,* p. 333.
14. Charles O. Jones, "Capitalizing on a Perfect Tie," in Greenstein, *The George W. Bush Presidency,* p. 194.
15. John C. Fortier and Norman J. Ornstein, "President Bush: Legislative Strategist," in Greenstein, *The George W. Bush Presidency,* p. 141.
16. Cooper, *By Order of the President;* and Mayer, *With the Stroke of a Pen.*
17. Jones, "Capitalizing on a Perfect Tie," p. 187.
18. Alexis Simendinger, "An Unused Veto Pen," *National Journal,* September 20, 2003, p. 2878.
19. Ibid., pp. 2878–2879.
20. Mark J. Rozell, "Executive Privilege in the Bush Administration: The Conflict Between Secrecy and Accountability," in Gregg and Rozell, *Considering the Bush Presidency,* p. 136.
21. Jones, *Passages to the Presidency,* p. 185.

Bibliography

Abshire, David, ed. 2000. *Report to the President-Elect 2000: Triumphs and Tragedies of the Modern Presidency.* Washington, D.C.: Center for the Study of the Presidency.

Bourne, Peter. 1997. *Jimmy Carter.* New York: Scribner.

Brauer, Carl. 1986. *Presidential Transitions: Eisenhower Through Reagan.* New York: Oxford University Press.

Bruni, Frank. 2002. *Ambling into History: The Unlikely Odyssey of George W. Bush.* New York: HarperCollins.

Burke, John P.. 2000. *The Institutional Presidency: Organizing and Managing the White House from FDR to Bill Clinton.* Baltimore: Johns Hopkins University Press.

———. 2000. *Presidential Transitions: From Politics to Practice.* Boulder: Lynne Rienner.

Burke, John P., and Fred I. Greenstein. 1989. *How Presidents Test Reality: Decisions on Vietnam, 1954 and 1965.* New York: Russell Sage.

Bush, George W. 1999. *A Charge to Keep.* New York: William Morrow.

Caeser, James W., and Andrew E. Busch. 2001. *The Perfect Tie: The True Story of the 2000 Presidential Election.* Lanham, Md.: Rowman and Littlefield.

Campbell, Colin, and Bert A. Rockman, eds. 2004. *The George W. Bush Presidency: Appraisals and Prospects.* Washington, D.C.: CQ Press.

Clarke, Richard A. 2004. *Against All Enemies: Inside America's War on Terror.* New York: Free Press.

Cooper, Phillip J. 2002. *By Order of the President: The Use and Abuse of Executive Direct Action.* Lawrence: University Press of Kansas.

Dionne, E. J., and William Kristol, eds. 2001. *Bush v. Gore: The Court Cases and Commentary.* Washington, D.C.: Brookings Institution Press.

Dionne, E. J., and Gerald M. Pomper, eds. 2001. *The Election of 2000: Reports and Interpretations.* New York: Chatham House.

Donley, Michael B., and Neal A. Pollard. 2002. "Homeland Security: The Difference Between a Vision and a Wish." *Public Administration Review* 62:138–144.

Drew, Elizabeth. 1997. *Whatever It Takes.* New York: Viking Books.

Dubose, Lou, Jan Reid, and Carl M. Cannon. 2003. *Boy Genius: Karl Rove, the Brains Behind the Remarkable Political Triumph of George W. Bush.* New York: PublicAffairs.

Dworkin, Ronald, ed. 2002. *A Badly Flawed Election: Debating Bush v. Gore, the Supreme Court, and American Democracy.* New York: New Press.

Edwards, George C., III. 2002. "Strategic Choices and the Early Bush Legislative Agenda." *PS: Political Science and Politics* 35:41–45.

Felzenberg, Alvin, ed. 2000. *The Keys to a Successful Transition.* Washington, D.C.: Heritage Foundation.

Frum, David. 2003. *The Right Man: The Surprise Presidency of George W. Bush.* New York: Random House.

George, Alexander L. 1980. *Presidential Decisionmaking in Foreign Policy: The Effective Use of Information and Advice.* Boulder, Colo.: Westview.

Greene, Abner. 2001. *Understanding the 2000 Election: A Guide to the Legal Battles That Decided the Presidency.* New York: New York University Press.

Greenstein, Fred I. 1982. *The Hidden-Hand Presidency: Eisenhower as Leader.* New York: Basic Books.

———. 2002. "The Changing Leadership of George W. Bush: A Pre- and Post-9/11 Comparison." *Presidential Studies Quarterly* 32:387–396.

———, ed. 2003. *The George W. Bush Presidency: An Early Assessment.* Baltimore: Johns Hopkins University Press.

———. 2004. *The Presidential Difference: Leadership Style from FDR to George W. Bush.* Princeton: Princeton University Press.

Gregg, Gary L., and Mark Rozell, eds. 2004. *Considering the Bush Presidency.* New York: Oxford University Press.

Henry, Lauren L. 1960. *Presidential Transitions.* Washington, D.C.: Brookings Institution.

Hughes, Karen. 2004. *Ten Minutes from Normal.* New York: Viking.

Jamieson, Kathleen Hall, and Paul Waldman, eds. 2001. *Electing the President, 2000: The Insiders' View.* Philadelphia: University of Pennsylvania Press.

Jeffords, James M. 2001. *My Declaration of Independence.* New York: Simon and Schuster.

———. 2003. *An Independent Man: Adventures of a Public Servant.* New York: Simon and Schuster.

Johnson, Clay. 2002. "The 2000–01 Presidential Transition: Planning, Goals, and Reality." *PS: Political Science and Politics* 35:51–53.

Jones, Charles O. 1998. *Passages to the Presidency: From Campaigning to Governing.* Washington, D.C.: Brookings Institution.

Kaplan, David A. 2001. *The Accidental President.* New York: William Morrow.

Kettl, Donald F. 2003. *Team Bush: Leadership Lessons from the Bush White House.* New York: McGraw-Hill.

Kumar, Martha Joynt. 2002. "Recruiting and Organizing the White House Staff." *PS: Political Science and Politics* 35:35–40.

———. 2003. "Communications Operations in the White House of President George W. Bush: Making News on His Terms." *Presidential Studies Quarterly* 33: 366–393.

———. 2003. "The White House and the Press: News Organizations as a Presidential Resource and as a Source of Power." *Presidential Studies Quarterly* 33:669–683.

Kumar, Martha Joynt, and Terry Sullivan, eds. 2003. *The White House World: Transitions, Organization, and Office Operations.* College Station: Texas A&M University Press.

Light, Paul C. 1995. *Thickening Government: Federal Hierarchy and the Diffusion of Accountability.* Washington, D.C.: Brookings Institution.

———. 1999. *The President's Agenda: Domestic Policy Choice from Kennedy to Clinton.* Baltimore: Johns Hopkins University Press.

Mackenzie, G. Calvin. 2002. "The Real Invisible Hand: Presidential Appointees in the Administration of George W. Bush." *PS: Political Science and Politics* 35:27–31.

Mann, James. 2004. *Rise of the Vulcans: The History of Bush's War Cabinet.* New York: Viking.

Mayer, Kenneth R. 2001. *With the Stroke of a Pen: Executive Orders and Presidential Power.* Princeton: Princeton University Press.

Moore, James, and Wayne Slater. 2003. *Bush's Brain: How Karl Rove Made George W. Bush Presidential.* Hoboken, N.J.: Wiley.

Morris, Roy, Jr. 2003. *Fraud of the Century.* New York: Simon and Schuster.

Newmann, William M. 2002. "Reorganizing for National Security and Homeland Security." *Public Administration Review* 62:126–137.

Ornstein, Norman, and John Fortier. 2002. "Relations with Congress." *PS: Political Science and Politics* 35:47–50.

Pfiffner, James P. 1996. *The Strategic Presidency: Hitting the Ground Running.* Lawrence: University Press of Kansas.

Pika, Joseph, and John Anthony Maltese. 2003. "George W. Bush: Challenges of a Wartime President." Paper prepared for delivery at the annual meeting of the American Political Science Association, Philadelphia, August 30.

Posner, Richard A. 2001. *Breaking the Deadlock: The 2000 Election, the Constitution, and the Courts.* Princeton: Princeton University Press.

Relyea, Howard C. 2002. "Homeland Security: The Concept and the Presidential Coordination Office—First Assessment." *Presidential Studies Quarterly* 32:397–411.

———. 2003. "Organizing for Homeland Security." *Presidential Studies Quarterly* 33:602–624.

Sabato, Larry J. 2002. *Overtime: The Election Thriller.* New York: Longman.

Sammon, Bill. 2002. *Fighting Back: The War on Terrorism—From Inside the Bush White House.* Washington, D.C.: Regnery.

Smith, Hedrick. 1988. *The Power Game: How Washington Works.* New York: Random House.

Sullivan, Terry. 2002. "Already Buried and Sinking Fast: Presidential Nominees and Inquiry." *PS: Political Science and Politics* 35:31–33.

———. 2002. "Nomination Forms Online." *PS: Political Science and Politics* 35:13–15.

Suskind, Ron. 2004. *The Price of Loyalty: George W. Bush, the White House, and the Education of Paul O'Neill.* New York: Simon and Schuster.

Tapper, Jake. 2001. *Down and Dirty: The Plot to Steal the Presidency.* Boston: Little, Brown.

Tenpas, Kathryn Dunn. 2002. "Can an Office Change a Country? The White House Office of Faith-Based and Community Initiatives: A Year in Review." Report prepared for the Pew Forum on Religion and Public Life.

Thompson, Carolyn B., and James W. Ware. 2003. *The Leadership Genius of George W. Bush.* Hoboken, N.J.: Wiley.

Toobin, Jeffrey. 2001. *Too Close to Call: The Thirty-six Day Battle to Decide the 2000 Election.* New York: Random House.

Wayne, Stephen J., and Clyde Wilcox, eds. 2002. *The Election of the Century and What It Tells Us About the Future of American Politics.* Armonk, N.Y.: M. E. Sharpe.

Wise, Charles R. 2002. "Organizing for Homeland Security." *Public Administration Review* 62:131–144.

Woodward, Bob. 2002. *Bush at War.* New York: Simon and Schuster.

Index

About the Book

How did a president-elect whose win was hardly convincing, and who had the narrowest margin of congressional support imaginable, create an advantage for himself that prevailed in the face of unexpected and unprecedented challenges? To answer this question, John Burke offers an in-depth account of George W. Bush's unconventional transition to power—and the significant developments that occurred during the early years of his presidency.

Burke argues convincingly that Bush had the organizational confidence to govern as if the election had delivered him a popular mandate. Examining the president's domestic and foreign policy initiatives, he also demonstrates that, contrary to conventional wisdom, decisions made early on—during the transition—shaped the evolution of Bush's leadership after September 11. History has yet to determine the legacy of Bush's presidency, but as Burke demonstrates, the Bush 2000 transition offers an enviable model for future administrations.

John P. Burke is professor of political science at the University of Vermont. His publications include *The Institutional Presidency* and *Presidential Transitions: From Politics to Practice*.